# Certificate Paper C3

## FUNDAMENTALS OF BUSINESS MATHEMATICS

For assessments under the 2006 new syllabus in 2006 and 2007

**Practice & Revision Kit**

CIMA

**In this June 2006 new edition**

- Banks of objective test questions on every syllabus area
- Answers with detailed feedback
- Two mock assessments
- Fully up to date as at 1 May 2006

BPP's **i-Pass** product also supports this paper

FOR ASSESSMENTS UNDER THE 2006 NEW SYLLABUS IN 2006 AND 2007

PROFESSIONAL EDUCATION

First edition June 2006
ISBN  0 7517 2654 0

British Library Cataloguing-in-Publication Data
A catalogue record for this book
is available from the British Library

Published by

BPP Professional Education
Aldine House, Aldine Place
London W12 8AW

www.bpp.com

Printed in Great Britain by
WM Print
45-47 Frederick Street
Walsall
WS2 9NE

We are grateful to the Chartered Institute of
Management Accountants for permission to reproduce
past examination questions. The answers to past
examination questions have been prepared by BPP
Professional Education.

# Contents

# Revising with this Kit

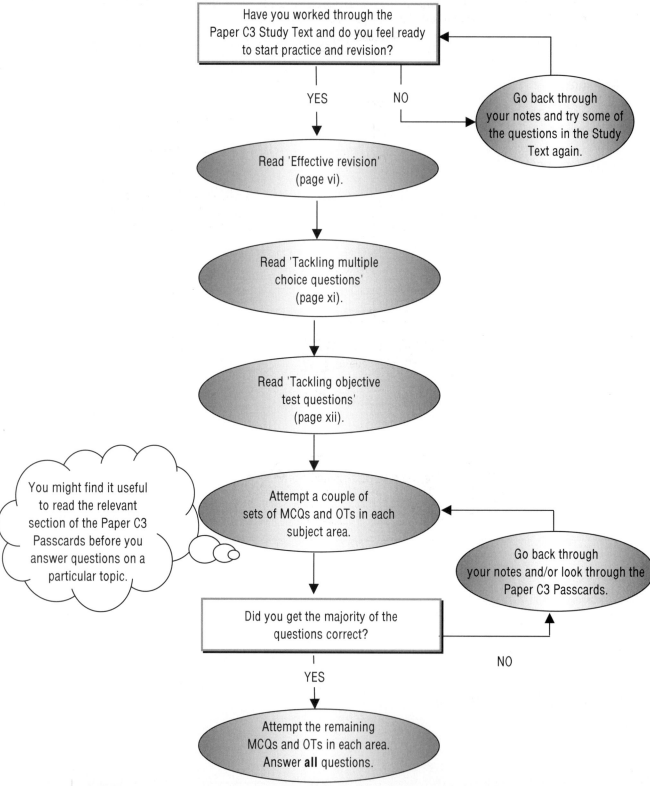

BPP
PROFESSIONAL EDUCATION

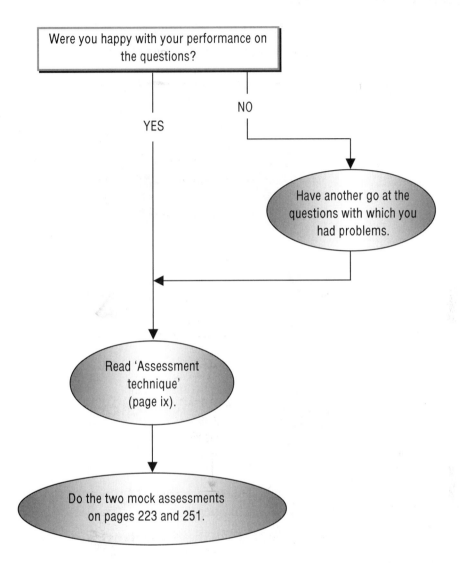

# Effective revision

This guidance applies if you have been studying for an exam over a period of time. (Some tuition providers are teaching subjects by means of one intensive course that ends with the assessment.)

## What you must remember

Time is very important as you approach the assessment. You must remember:

> **Believe in yourself**
>
> **Use time sensibly**

### Believe in yourself

**Are you cultivating the right attitude of mind?** There is absolutely no reason why you should not pass this **assessment** if you adopt the correct approach.

- **Be confident** – you've passed exams before, you can pass them again

- **Be calm** – plenty of adrenaline but no panicking

- **Be focused** – commit yourself to passing the assessment

### Use time sensibly

1. **How much study time do you have?** Remember that you must **eat**, **sleep**, and of course, **relax**.

2. **How will you split that available time between each subject?** A revision timetable, covering what and how you will revise, will help you organise your revision thoroughly.

3. **What is your learning style?** AM/PM? Little and often/long sessions? Evenings/ weekends?

4. **Do you have quality study time?** Unplug the phone. Let everybody know that you're studying and shouldn't be disturbed.

5. **Are you taking regular breaks?** Most people absorb more if they do not attempt to study for long uninterrupted periods of time. A five minute break every hour (to make coffee, watch the news headlines) can make all the difference.

6. **Are you rewarding yourself for your hard work?** Are you leading a **healthy lifestyle?**

# What to revise

## Key topics

You need to spend **most time** on, and practise **lots of questions** on, topics that are likely to yield plenty of questions in your assessment.

You may also find certain areas of the syllabus difficult.

Difficult areas are

- Areas you find dull or pointless
- Subjects you highlighted as difficult when you studied them
- Topics that gave you problems when you answered questions or reviewed the material

**DON'T** become depressed about these areas; instead do something about them.

- Build up your knowledge by **quick tests** such as the quick quizzes in your BPP Study Text and the batches of questions in the I-Pass CD ROM.

- Work carefully through **examples** and **questions** in the Text, and refer back to the Text if you struggle with questions in the Kit.

## Breadth of revision

Make sure your revision covers all areas of the syllabus. Your assessment will test your knowledge of the whole syllabus.

# How to revise

There are four main ways that you can revise a topic area.

> Write it!
>
> Read it!
>
> Teach it!
>
> Do it!

## Write it!

Writing important points down will help you recall them, particularly if your notes are presented in a way that makes it easy for you to remember them.

## Read it!

You should read your notes or BPP Passcards actively, testing yourself by doing quick quizzes or Kit questions while you are reading.

## Teach it!

Assessments require you to show your understanding. Teaching what you are learning to another person helps you practise explaining topics that you might be asked to define in your assessment. Teaching someone who will challenge your understanding, someone for example who will be taking the same assessment as you, can be helpful to both of you.

## Do it!

Remember that you are revising in order to be able to answer questions in the assessment. Practising questions will help you practise **technique** and **discipline**, which can be crucial in passing or failing assessments.

1   Start your question practice by doing a couple of sets of objective test questions in a subject area. Note down the questions where you went wrong, try to identify why you made mistakes and go back to your Study Text for guidance or practice.

2   The **more questions** you do, the more likely you are to pass the assessment. However if you do run short of time:

   •   Make sure that you have done at least some questions from every section of the syllabus

   •   Look through the banks of questions and do questions on areas that you have found difficult or on which you have made mistakes

3   When you think you can successfully answer questions on the whole syllabus, attempt the **two mock assessments** at the end of the Kit. You will get the most benefit by sitting them under strict assessment conditions, so that you gain experience of the vital assessment processes.

   •   Managing your time
   •   Producing answers

---

BPP's *Learning to Learn Accountancy* gives further valuable advice on how to approach revision.
BPP has also produced other vital revision aids.

•   **Passcards** – Provide you with clear topic summaries and assessment tips
•   **i-Pass CDs** – Offer you tests of knowledge to be completed against the clock
•   **Success Tapes and Success CDs** – Help you revise on the move

You can purchase these products by completing the order form at the back of this Kit or by visiting www.bpp.com/cima

---

BPP
PROFESSIONAL EDUCATION

# Assessment technique

## Format of the assessment

The assessment will contain 45 questions to be completed in 2 hours. The questions will be a combination of multiple choice questions and other types of objective test questions.

## Passing assessments

Passing assessments is half about having the knowledge, and half about doing yourself full justice in the assessment. You must have the right approach to two things.

> **The day of the assessment**
>
> **Your time in the assessment room**

### The day of the assessment

1   Set at least one **alarm** (or get an alarm call) for a morning assessment.

2   Have **something to eat** but beware of eating too much; you may feel sleepy if your system is digesting a large meal.

3   Allow plenty of **time to get to the assessment room**; have your route worked out in advance and listen to news bulletins to check for potential travel problems.

4   **Don't forget** pens and watch. Also make sure you remember **entrance documentation** and **evidence of identity**.

5   Put **new batteries** into your calculator and take a spare set (or a spare calculator).

6   **Avoid discussion** about the assessment with other candidates outside the assessment room.

### Your time in the assessment room

1   **Listen carefully to the invigilator's instructions**

Make sure you understand the formalities you have to complete.

2   **Ensure you follow the instructions on the computer screen**

In particular ensure that you select the correct assessment (not every student does!), and that you understand how to work through the assessment and submit your answers.

3    **Keep your eye on the time**

In the assessment you will have to complete 45 questions in 120 minutes. That will mean that you have roughly 2½ minutes on average to answer each question. You will be able to answer some questions instantly, but others will require thinking about. If after a minute or so you have no idea how to tackle the question, leave it and come back to it later.

4    **Label your workings clearly with the question number**

This will help you when you check your answers, or if you come back to a question that you are unsure about.

5    **Deal with problem questions**

There are two ways of dealing with questions where you are unsure of the answer.

(a)    **Don't submit an answer.** The computer will tell you before you move to the next question that you have not submitted an answer, and the question will be marked as not done on the list of questions. The risk with this approach is that you run out of time before you do submit an answer.

(b)    **Submit an answer**. You can always come back and change the answer before you finish the assessment or the time runs out. You should though make a note of answers that you are unsure about, to ensure that you do revisit them later in the assessment.

6    **Make sure you submit an answer for every question**

When there are ten minutes left to go, concentrate on submitting answers for all the questions that you have not answered up to that point. You won't get penalised for wrong answers so take a guess if you're unsure.

7    **Check your answers**

If you finish the assessment with time to spare, check your answers before you sign out of the assessment. In particular revisit questions that you are unsure about, and check that your answers are in the right format and contain the correct number of words as appropriate.

BPP's *Learning to Learn Accountancy* gives further valuable advice on how to approach the day of the assessment.

# Tackling multiple choice questions

The MCQs in your assessment contain a number of possible answers. You have to **choose the option(s) that best answers the question**. The three incorrect options are called distracters. There is a skill in answering MCQs quickly and correctly. By practising MCQs you can develop this skill, giving you a better chance of passing the assessment.

You may wish to follow the approach outlined below, or you may prefer to adapt it.

**Step 1**    **Note down how long** you should allocate to each MCQ. For this paper you will be answering 45 questions in 120 minutes, so you will be spending on average just over two and a half minutes on each question. Remember however that you will not be expected to spend an equal amount of time on each MCQ; some can be answered instantly but others will take time to work out.

**Step 2**    **Attempt each question**. Read the question thoroughly.

You may find that you recognise a question when you sit the assessment. Be aware that the detail and/or requirement may be different. If the question seems familiar read the requirement and options carefully – do not assume that it is identical.

**Step 3**    Read the four options and see if one matches your own answer. Be careful with numerical questions, as the distracters are designed to match answers that incorporate **common errors**. Check that your calculation is correct. Have you followed the requirement exactly? Have you included every stage of a calculation?

**Step 4**    You may find that none of the options matches your answer.

- **Re-read the question** to ensure that you understand it and are answering the requirement

- **Eliminate any obviously wrong answers**

- **Consider which of the remaining answers** is the **most likely** to be correct and select the option

**Step 5**    If you are still unsure, **continue to the next question**. Likewise if you are nowhere near working out which option is correct after a couple of minutes, leave the question and come back to it later. Make a note of any questions for which you have submitted answers, but you need to return to later. The computer will list any questions for which you have not submitted answers.

**Step 6**    **Revisit questions** you are uncertain about. When you come back to a question after a break you often find you are able to answer it correctly straight away. If you are still unsure have a guess. You are not penalised for incorrect answers, so **never leave a question unanswered!**

# Tackling objective test questions

## What is an objective test question?

An objective test (**OT**) question is made up of some form of **stimulus**, usually a question, and a **requirement** to do something.

- **MCQs.** Read through the information on page (xi) about MCQs and how to tackle them.

- **True or false**. You will be asked if a statement is true or false.

- **Data entry**. This type of OT requires you to provide figures such as the correct figure for creditors in a balance sheet, or words to fill in a blank.

- **Hot spots**. This question format might ask you to identify which cell on a spreadsheet contains a particular format or where on a graph marginal revenue equals marginal cost.

- **Multiple response.** These questions provide you with a number of options and you have to identify those that fulfil certain criteria.

- **Matching.** This OT question format could ask you to classify particular costs into one of a range of cost classifications provided, to match descriptions of variances with one of a number of variances listed, and so on.

## OT questions in your assessment

CIMA is currently developing different types of OTs for inclusion in computer-based assessments. The timetable for introduction of new types of OTs is uncertain, and it is also not certain how many questions in your assessment will be MCQs, and how many will be other types of OT. Practising all the different types of OTs that this Kit provides will prepare you well for whatever questions come up in your assessment.

## Dealing with OT questions

Again you may wish to follow the approach we suggest, or you may be prepared to adapt it.

Step 1    Work out **how long** you should allocate to each OT. Remember that you will not be expected to spend an equal amount of time on each one; some can be answered instantly but others will take time to work out.

Step 2    **Attempt each question**. Read the question thoroughly, and note in particular what the question says about the **format** of your answer and whether there are any **restrictions** placed on it (for example the number of words you can use).

You may find that you recognise a question when you sit the assessment. Be aware that the detail and/or requirement may be different. If the question seems familiar read the requirement and options carefully – do not assume that it is identical.

**Step 3**    Read any options you are given and select which ones are appropriate. Check that your calculations are correct. Have you followed the requirement exactly? Have you included every stage of the calculation?

**Step 4**    You may find that you are unsure of the answer.

- Re-read the question to ensure that you understand it and are answering the requirement

- Eliminate any obviously wrong options if you are given a number of options from which to choose

**Step 5**    If you are still unsure, **continue to the next question**. Make a note of any questions for which you have submitted answers, but you need to return to later. The computer will list any questions for which you have not submitted answers.

**Step 6**    Revisit questions you are uncertain about. When you come back to a question after a break you often find you are able to answer it correctly straight away. If you are still unsure have a guess. You are not penalised for incorrect answers, so **never leave a question unanswered!**

# Formulae to learn

You will be provided with certain formulae and mathematical tables in your assessment but the following formulae are not provided and you may need to use them in the assessment. **Learn them.**

- Sum of a geometric progression, $S = \dfrac{A(R^n - 1)}{R - 1}$

- 1f $ax^2 + bx + c = 0$ then $x = \dfrac{-b \pm \sqrt{(b^2 - 4ac)}}{2a}$

- Arithmetic mean of ungrouped data $= \dfrac{\text{Sum of values of items}}{\text{Number of items}}$

- Mean deviation $= \dfrac{\sum f(x - \bar{x})}{n}$

- Coefficient of variation (coefficient of relative spread) $= \dfrac{\text{Standard deviation}}{\text{Mean}}$

- Price index $= 100 \times \dfrac{P_1}{P_0}$

- Quantity index $= 100 \times \dfrac{Q_1}{Q_0}$

- Average price relatives index $= 100 \times \dfrac{1}{n} \times \sum (P_1/P_0)$

- Average quantity relatives index $= 100 \times \dfrac{1}{n} \times \sum (Q_1/Q_0)$

- Probability of achieving the desired result
  $= \dfrac{\text{Number of ways of achieving desired result (heads)}}{\text{Total number of possible outcomes (heads or tails)}}$

- $P(\bar{A}) = 1 - P(A)$ where $\bar{A}$ is 'not A'

- Simple interest, $S = X + nrX$

- Compound interest (when there are changes in the rate of interest), $S = X(1 + r_1)^y (1 + r_2)^{n-y}$

- Effective Annual Rate of Interest $= [(1 + r)^{\frac{12}{n}} - 1] \text{ or } [(1 + r)^{\frac{365}{y}} - 1]$

- Discounting formula, $X = S \times \dfrac{1}{(1 + r)^n}$

- $IRR = a\% + \left[ \dfrac{A}{A - B} \times (b - a) \right]\%$

- Annuity (a) $= \dfrac{\text{Present value of an annuity}}{\text{Annuity factor}}$

PROFESSIONAL EDUCATION

## Use of computer notation in the computer based assessment

Make sure that you understand and are able to write formulae in computer notation. For example, you can use * on a computer instead of a multiplication sign, or ∧ if you wish to introduce a power.

# Useful websites

The websites below provide additional sources of information of relevance to your studies for *Business Mathematics*.

- BPP                                   www.bpp.com

    For details of other BPP material for your CIMA studies

- CIMA                                  www.cimaglobal.com

    The official CIMA website

# Question and Answer checklist/index

# Questions

## Basic mathematics

Questions 1 to 5 cover basic mathematics, the subject of Part A of the BPP Study Text for C3

# 1 Basic mathematics 1

1    A square-ended rectangular box has a volume of 1,458cm³. The length of the box is twice that of one side of the square end.

One side of the square end therefore measures

[    ]    cms

2    The expression $\frac{(x^2)^3}{x^5}$ equals    $= \frac{x^5}{x^5} = 1$

A   0          (B) 1 †          $\widehat{C}$ x          D   $x^2$

3    A radio which was priced at $56.99 has been reduced to $52.49. To two decimal places, the percentage reduction in price is

[    ]    %

4    The expression $(x^3)^4$ equals

A   $x^7$          B   $x^{12}$          C   7x          D   x/7

5    A buyer has spent $30,151 on 550 units of a particular item. The first 100 units cost $50 each, the next 150 units cost $8,250 in total, the next batch cost $11,200 in total and the final 100 cost $x each. The value of x is

A   $57.01          B   $107.01          C   $139.51          D   $169.01

6    The term $x^{-1}$ equals

A   −x          (B)   1/x          C   $x^2$          D   x − 1

7    A coat which was priced at $45.99 last year is now $53.99.

What is the percentage increase in price to three decimal places?

[    ]

8    The expression $(y^2)^3$ equals

A   $\sqrt[3]{y}$          B   $y^6$          C   $y^5$          D   $y^{\frac{2}{3}}$

*[Handwritten at top: S.p = 50, C.p = 10, 100%, 80%, profit = 10, 20% ∴ SP = 40 × 100/80 = 50, profit = 40/80 × 70 = 10]*

9  A jacket which cost the retailer $40 is sold at a profit of 20% on the selling price. The profit is therefore

$ 10

10  The term $x^{-\frac{3}{4}}$ equals

A $\dfrac{1}{\sqrt[4]{x^3}}$  B $\dfrac{3}{x^4}$  C $\dfrac{1}{\sqrt[3]{x^4}}$  D $\dfrac{4}{x^3}$

# 2 Basic mathematics 2

1  The expression $\dfrac{x^8}{x^7}$ can be expressed as

A −1  B $x^{-1}$   C x  D $x^{8/7}$

2  A product was previously sold for $2.60 per kg, but is now sold for $4 for 2 kgs. The percentage reduction per kg is closest to

A 23  B 30  C 35  D 53

3  The graph of Y = 2X is shown by which of the following lines?

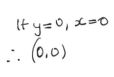
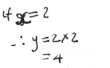

*[Handwritten: If y = 0, x = 0 ∴ (0,0); If x = 2 ∴ y = 2×2 = 4 ∴ (2,4); x y ∴ ans (0,0) (2,4)]*

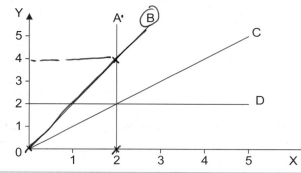

4  In which of the following ways could the expression $(x^4)^{-4}$ be written?

☐ $4\sqrt{x^4}$

☐ $\dfrac{1}{x^{16}}$

☐ $16\sqrt{x}$

☐ $x^{16}$

5  In the formula $Q = \sqrt{\dfrac{2CD}{Ch}}$ , if C = $20, D = 24,000 and Q = 400, then Ch is closest in value to

A $1.73  B $2.45  C $6.00  D $12.00

BPP PROFESSIONAL EDUCATION

6   A store sells oranges either for 39c per kg, or in bulk at $7 per 22 kg bag. The percentage saving (per kg) from buying a 22 kg bag is closest to

    A 7.2%          B 17.9%          C 18.4%          D 22.6%

7   Fred makes a number of deliveries in a week. In a week where his average journey was 267 miles, his individual journey distances, in miles, were

286, 192, x, 307, 185, y, 94

When x = 4y, the value of x is [         ]

*[handwritten: 1st mlc = 6/10 × 100 = 60; 2nd mlc = 3/10 × 100 = 30; 3rd mlc = 1/10 × 100 = 10 / 100]*

8   A company uses any one of three machines to produce 'identical' hinges. The output of hinges from the three machines is in the ratio 6:3:1. The percentage of defects is 5, 20 and 10 respectively. The overall percentage of defects is closest to

*[handwritten: 6+3+1 = 10; 5+20+10 = 35]*

    A 8            B 9            C 10            D 11

9   X% of 200 equals

*[handwritten: 1st mlc: over 60 hinges, 5% defect = 60 × 3/100 = 3; 20% defect 2nd mlc = 30 × 20/100 = 6; 10% defect of 3rd mlc = 10 × 10/100 = 1 / 10]*

    A $\dfrac{X}{20,000}$          B $\dfrac{X}{200}$          C $\dfrac{X}{2}$          D 2X

10   Sylvia pays no tax on the first $3,500 of her earnings and then

[ *770* ] 22%

[      ] 23%

[      ] 24%

[      ] 25%

tax on the remainder of her earnings. She wishes to have gross earnings of $18,435 and wishes to have $15,000 net of tax earnings.

# 3 Basic mathematics 3

1   If cost = 3,800 − 24P and revenue = 410P − 22P², where P = price per unit, how would you express profit per unit (in terms of price)?

(Profit = Revenue − cost)

    A       $434P - 22P^2 - 3,800$

    B       $434P - 22P^2 + 3,800$

    C       $22P^2 - 434P + 3,800$

    D       $386P - 22P^2 - 3,800$

2     If demand D = 60 – 5P, how is price (P) expressed in terms of D?

A     P = 12 – D
B     P = 12 – D/5
C     P = 12 + D/5
D     P = D/55

3     If $y^2 = x^2 - 3x + 25$, what is the value of y if x = 3?

        [      ]

4     If the price of a product (P) = 250 – D/1.2 where D = demand of the product, how is the demand of the product expressed in terms of P, the price?

A     D = 300 + 1.2P
B     D = 300 – P
C     D = 1.2P – 300
D     D = 300 – 1.2P

5     If $y^{1/3} = x^3 - 3x^2 + 22x - 102$, what is the value of y when x = 4?

        [      ]

6     When x = 3, what is the value (to two decimal places) of the expression below?

     $(X^{-0.5})^{-5}$

        [      ]

7     The expression $(x^{-3})^{-4}$ equals

A $1/x^{12}$          B $4\sqrt{x^{-3}}$         C $x^{-1}$         D $x^{12}$

8     An article in a sales catalogue is priced at $125 including sales tax at 17.5%. The price excluding sales tax to the nearest cent is

     [ $     ]

9     Three years ago a retailer sold product TS for $30 each. At the end of the first year he increased the price by 5% and at the end of the second year by a further 6%. At the end of the third year the selling price was $35.73 each. The percentage price change in year 3 was

     [      ] %

10    The expression $\dfrac{x^3}{x^4}$ can be expressed as

A –1          B $x^{-1}$         C x         D $x^{3/4}$

# 4 Basic mathematics 4

1    When x = 3 the value (to 2 decimal places) of $(x^{-0.75})^{-7}$ = [ ]

2    An item priced at $90.68, including local sales tax at 18%, is reduced in a sale by 20%. The new price before sales tax is added is $61.50 (to 2 decimal places).

   True  [ ]

   False [ ]

3    Total sales of Company A are $350,000 and total sales of Company B are $700,000. The ratio of Company A sales to Company B sales (to the nearest whole number) is [ ] to [ ].

4    An article in a sales catalogue is priced at $289, including sales tax at 17.5%. The price, excluding sales tax, to the nearest cent, is $ [ ]

5    The numeric value of the expression $\dfrac{(x^3)^4}{x^7}$ when    x = 3 is [ ]

                                                        x = 4 is [ ]

6    Three years ago a garden centre sold hanging baskets for $27.50 each. At the end of the first year they increased the price by 8% and at the end of the second year by a further 4%. At the end of the third year the selling price was $30.27 each. The percentage price change in year three was [ ] %.

7    At a sales tax rate of 12½%, an article sells for 48c, including sales tax. If the sales tax rate increases to 17½%, which of the following are true?

   A    The new selling price to the nearest cent is 50p
   B    The new selling price to the nearest cent is 51c
   C    The cost of the article is 42c
   D    The cost of the article is 45c

8    In the formula $Q = \sqrt{\dfrac{2DC}{PR}}$ , if Q = 80, C = 10, P = 6 and R = 0.2, then D, to the nearest unit, is [ ]

9    The expression $\dfrac{x^7}{x^8}$ can be expressed in which of the following ways?

   A    −1
   B    $x^{-1}$
   C    $1/x^2$
   D    7/8

10    The solution to the simultaneous equations:

5x + 3y = 13
3x − y = 12

| x | y |
|---|---|
|   |   |

# 5 Basic mathematics 5

1    An article in a sales catalogue is priced at $500 including sales tax at 17.5%. The price excluding sales tax to the nearest cent is $ [          ]

2    A greengrocer sells apples either for 35c per kg, or in bulk at $7 per 25 kg bag. The percentage saving (per kg) from buying a 25 kg bag is closest to

A    7.0%
B    8.8%
C    20.0%
D    25.0%

The correct answer is option [          ]

3    If $y^2 = x^2 − 4x + 36$ and if $x = 4$, the value of y is [          ]

4    A skirt which cost the retailer $200 is sold at a profit of 25% on the selling price. The profit (to 2 decimal places) is $ [          ]

5    The telephone costs of a company last year were $10,000, **including** sales tax at 17.5%. It has been decided to allocate 60% of these telephone costs, **excluding** sales tax, to Central Administration and to allocate 30% **of the remainder, excluding** sales tax, to Finance.

The telephone costs (to the nearest $) to be allocated to Finance will be closest to $ [          ]

6    The formula $Q = \sqrt{\dfrac{2CD}{H}}$ is used in stock control.

When the formula is rearranged, with H as the subject, H equals

A    $\dfrac{2CD}{Q^2}$

B    $\dfrac{4CD}{Q^2}$

C    $\sqrt{\dfrac{2CD}{Q}}$

D    $\dfrac{2CD}{Q}$

7 The equations of two straight lines are given below:

$Y = 7 + X$
$Y = 9 + 3X$

These lines intersect where the (X, Y) co-ordinates are equal to

| X | Y |
|---|---|
|   |   |

8 Katie and Jamie share out a certain sum of money in the ratio 3:5 and Katie ends up with $9.

How much money was shared out in the first place? $ [        ]

How much would have been shared out if Katie had got $9 and the ratio had been 5:3 instead of 3:5? $ [        ]

State your answers to 2 decimal places.

9 There are 45 students in a classroom, 24 of whom have dark hair. What proportion of the students (to 4 decimal places) do **not** have dark hair?

A    0.4667
B    0.5334
C    0.4666
D    0.5333

10 The sum of the squares of two numbers is 740 and the difference between the 2 numbers is 4.

x = [        ] or [        ]

y = [        ] or [        ]

State your answers to 2 decimal places.

> ## Probability
>
> Questions 6 to 12 cover probability, the subject of Part B of the BPP Study Text for C3

# 6 Probability 1

1   In a student survey, 40% of the students are male and 80% are CIMA candidates.  The probability that a student chosen at random is either female or a CIMA candidate is

  A  0.48            B  0.52            C  0.60            D  0.92

2   A sample of 100 companies has been analysed by size and whether they pay invoices promptly. The sample has been cross-tabulated into *large/small* against *fast payers/slow payers*. 60 of the companies are classified as *large* of which 40 are *slow payers*. In total, 30 of all the companies are *fast payers*.

  The probability that a company chosen at random is a *fast paying small company* is

  A 0.10             B 0.20             C 0.30             D 0.40

3   Next year, sales may rise, fall or remain the same as this year, with the following respective probabilities: 0.56, 0.23 and 0.21.

  The probability of sales remaining the same or falling is

  A  0.05            B  0.12            C  0.13            D  0.44

4   In a group of 100 CIMA students, 30 are male, 55 are studying for the Certificate Level and 6 of the male students are not studying for the Certificate Level. A student chosen at random is female. What is the probability that she is not studying for the Certificate Level?

  A  0.70            B  0.56            C  0.20            D  0.45

5   In a survey of a housing estate, 30% of tenants had satellite television and 80% had video recorders. The probability that a household chosen at random had either a satellite television or a video recorder is

  A  0.24            B  0.30            C  0.80            D  0.86

6   In a survey, 60% of households have a digital camera and 80% have a DVD player.

  The probability that a household chosen at random has either a digital camera or a DVD player is

  [        ]  (to 2 decimal places)

7   From past records it is known that 15% of items from a production line are defective. If two items are selected at random, the probability (to 2 decimal places) that only one is defective is [        ]

8   A sales representative makes calls to three separate unrelated customers. The chance of making a sale at any one of them is 80%. The probability (to the nearest percent) that a sale is made on the third call only is [        ] %.

9   A sales representative visits two independent firms – L and W. The probability of making a sale at L is 0.3 and the probability of making a sale at W is 0.4.

The probability (to 2 decimal places) of making no sale at all is [        ]

10  Invoices produced within a firm are known to contain errors: 3% contain a very serious error, 6% a serious error and 12% a minor error.

The probability that a randomly-chosen invoice will have a serious error or a minor error is

A    0.21
B    0.18
C    0.09
D    0.06

# 7 Probability 2

$\frac{1}{2} \times 50,000 = 25000$
$\frac{1}{3} \times 90,000 = 30,000$
$\frac{1}{5} \times 100,000 = 20,000$
$\overline{75,000}$

1   A company is bidding for three contracts which are awarded independently of each other. The board estimates its chances of winning contract X as 50%, of winning contract Y as 1 in 3, and of winning contract Z as 1 in 5. The profits from X, Y and Z are estimated to be $50,000, $90,000 and $100,000 respectively.

The **expected value** to the company of the profits from all three contracts will be ($'000) E note  .sm=75.

[ 75 000 ]

2   A company recommends its employees to have free influenza vaccinations but only 50% do so. The effectiveness of the vaccine is known to be 90%. The probability of any non-vaccinated employee getting influenza by chance is 0.3. An employee catches influenza. What is the probability that she was vaccinated?

A    0.05
B    0.10
C    0.25
D    None of the values

3   Because of the nature of a process, only two outputs are possible from a process.  Probabilities of the outputs are as follows:

| Output | Probability |
|--------|-------------|
| 10     | 0.4         |
| 16     | 0.6         |

Daily production is independent.

The probability that over a two-day period, the total output will be 26 is [        ]

State your answer to 2 decimal places.

4    Three sales representatives – J, K and L – rate their (independent) chances of achieving certain levels of sales as follows.

| Possible sales | | $10,000 | $20,000 | $30,000 | |
| --- | --- | --- | --- | --- | --- |
| J | Probability | 0.3 | 0.5 | 0.2 | 3000 |
| K | Probability | 0.3 | 0.4 | 0.3 | 3000 |
| L | Probability | 0.2 | 0.6 | 0.2 | 2000 |

(For example, J rates her chances of selling $20,000 worth of business as 'fifty-fifty' and K has a 30% chance of selling $30,000 worth.)

On this evidence, the highest expected sales will be from

A    J alone
B    K alone
C    L alone
D    K and L

5    If one card is drawn from a normal pack of 52 playing cards, what is the probability of getting a king or a heart?

A    1/52
B    1/13
C    1/4
D    4/13

6    A die is thrown and a coin is tossed simultaneously. What is the probability of throwing a 3 and getting tails on the coin?

A    1/2
B    1/3
C    1/6
D    1/12

# The following data is required for questions 7, 8 and 9

A cosmetics company has developed a new anti-dandruff shampoo which is being tested on volunteers. 70% of the volunteers have used the shampoo whereas the others have used a normal shampoo, believing it to be the new anti-dandruff shampoo. 2/7 of those using the new shampoo showed no improvement whereas 1/3 of those using the normal shampoo has less dandruff.

7    A volunteer shows some improvement. What is the probability that he used the normal shampoo?

A    10/60
B    10/100
C    50/60
D    10/30

8 A volunteer shows no improvement. What is the probability that he used the new shampoo?

A  20/70
B  20/40
C  20/100
D  20/30

9 A volunteer used the new shampoo. What is the probability that he shows some improvement?

A  50/70
B  50/100
C  50/60
D  60/100

10 In a student survey, 70% of the students are female and 60% are CIMA candidates. The probability that a student chosen at random is either female or a CIMA candidate is

A  0.42
B  0.70
C  0.88
D  1.00

# 8 Probability 3

1 A company must decide between two projects – Project A and Project B. The profits that might be generated from each project are as follows.

| | Project A | | | Project B | |
|---|---|---|---|---|---|
| | Probability | Profit | | Probability | Profit/(loss) |
| | | $ | | | $ |
| | 0.45 | 4,000 | | 0.64 | 8,000 |
| | 0.55 | 2,000 | | 0.36 | (1,000) |

Which project should be chosen and what is the associated expected value of profit?

| | Project | Expected profit |
|---|---|---|
| | | $ |
| A | A | 2,900 |
| B | A | 3,000 |
| C | B | 4,760 |
| D | B | 5,480 |

proj A $= (0.45 \times 4000) + (0.55 \times 2000) = 2900$

proj B $= (0.64 \times 8000) + (0.36 \times -1,000) = 5120$
$-360$
$4760$

∴ B has a > EPv than A.

Ans C.

# The following data is required for questions 2, 3 and 4

A pharmaceutical company has developed a new migraine headache tablet which is being tested on volunteers. 80% of the volunteers have been given the new tablets whilst the others have been given a placebo (a 'blank' tablet), believing it to be the new tablet. ¼ of those using the new tablet reported no improvement in their headaches whereas 1/10 of those using the placebo had less headaches.

2    A volunteer shows no improvement. What is the probability that he used the placebo? State your answer to two decimal places.

   A  0.18             B  0.47             C  0.90             D  0.53

3    A volunteer has less headaches. What is the probability that he used the new tablets? (Answer to two decimal places.)

   A  0.60             B  0.75             C  0.97             D  1.00

4    A volunteer used the placebo. What is the probability that he had less headaches? (Answer to two decimal places.)

   A  0.02             B  0.03             C  0.10             D  0.20

5    A company is about to launch a new product. It has been predicted that, in each of the first two years, there are two possible levels of sales, high or low. The probability of sales being high in the first year is 0.3. If the first year's sales are high, the probability of high sales in the second year is 0.8. If sales are low in the first year, the probability of high sales in the second year is 0.3.

   The probability of low sales in both years is [          ] (to 2 decimal places)

6    A company is deciding which one of four products to launch. The expected payoff from each of the products is shown below.

|        |             | Profit          |                   |                    |                   |
|--------|-------------|-----------------|-------------------|--------------------|-------------------|
| Demand | Probability | Type I $'000    | Type II $'000     | Type III $'000     | Type IV $'000     |
| High   | 0.5         | 20              | 50                | 40                 | 30                |
| Medium | 0.3         | 20              | 0                 | 20                 | 20                |
| Low    | 0.2         | 20              | (50)              | 0                  | 10                |

   Complete the following table.

| Type | Expected profit $'000 |
|------|-----------------------|
| I    |                       |
| II   |                       |
| III  |                       |
| IV   |                       |

   If the company wants to maximise the expected profit it should launch Type [          ]

7     With reference to events A and B, how would you best describe mutually exclusive outcomes?

     A     A and B are dependent events
     B     A and B are independent events
     C     The occurrence of event A excludes the possibility of event B from happening
     D     Events A and B happen at the same time

8     Which of the following formulae represent the general rule of multiplication?

     A     $P(A \text{ and } B) = P(A) \times P(B/A)$
     B     $P(A \text{ and } B) = P(A) \times P(B)$
     C     $P(A \text{ or } B) = P(A) + P(B) - P(A \text{ and } B)$
     D     $P(A \text{ or } B) = P(A) + P(B)$

9     In a survey of people living in a town, 40% of residents went abroad on holiday last year and 55% of residents bought a new car. The probability that a resident chosen at random either went abroad on holiday or bought a new car is

     A     0.22
     B     0.55
     C     0.73
     D     0.95

10    Next year, sales at Company X may rise, fall or remain the same as this year, with the following respective probabilities: 0.44, 0.38 and 0.18. The probability of sales remaining the same or rising is

     A     0.08
     B     0.54
     C     0.56
     D     0.62

# 9 Probability 4

## The following data is required for questions 1, 2 and 3

High Street Shoe Store has analysed the expenditure habits of a random sample of 500 of its customers and produced the following table showing the number of customers in each category:

|  | Age of customer | | |
|---|---|---|---|
|  | Under 21 | 21 and over | Total |
| Expenditure |  |  |  |
| Under $25 | 55 | 205 | 260 |
| $25 to $50 | 125 | 80 | 205 |
| Over $50 | 10 | 25 | 35 |
|  | 190 | 310 | 500 |

1    The probability that a customer is aged under 21 *and* spent between $25 and $50 is [                    ]

State your answer to 2 decimal places.

2    If a customer is aged under 21, the probability that he spent between $25 and $50 is:

[                    ]

State your answer to 2 decimal places.

3    The probability that a customer who spent between $25 and $50 is aged under 21 is: [                    ]

State your answer to 2 decimal places.

4    The independent probabilities that the three sections of an accounts department will encounter one computer error in a week are 0.2, 0.4 and 0.6 respectively. There is never more than one computer error encountered by any one section in a week.

The probability that there will be one and only one computer error is

A  0.192              B  0.400              C  0.464              D  0.808

5    The probability of rain tomorrow is 0.3. The probability of rain the day after is 0.6 if it rains tomorrow, but 0.2 if it does not rain tomorrow. What is the probability that it will be dry the day after tomorrow?

A  0.24               B  0.40               C  0.56               D  0.68

6    Product Beta is made in two stages. At the first stage it is processed by one of four machines – T, V, W, or X – with equal probability. At the second stage it is processed by one of two machines – Y or Z – and is twice as likely to go through Z as this machine works twice as quickly.

The probability that an item is processed on T or Y is:

A    $\frac{1}{12}$

B    $\frac{2}{7}$

C    $\frac{1}{2}$

D    $\frac{7}{12}$

7    A company must decide between two projects – Project Alpha and Project Beta. The profits that might be generated from each project are as follows.

| Project Alpha | | Project Beta | |
|---|---|---|---|
| *Probability* | *Profit* | *Probability* | *Profit* |
| 0.5 | $50,000 | 0.6 | $60,000 |
| 0.5 | $20,000 | 0.4 | $10,000 |

Which project should the company choose?

A    Project Alpha
B    Project Beta
C    Both projects
D    Neither project

8    In a consumer survey, 80% of the consumers are female and 30% go shopping every Saturday. The probability that a consumer chosen at random is either male, or goes shopping every Saturday is [      ] to 2 decimal places.

9    A company is bidding for three contracts which are awarded independently of each other. The board estimates its chances of winning Contract A as 50%, of winning Contract B as 1 in 5 and of winning Contract C as 1 in 3. The profits from A, B and C are estimated to be $500,000, $800,000 and $900,000 respectively.

The expected value to the company of the profits from all three contracts will be closest to:

A    $300,000
B    $710,000
C    $733,000
D    $900,000

10    In a large business school, 55% of the students are women and 10% of the students are mathematicians. There is no correlation between gender and subject. If two students are chosen at random, the probability that each of them is a woman or a mathematician (to the nearest percent) is [      ] %

# 10 Probability 5

1    Production next year may increase, stay the same or decline, with probabilities 0.55, 0.30 and 0.15 respectively. What is the probability of production remaining the same or falling?

A    0.45
B    0.045
C    0.405
D    0.55

2    The train you need to catch is in the station, waiting to leave. The probabilities of when it will leave are shown below.

|  | Probability |
|---|---|
| On time | 0.30 |
| 1 minute late | 0.25 |
| 2 minutes late | 0.20 |
| 3 minutes late | 0.15 |
| 4 minutes late | 0.10 |
|  | 1.00 |

You are running late for the train and you are going to arrive at the train two minutes late. What is the probability you will miss the train?

A    0.20
B    0.45
C    0.55
D    0.75

3    If two outcomes, X and Y are both mutually exclusive and outcomes of independent events, it follows that

A    At least one of them is impossible
B    At least one of them must happen
C    They are both impossible
D    Their probabilities add up to 1

4    Singers Ltd is launching a new sewing machine. With television advertising, sales are estimated to achieve the following levels, with associated probabilities.

| Sales Units | Probability |
|---|---|
| 1,000 | 0.3 |
| 4,000 | 0.5 |
| 8,000 | 0.2 |

What is the expected level of sales?

A  4,000          B  4,333          C  13,000          D  3,900

5    A saleswoman visits areas A, B and C in the ratio 2:1:1. The probabilities that her visits will be successful are 0.35, 0.15 and 0.12 respectively. Find the expected probability that any given visit is successful.

A  0.62          B  0.2067          C  0.0063          D  0.2425

6    A firm employs three sales staff and the probabilities that they will make a sale on a given day are 0.4, 0.45 and 0.5 respectively. Each person never makes more than one sale per day and acts independently of the others. Find the probability that at least one sale is made on a particular day.

A  0.09          B  0.165          C  0.835          D  0.5

7    Four coins are tossed. The probability of getting precisely three heads is [        ] to 2 decimal places.

8    A project is thought to have a 0.6 probability of making a profit of $3,000 and a 0.4 probability of making a profit of $1,500. Find the change in expected profit if the probabilities actually turn out to be 0.55 and 0.45 respectively.

    A     A gain of $75
    B     A fall of $150
    C     A fall of $75
    D     A fall of $225

9    The number of units of a particular product sold every day varies, with 100, 200, 300 or 400 units being sold with probabilities 0.23, 0.29, 0.42 and 0.06 respectively. Find the expected daily sales.

    A  231                 B  250                 C  126                 D  300

10   The independent probabilities that an error will be made on any one day by three different workers are 15%, 20% and 25% respectively.

The probability that there will be one error made on any particular day is [          ] %

State your answer to 1 decimal place.

# 11 Probability 6

1    Three independent experts have estimated the probability of a company's future annual sales:

| Sales | High ($1m) | Medium ($0.5m) | Low ($0.25m) |
|-------|-----------|----------------|--------------|
| Expert W | 0.2 | 0.3 | 0.5 |
| Expert X | 0.1 | 0.4 | 0.5 |
| Expert Y | 0.1 | 0.6 | 0.3 |

The highest expected value for the company's estimated annual sales is given by

| | |
|---|---|
| [     ] | W only |
| [     ] | X only |
| [     ] | Y only |
| [     ] | Both W and Y |

2    Three people are carrying out independent functions during an internal audit. It is known that in each of the three separate areas being investigated there is a serious error. From past experience, it is estimated that the (independent) chances of the individuals finding the serious error in their area are 0.8, 0.7 and 0.6.

The probability that **at least one** of the serious errors will be found is [          ] (to 3 decimal places)

3    If one card is drawn from a normal pack of 52 playing cards, what is the probability of getting a queen or a heart?

Probability

| Queen | Heart | Queen of hearts | Queen or heart |
|-------|-------|-----------------|----------------|
|       |       |                 |                |

## The following information relates to questions 4 – 6

A company sells and manufactures product SX. The selling price of the product is $10 per unit and estimates of demand and variable costs of sales are as follows.

| Probability | Demand | Probability | Variable cost per unit |
|-------------|--------|-------------|------------------------|
|             | Units  |             | $                      |
| 0.1         | 5,000  | 0.1         | 3.00                   |
| 0.6         | 6,000  | 0.5         | 3.50                   |
| 0.3         | 8,000  | 0.3         | 4.00                   |
|             |        | 0.1         | 4.50                   |

The unit variable costs do not depend on the volume of sales.

Fixed costs will be $30,000.

4    EV of demand = [          ] units

5    EV of unit variable costs = $ [          ] (to 2 decimal places)

6    EV of profit = $ [          ]

7    A sales manager has recorded the following demand for a product over the last 100 days.

| Daily demand | Number of days |
|--------------|----------------|
| Units        |                |
| 500          | 14             |
| 510          | 18             |
| 520          | 19             |
| 530          | 21             |
| 540          | 28             |

If these data are representative of the normal pattern of sales, the probability of a daily demand of 520 units is [          ] % (to 1 decimal place).

## The following data relate to questions 8, 9 and 10

A pet food company has developed a low-fat dog food designed to make overweight dogs lose weight. In field tests on 1,000 dogs, some dogs ate the new food and some a normal dog food. The results of the tests were as follows.

|  | Given low-fat food | Given normal food |
|---|---|---|
| Lost weight | 200 | 250 |
| No weight loss | 300 | 250 |

8  The probability that a dog has lost weight is [_____] (to 2 decimal places).

9  The conditional probability that a dog has lost weight, given that it received low-fat food is [_____] (to 2 decimal places).

10  The conditional probability that a dog was given the normal food, given that it lost weight is [_____] (to 2 decimal places).

# 12 Probability 7

## The data below relate to questions 1 and 2

A porcelain manufacturer has three assembly lines (X, Y and Z) producing decorative plates. An inspector samples finished plates from the assembly lines in the ratio 1X, 2Y, 3Z.

Analysis of past inspection records suggests that the defective rates from the assembly lines are:

| X | Y | Z |
|---|---|---|
| 5% | 10% | 30% |

During a shift the inspector examines 240 plates.

1  Complete the following table which shows the number of plates the inspector samples from each assembly line.

| Assembly line | Number of plates sampled |
|---|---|
| X | [_____] |
| Y | [_____] |
| Z | [_____] |

2  The probability that a plate sampled is defective is [_____] (to 3 decimal places).

## The following data relate to questions 3 and 4

A pharmaceutical company has developed a new headache treatment which is being field tested on 1,000 volunteers. In a test some volunteers have received the treatment and some a placebo (a harmless neutral substance). The results of the test are as follows.

|  | Treatment received | Placebo received | Total |
|---|---|---|---|
| Some improvement | 600 | 125 | 725 |
| No improvement | 150 | 125 | 275 |
|  | 750 | 250 | 1,000 |

3   The probability that a volunteer has shown some improvement is [          ] (to 3 decimal places)

4   The conditional probability that a volunteer has received the treatment given that no improvement has been observed is [          ] (to 3 decimal places)

## The following data relate to questions 5 and 6

A travel agent keeps a stock of holiday brochures. Currently there is a total of 500 brochures in stock, as follows: 285 for European holidays, 90 for American holidays, 110 for Asian holidays and 15 for African holidays. A brochure is selected at random.

5   The probability that an African brochure is **not** selected is [          ] %

6   The probability that neither an American nor an Asian brochure is selected is [          ] %

7   A company sells much of its output on credit. It employs a credit rating agency and experience shows that of those customers rated a good credit risk, 90% settle their debts without difficulty. The company does not extend credit to those rated a bad credit risk.

The credit rating agency does not have information on all would-be customers, however. Experience shows that of those customers who are given credit without a check from the credit rating agency, 80% settle their debts without difficulty. 60% of customers are not checked by the credit rating agency.

The probability that a customer who defaults was actually checked by a credit rating agency is [          ] (to 2 decimal places).

8   A company is about to launch a new product. It has been predicted that, in each of the first two years, there are two possible levels of sales, high or low. The probability of sales being high in the first year is 0.3. If the first year's sales are high, the probability of high sales in the second year is 0.9. If sales are low in the first year, the probability of high sales in the second year is 0.2.

The probability of low sales in both years is:

A    0.8
B    0.56
C    0.90
D    1.5

9    A company is deciding which one of four products to launch. The expected payoff from each of the products is shown below.

| Demand | Probability | Type W $000 | Profit Type X $000 | Type Y $000 | Type Z $000 |
|--------|-------------|-------------|--------------------|-------------|-------------|
| High   | 0.5         | 20          | 50                 | 40          | 30          |
| Medium | 0.3         | 20          | 0                  | 20          | 20          |
| Low    | 0.2         | 20          | (50)               | 0           | 10          |

If the company wants to maximise the expected profit it should launch:

A    Type W
B    Type X
C    Type Y
D    Type Z

10  What is illustrated in this diagram?

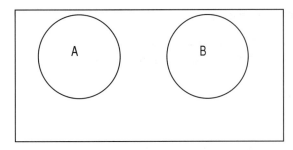

A    A Venn diagram illustrating complementary outcomes
B    A pie chart
C    A Venn diagram illustrating two mutually exclusive outcomes
D    A Pareto chart

## Summarising and analysing data

Questions 13 to 21 cover summarising and analysing data, the subject of Part C of the BPP Study Text for C3

# 13 Summarising and analysing data 1

1    When forecasting future costs, a manager puts a margin of 5% either side of each cost. If the upper estimate of a particular cost is stated as $21.50, then the mid-point of the estimate, to two decimal places, is

2    In 1994, a price index based on 1980 = 100 stood at 126. In that year it was re-based at 1994 = 100. By 1996, the new index stood at 109. For a continuous estimate of price changes since 1980, the new index may be expressed, to two decimal places, in terms of the old as

A    85.51
B    100
C    135.00
D    137.34

3    The price index for a commodity in the current year is 135 (base year = 100). The current price for the commodity is $55.35 per kg.

What was the price per kg in the base year?

4    Over a period a firm made purchases of $400, $500, $550 and $600 on items, the unit costs of which were $10.00, $12.50, $11.00 and $12.00 respectively.

To the nearest cent, the average price paid per item was

$$\frac{\Sigma tp}{\Sigma t}$$

$= 10x$

| Purchases | Unit cost |
|-----------|-----------|
| 400       | 10.00     |
| 500       | 12.50     |
| 550       | 11.00     |
| 600       | 12.00     |

5    The following scores are observed for the times taken to complete a task, in minutes.

12, 34, 14, 15, 21, 24, 9, 17, 11, 8

The median score is

8, 9, 11, 12, 14, 15, 17, 21, 24, 34

$= \frac{10}{2} = 5$

A·    14.00
B     14.10
C     14.50
D     16.50

6   Sales for the first five months of the year averaged $8,200 per month.

For the last four months of the year sales averaged $8,500 per month.

If sales for the year totalled $102,000, the average for the sixth, seventh and eighth months must be

A   $8,500
B   $9,000
C   $9,500
D   $10,200

7   The median of the scores 34, 23, 78, 12, 56, 43, 28, 9, 24 and 87 is

A   26
B   28
C   31
D   34

8   In a histogram, one class is three quarters of the width of the remaining classes.

If the score in that class is 21, the correct height to plot on the histogram is

9   In a histogram in which one class interval is one and a half times as wide as the remaining classes, the height to be plotted in relation to the frequency for that class is

Ⓐ   × 0.67      $1\frac{1}{2} \times width$
B   × 0.75      ie $\frac{1}{1.5} = 0.67$.
C   × 1.00
D   × 1.50

10  When the mean purchase price of 10 units at 50c, 10 units at 70c, and 20 units at Xc is 80c, the value of X is

A   60        $\bar{x} = \frac{\Sigma fx}{\Sigma f}$      10   50   500
B   67                                                    10   70   700
C   75        $80 = \frac{1200 + 20x}{40}$               20   xc   20xc
Ⓓ   100                                                        80c

∴  3200 = 1200 + 20x
   2000 = 20x   ∴ x = 100¢

# 14 Summarising and analysing data 2

1   The common class width in a histogram is $20. One class has a non-standard class width and an actual frequency of 100. If the score plotted is 80, what is the width of the non-standard class?

A   $4
B   $16
C   $20
D   $25

2    An ogive is another name for a histogram.

    True    [                ]
    False   [                ]

3    A histogram uses a set of rectangles to represent a grouped frequency table. To be correctly presented, the histogram must show the relationship of the rectangles to the frequencies by reference to the

    A    Height
    B    Area
    C    Width
    D    Diagonal

    of each rectangle.

4    In a histogram, the common class width is $10.00.  For analysis purposes, the analyst has set one class at $12.50 and the frequency recorded is 50 respondents.  To maintain the accuracy of the histogram identify the frequency which must be plotted on the y axis of the histogram shown below.

    [                ]

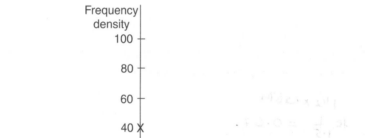

5    The following table shows the typical salary of part qualified management accountants in five different regions of England.

| Area | Typical salary |
| --- | --- |
|  | $ |
| South-east | 21,500 |
| Midlands | 20,800 |
| North-east | 18,200 |
| North-west | 17,500 |
| South-west | 16,700 |

    The best diagram to draw to highlight the differences between areas is

    A    A pie diagram
    B    A multiple bar chart
    C    A percentage component bar chart
    D    A simple bar chart

6    An index-linked pension of $10,000 a year became payable on 1 January 1998. Details of the index of Retail Prices are shown below.

*Index of Retail Prices each January (January 1993 = 100)*

| 1993 | 1997 | 1998 | 1999 | 2000 |
|------|------|------|------|------|
| 100  | 130.2 | 135.6 | 137.9 | 142.0 |

The annual pension payable from 1 January 2000 is closest to

A  $10,297          B  $10,472          C  $10,906          D  $13,560

7    The arithmetic mean of the following ten invoice values is $20:

$X,  $15,  $22,  $14,  $21,  $15,  $20,  $18,  $27,  $X.

Therefore $X equals

A  $15          B  $19          C  $24          D  $48

8    A factory employs staff in four departments for which the average (mean) wage per employee per week is as follows.

| Department | W | X | Y | Z |
|------------|-----|------|-----|-----|
| Mean wage | $50 | $100 | $70 | $80 |
| Number of employees | 20 | 5 | 10 | 5 |

The average (mean) wage per employee per week in this factory is

A  $50          B  $65          C  $70          D  $75

9    A car travels 20 miles at 30 mph, then 10 miles at 60 mph.

The mean speed for the whole journey of 30 miles is closest to (mph)

A  36          B  40          C  42          D  45

10   The average (mean) cost of producing 10 units of X is $1, of producing 20 units of Y is $2 and of producing 30 units of Z is $3. The average (mean) unit cost of producing all items is closest to:

A  $2          B  $2.25          C  $2.33          D  $2.50

# 15 Summarising and analysing data 3

1    A Normal distribution has a mean of 55 and a variance of 14.44. The probability of a score of 59 or more is approximately

A    0.15
B    0.35
C    0.50
D    0.85

## QUESTIONS

**2** A normal distribution has a mean of 75 and a variance of 25.

The upper quartile of this distribution is therefore

A 58.25
B 71.65
C 78.35
D 91.75

**3** A normal distribution has a mean of 150, and a standard deviation of 20. 80% of the distribution is below (approximately)

A 158
B 170
C 161
D 167

*note* $= 150$
$\underline{-\ 20}$
$130$
$= \underline{-100}$
$30$

↗80%

$\therefore 0.3 \text{ or } 30\% = 0.84 \text{ i.e } z\text{-score}$

$z = \dfrac{x - u}{\sigma} = 0.84 = \dfrac{x - 150}{20}$

$0.84 \times 20 = x - 150$
$0.84 \times 20 + 150 = x$
$\therefore x = 166.8 \doteq 167$

**4** A normal distribution is to be split into four equal areas, two to the right of Z = 0 and two to the left of Z = 0 (Z = 0 at the mean). Using normal distribution tables, the |Z| value that splits the area in this way is closest to

A 0.0987
B 0.1915
C 0.3333
D 0.675099

**5** Production of aluminium tubes is normally distributed with a mean length of 50 cm and a standard deviation of 5 cm. The percentage of tubes at least 57 cm long is closest to

A 8%
B 42%
C 58%
D 92%

$z = \dfrac{x - \mu}{\sigma} \quad \dfrac{57 - 50}{5} = \dfrac{7}{5} = 1.4$

**6** A normal distribution has a mean of 60 and a variance of 25. The probability of a score of 72 or more is approximately (to 4 decimal places)

**7** A normal distribution has a mean of 150 and a variance of 6,944. What percentage of the population is less than 210? (Give your answer to two decimal places.)

A 23.58%     B 26.42%     C 72.00%     D 76.42%

**8** A normal distribution has a mean of 650 and a variance of 100.

The upper quartile of this distribution is therefore

A 643.3     B 656.7     C 717.0     D 812.5

BPP
PROFESSIONAL EDUCATION

9 A normal distribution is to be split into eight equal areas, four to the right of Z = 0 and four to the left of Z = 0 (Z = 0 at the mean). Using normal distribution tables, the IZI value that splits the area in this way is closest to

A  0.28              B  0.30              C  0.32              D  0.34

10 The weights of elephants are normally distributed. The mean weight is 5,200kg and the standard deviation is 430kg. What is the probability of an elephant weighing more than 6,000kg?

A  0.0314            B  0.2343            C  0.4686            D  0.9686

# 16 Summarising and analysing data 4

1 The following series has a base date of 20X0.

|        | 20X0 | 20X1 | 20X2 | 20X3 | 20X4 | 20X5 |
|--------|------|------|------|------|------|------|
| Index  | 100  | 104  | 107  | 109  | 110  | 111  |

The base date of 20X0 is now considered to be out of date and when the time series is rebased so that it has a base date of 20X4, the index for the year 20X2 is:

2 You have just calculated for the last two six-monthly periods, the running costs of a factory, broken down into five categories. You are using a computer package which can produce ogives, pie-charts, time series graphs and scatter diagrams, amongst others. The graphics to illustrate best the relative sizes of the cost categories in this situation will be

A     Ogives
B     Pie-charts
C     Time series graphs
D     Scatter diagrams

3 Quality control of four independent production processes reveals the length of certain parts (in mm) to be as follows.

| Process | Mean | Standard deviation |
|---------|------|--------------------|
| W       | 100  | 10                 |
| X       | 40   | 5                  |
| Y       | 80   | 8                  |
| Z       | 150  | 12                 |

The process(es) with the largest relative variation, as measured by the coefficient of variation, is/are

A     X only
B     Z only
C     X and Y
D     W and Y

4   An accountant is selecting a sample of invoices for checking. The invoices are numbered 8, 13, 18, 23 and 28. What sampling interval was the accountant using?

A   5
B   8
C   10
D   18

5   A frequency distribution has a common class width of $5.00. For analysis purposes, the analyst has set one class at $7.50, this class has a corresponding frequency of 60. When drawing a histogram, the height of this class should be

    ┌──────────────┐
    │              │
    └──────────────┘

6   Eight people have the following individual weights, in kilograms:

| Person | kg |
|--------|-----|
| 1 | 97 |
| 2 | 105 |
| 3 | 53 |
| 4 | 69 |
| 5 | 84 |
| 6 | 59 |
| 7 | 94 |
| 8 | x |

    If the median weight is 88kgs, then x is ┌────────────┐ (to the nearest whole number).
                                             └────────────┘

7   The graph below is an ogive showing the value of invoices selected in a sample.

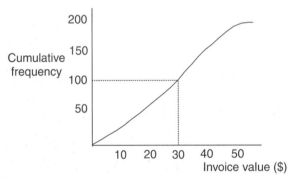

    Which of the following statements is true?

    A   There are 100 invoices with values of $30

    B   There are more than 100 invoices with values of $30 or more

    C   There are 100 invoices with values of less than $30

    D   There are more than 100 invoices with values of $30 or more and there are 100 invoices with values of less than $30

8   A company has recorded the following data on days lost through employee sickness in a year.

| Days lost per employee | | Number of employees |
| --- | --- | --- |
| At least | Less than | |
| 0 | 6 | 18 |
| 6 | 8 | 30 |
| 8 | 10 | 18 |
| 10 | 14 | 12 |

Which of the following histograms represents the data most accurately?

Graph 1

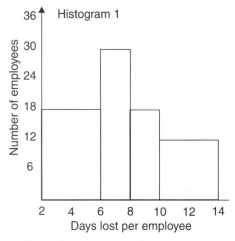

Graph 2

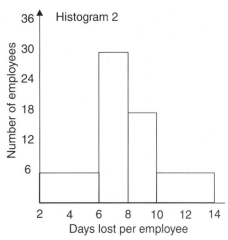

Graph 3

Graph 4

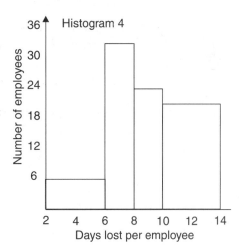

9   The arithmetic mean of nineteen numbers is 5. When a twentieth number, x, is added the overall mean becomes 7. What is the value of x?

```
┌──────────┐
│          │
└──────────┘
```

10    The number of responses from nine different direct mail advertisements is as follows.

35, 35, 10, 30, 35, 10, 15, 20, 35

The median number of responses from an advertisement was

[                    ]

# 17 Summarising and analysing data 5

1    The number of books read in the last month by a sample of the public interviewed is shown below.

| Number of books | Frequency<br>Number of people |
|:---:|:---:|
| 0 | 1 |
| 1 | 11 |
| 2 | 16 |
| 3 | 1 |
| 4 | 17 |
| 5 | 3 |
| 6 | 6 |
| | 55 |

What is the median number of books read in the last month?

[                    ]

2    A distribution where the mode has a lower value than the median and the median is less than the mean is known as

A    Positively skewed distribution
B    Normal distribution
C    Negatively skewed distribution
D    Continuous distribution

3    In a histogram in which one class interval is one and two thirds times as wide as the remaining classes, the height to be plotted (to 1 decimal place) in relation to the frequency for that class is [                    ]

4    An ogive is

A    a graph of a cumulative frequency distribution
B    a chart showing a non-linear relationship
C    another name for a histogram
D    a chart showing any linear relationship

5    A driver makes a number of deliveries in a week. In a week where his average journey was 267 miles, his individual journey distances, in miles, were

286, 192, x, 307, 185, y, 94

When y = 2.5x, the value of x is [         ]

---

6    The quartile deviation is half the difference between the lower and upper quartiles and is also known as the

    A     Inter-quartile range
    B     Semi-interquartile range
    C     Standard deviation
    D     Mode

---

7    In a positively skewed distribution

    A     the mean is larger than the median
    B     the mean is smaller than the median
    C     the mean is the same as the median
    D     the mean lies between the median and the mode

---

8    A buyer purchases 40 cases of Product A at $7.84 per case, 20 cases of Product B at $8.20 per case, 24 cases of Product C at $8.50 per case and a number of cases of Product D at $8.60 per case. He spends $939.60 in total.

If there are 12 items in each case of Product D, how many **items** of Product D does he buy?

[         ]

---

9    In 1998, a price index based on 1984 = 100 stood at 129. In that year it was rebased at 1998 = 100. By 2000, the new index stood at 110. For a continuous estimate of price changes since 1984, the new index may be expressed, to two decimal places, in terms of the old as

*Splicing*

| | Old index | New index |
|---|---|---|
| 1984 | 100 | |
| 1998 | 129 | 100 |
| 2000 | | 110 |

$= \dfrac{129 \times 110}{100} = 141.90$

    A    58.10
    B    100.00
    Ⓒ    141.90
    D    139.00

---

10    In a histogram, one class is two thirds of the width of the remaining classes. If the score in that class is 25, the correct height to plot on the histogram is

    A    16.67
    B    25.00
    C    37.50
    D    41.67

# 18 Summarising and analysing data 6

1   In a histogram in which one class interval is one and a quarter times as wide as the remaining classes, the height to be plotted in relation to the frequency for that class is (to two decimal places)

   A   × 0.25
   B   × 0.63
   C   × 0.80
   D   × 1.25

2   A factory employs 100 people and is divided into three departments. The mean (arithmetic) output per employee per month for all employees is 139 units. What is the mean output per employee per month for department 2?

| Department | Number of employees in department | Mean output per employee per month Units |
|:---:|:---:|:---:|
| 1 | 54 | 130 |
| 2 | ? | ? |
| 3 | 24 | 140 |

   [          ]

3   When the mean purchase price of 20 units at 50c, 10 units at 60c and 25 units at Xc is 80c, the value of X is

   [          ]

4   The number of new orders received by five sales staff last week is as follows.

   2, 4, 6, 8, 10

   The variance of the number of new orders received is

   A   1.33
   B   2.83
   C   6
   D   8

5   Which of the following sets of data have the widest spread?

|  | A | B | C | D |
|---|:---:|:---:|:---:|:---:|
| Mean | 150 | 175 | 200 | 250 |
| Standard deviation | 25 | 20 | 25 | 30 |

   A   Data A
   B   Data B
   C   Data C
   D   Data D

6  The following information relates to Population Zeta.

Lower quartile   = 438
Upper quartile   = 621
Median           = 531

What is the value of the semi-interquartile range?

A    90.0
B    91.5
C    93.0
D    183.0

7  The average prices of three commodities and the number of units used annually by a company are given below.

| Commodity | 20X1 Price per unit ($P_0$) $ | 20X2 Price per unit ($P_1$) $ | w Quantity Units | $P_1/P_0$ | $w \times P_1 P_0$ |
|---|---|---|---|---|---|
| A | 16 | 20 | 20 | 1·25 | 25 |
| B | 40 | 50 | 2 | 1·25 | 2·5 |
| C | 100 | 105 | 10/32 | 0·05 | 10·5/38 |

The price for 20X2 based on 20X1 calculated using the weighted average of relatives method is (to the nearest whole number)

$$\frac{\Sigma \left( w \times P_1/P_0 \right)}{\Sigma w} \times 100 = \frac{\Sigma (38)}{32} \times 100 = 118·75$$

A    117
B    118
C    119
D    120

≈ 119·

8  A frequency distribution has a common class width of $12. For analysis purposes, the analyst has set one class at $18, this class has a corresponding frequency of 180. When drawing a histogram, the height of this class should be (ring the correct value on the y axis of the graph shown below).

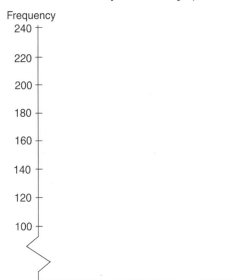

Frequency
240
220
200
180
160
140
120
100

9   A distribution where the mode is greater than the median and the median is greater than the mean is known as a

A   Positively-skewed distribution
B   Normal distribution
C   Negatively-skewed distribution
D   Continuous distribution

10  Quality control of four independent production processes reveals the length of certain parts (in mm) to be as follows.

| Process | Mean | Standard deviation |
|---------|------|--------------------|
| W       | 100  | 10                 |
| X       | 40   | 5                  |
| Y       | 80   | 8                  |
| Z       | 150  | 12                 |

The process(es) with the smallest relative variation, as measured by the coefficient of variation, is/are

A   X only
B   Z only
C   X and Y
D   W and Y

# 19 Summarising and analysing data 7

1   In a supermarket, the number of employees and the annual earnings per employee are shown as follows.

| Annual earnings $ | Number employed |
|-------------------|-----------------|
| 6,000             | 3               |
| 7,000             | 5               |
| 10,000            | 3               |
| 11,000            | 1               |
| 12,000            | 2               |
| 15,000            | 1               |

The median value of annual earnings is

┌─────────┐
│         │
└─────────┘

2   In 1990, a price index based on 1980 = 100 had a value of x.

During 1990, it was re-based at 1990 = 100, and in 1998 the new index stood at 112.

If the total price movement between 1980 and 1998 was an increase of 30%, the value of x (to the nearest whole number) in 1990 (ie before re-basing) was ┌─────────┐
                                                                                          └─────────┘

3    The number of sales achieved by a sales manager each week has a mean of 400 and a standard deviation of 60. 99% of sales achieved each week lie in the range

Low                    High

[            ]    to    [            ]

Calculate your answer correct to 1 decimal place.

---

4    In a negatively-skewed distribution,

[        ]    the mean is larger than the median

[        ]    the mean is smaller than the median

[        ]    the mean is the same as the median

[        ]    the mean lies between the median and the mode

---

5    The weights of three items, A, B and C vary independently and have the following means and standard deviations.

|     | Mean weight kg | Standard deviation kg |
|-----|----------------|------------------------|
| A   | 120            | 20                     |
| B   | 100            | 20                     |
| C   | 80             | 10                     |

The three items are sold together in a single packet.

What is the mean weight of a packet of one unit each of A, B and C, and the standard deviation of the weights of packets?

|     | Mean kg | Standard deviation kg |
|-----|---------|------------------------|
| A   | 100     | 30                     |
| B   | 100     | 900                    |
| C   | 300     | 30                     |
| D   | 300     | 900                    |

---

6    A survey of heights of lampposts is carried out in Britain to find out if there is any variation across the country.

What sort of data is being collected in such a survey?

|     |              |            |
|-----|--------------|------------|
| A   | Quantitative | Discrete   |
| B   | Qualitative  | Discrete   |
| C   | Quantitative | Continuous |
| D   | Qualitative  | Continuous |

7    A group of shoppers were interviewed and asked how many loaves of bread they would need to buy from the bakers over a one-week period. The results are as follows.

| Number of loaves | Number of shoppers |
|---|---|
| 0 | 2 |
| 1 | 22 |
| 2 | 32 |
| 3 | 2 |
| 4 | 34 |
| 5 | 6 |
| 6 | 12 |

What is the mode of the number of loaves needed per shopper in a one-week period?

[          ]

---

8    In a normal distribution with a mean of 80, and a standard deviation of 15.75, what percentage of the population is less than 60?

A  10.2%              B  19.9%              C  39.8%              D  89.8%

---

9    Production of lead pipes is normally distributed with a mean length of 500cm and a variance of 484cm. The percentage of pipes between 470cm and 550cm long is closest to:

A  6.37%              B  41.31%              C  48.84%              D  90.15%

---

10   A histogram uses a set of bars to represent a grouped frequency table. To be correctly presented, the histogram must show the relationship of the rectangles to the frequencies by reference to the

A     height of each bar
B     width of each bar
C     area of each bar
D     diagonal of each bar

---

# 20 Summarising and analysing data 8

1    The mean of the following set of data is [          ]

13, 42, 7, 51, 69, 28, 33, 14, 8, 15

---

2    A group of people have the following ages:

21, 32, 19, 24, 31, 27, 17, 21, 25 and 42 years.

The median age of the group is [          ] to 1 decimal place.

---

3    The mean weight of ten containers is 20 kgs.

If the individual weights in kgs are

15, ×, 22, 14, 21, 15, 20, ×, 28 and 27,

then the value of x is [          ] kgs.

---

4    A buyer purchases 20 cases of Alpha at $7.84 per case, 10 cases of Beta at $8.20 per case, 12 cases of Gamma at $8.50 per case and a number of cases of Delta at $8.60 per case. He spends $512.80 in total.

If there are 12 items in each case of Delta, how many *items* of Delta does he buy?

Answer [          ]

---

5    The number of new orders received by five salesmen last week is: 2, 4, 6, 8, 10. The variance of the number of new orders received is [          ]

---

6    The exam marks for nine students were:

65, 86, 37, 56, 72, 65, 64, 70, 45

The mode of the exam marks is [          ]

---

7    The exam marks for nine students were:

55, 86, 37, 59, 72, 55, 64, 70, 45

The median of the exam marks is [          ]

---

8    The coefficient of variation is used to measure

[          ] the correlation between two variables.

[          ] the percentage variation in one variable caused by variation in another.

[          ] the strength of a relationship between two variables.

[          ] relative dispersion.

---

9    The average prices of four commodities along with the number of units used annually by a company, are given in the following table:

| Commodity | Year 1<br>Price per unit<br>$ | Year 2<br>Price per unit<br>$ | Quantity<br>Units |
|-----------|-------------------------------|-------------------------------|-------------------|
| A | 10 | 11 | 10 |
| B | 20 | 24 | 1 |
| C | 50 | 52 | 5 |
| D | 100 | 105 | 4 |

Complete the following table (to 2 decimal places).

| Commodity | Price relative | Weight | Relative weight |
|-----------|----------------|--------|-----------------|
| A | | | |
| B | | | |
| C | | | |
| D | | _____ | _____ |
| | | _____ | _____ |

Price index for year 2 based on year 1 (using weighted average of relatives method) =

[          ] to the nearest whole number.

10 In January 2002 the average pay for Grade B workers was $200 per week. There was a contract in force index-linking the pay for the next five years, with increases effective from 1 January each year, starting in 2003. Details of the relevant price index for the last four years are:

| | Index of prices each January (January 1990 = 100) | | | | |
|---|---|---|---|---|---|
| Year | 2002 | 2003 | 2004 | 2005 | 2006 |
| Price index | 124 | 131 | 136 | 140 | 148 |

The average weekly pay for Grade B workers during 2006 was (to the nearest $)

$ [          ]

# 21 Summarising and analysing data 9

1 The number of times members of the public (who were questioned) ate out last week is shown below.

| Number of meals eaten out | Frequency (number of people) |
|---|---|
| 0 | 10 |
| 1 | 110 |
| 2 | 10 |
| 3 | 160 |
| 4 | 170 |
| 5 | 30 |
| 6 | 9 |
| | 499 |

The median number of meals eaten out last week is [          ]

2    In a merchant bank, the number of employees and the annual earnings per employee are shown as follows.

| Annual earnings | Number employed |
|---|---|
| $ | |
| 60,000 | 3 |
| 70,000 | 3 |
| 100,000 | 5 |
| 110,000 | 1 |
| 120,000 | 2 |
| 150,000 | 1 |

The median value of annual earnings is $ [          ]

3    The following table shows the values of deliveries made to customers last week:

| Value of delivery ($) | | Frequency |
|---|---|---|
| at least | less than | |
| 1 | 10 | 3 |
| 10 | 20 | 6 |
| 20 | 30 | 11 |
| 30 | 40 | 15 |
| 40 | 50 | 12 |
| 50 | 60 | 7 |
| 60 | 70 | 6 |

The value of the lower quartile in this frequency distribution (to 2 decimal places) is [          ]

4    The following table shows the values of deliveries made to customers last week:

| Value of delivery ($) | | Frequency |
|---|---|---|
| at least | less than | |
| 1 | 10 | 3 |
| 10 | 20 | 6 |
| 20 | 30 | 11 |
| 30 | 40 | 15 |
| 40 | 50 | 12 |
| 50 | 60 | 7 |
| 60 | 70 | 6 |

The value of the upper quartile in this frequency distribution (to the nearest $) is

[          ]

5    A large publishing company awards a 14% salary increase to every employee. Which of the following statements about the distribution of the company's salaries is/are correct?

Statement

| | |
|---|---|
| ☐ | The standard deviation will remain unaltered |
| ☐ | The standard deviation will increase by 14% |
| ☐ | The coefficient of variation will remain unaltered |

6    The price index for a commodity in the current year is 125 (base year = 100). The current price for the commodity is $160.

The price (to the nearest $) in the base year was therefore $ [          ]

7    The average prices of three commodities and the number of units used annually by a company are given below.

| Commodity | 20X1 Price per unit ($P_0$) $ | 20X2 Price per unit ($P_1$) $ | Quantity Units |
|---|---|---|---|
| Brighton | 32 | 40 | 40 |
| Eastbourne | 80 | 100 | 4 |
| Worthing | 100 | 210 | 20 |

Complete the following table (correct to 2 decimal places).

| Commodity | Price relative | Weight | Relative weight |
|---|---|---|---|
| Brighton | | | |
| Eastbourne | | | |
| Worthing | | _____ | _____ |
| | | ══════ | ══════ |

The price for 20X2 based on 20X1 calculated using the weighted average of relatives method is (to 2 decimal places) $ [          ]

8    An inflation index and index numbers of a company's sales ($) for the last year are given below.

| Quarter | 1 | 2 | 3 | 4 |
|---|---|---|---|---|
| Sales ($) index | 109 | 120 | 132 | 145 |
| Inflation index | 109 | 110 | 111 | 113 |

'Real' sales, ie adjusted for inflation, are

(a)    Growing steadily

True    [          ]

False    [          ]

(b)    Keeping up with inflation

True    [          ]

False    [          ]

9    The numbers of rejects from 50 samples of the same size is as follows:

| Number of rejects in each sample: | 0 | 1 | 2 | 3 | 4 | 5 |
|---|---|---|---|---|---|---|
| Number of samples (frequency of rejects): | 5 | 10 | 10 | 20 | 5 | 0 |

The arithmetic mean number of rejects per sample (to 1 decimal place) is [          ]

---

10    The unit price of Brand X in May 2000 and May 2001 was as follows:

| Year | 2000 | 2001 |
|---|---|---|
| Unit price of Brand X | $1.40 | $1.75 |

The price relative for Brand X in May 2001, with base May 2000 = 100 is [          ]

> ### Inter-relationships between variables
>
> Questions 22 to 26 cover inter-relationships between variables, the subject of Part D of the BPP Study Text for C3

# 22 Inter-relationships between variables 1

1   If $\Sigma x = 440$, $\Sigma y = 330$, $\Sigma x^2 = 17,986$, $\Sigma y^2 = 10,366$, $\Sigma xy = 13,467$ and $n = 11$, then the value of r, the coefficient of correlation, to 2 decimal places, is

   ┌─────────────┐
   │             │
   └─────────────┘

2   A rank correlation coefficient is being calculated, using the formula

   $R = 1 - \dfrac{6\Sigma d^2}{n(n^2 - 1)}$. If $\Sigma d^2 = 50$ and $n = 10$, R will (to 2 decimal places) be

   A  −0.30              B  0.69               C  0.30               D  0.70

3   A company's weekly costs ($C) were plotted against production level (P) for the last 50 weeks and a regression line calculated to be C = 1,000 + 250P. Which statement about the breakdown of weekly costs is true?

   A    Fixed costs are $1,000. Variable costs per unit are $5.
   B    Fixed costs are $250. Variable costs per unit are $4.
   C    Fixed costs are $250. Variable costs per unit are $1,000.
   D    Fixed costs are $1,000. Variable costs per unit are $250.

4   The following four data pairs have been obtained: (1, 5), (2, 6), (4, 9), (5, 11). Without carrying out any calculations, which of the following Pearons's correlation coefficients best describes the relationship between x and y?

   A  −0.98              B  −0.25              C  0.98               D  0.25

5   Monthly sales of overcoats (Y in $'000s) are found to be related to the average monthly daytime temperature (X in degrees C) by the regression equation Y = 32 − 1.6X. Which of the following is true?

   A    When temperature increases by 1 degree, sales fall by $3,200
   B    When temperature increases by 1 degree, sales fall by $1,600
   C    When temperature increases by 1 degree, sales fall by $1.60
   D    When temperature increases by 1 degree, sales increase by $1,600

6   The value of the correlation coefficient between x and y is 0.9. Which of the following is correct?

   A    There is a weak relationship between x and y
   B    x is 90% of y
   C    If the values of x and y were plotted on a graph, the line relating them would have a slope of 0.9
   D    There is a very strong relationship between x and y

7    The correlation coefficient between advertising expenditure and sales revenue is calculated to be 0.85. Which of the following statements is true?

    A    There is a weak relationship between advertising expenditure and sales revenue

    B    85% of the variation in sales revenue can be explained by the corresponding variation in advertising expenditure

    C    72% of the variation in sales revenue can be explained by the corresponding variation in advertising expenditure

    D    Sales revenue will increase by 85% more than advertising expenditure will increase

8    If $\sum x = 12$, $\sum y = 42$, $\sum x^2 = 46$, $\sum y^2 = 542$, $\sum xy = 157$ and $n = 4$, find the correlation coefficient.

9    If X denotes advertising expenditure in one period and Y denotes sales revenue in the next period, the regression equation linking X and Y has been found to be $Y = 40 + 10X$. Interpret the value '40'.

    A    When advertising expenditure increases by $1, sales will increase by $40 on average

    B    If nothing is spent on advertising, sales will be $40 on average

    C    If $10 is spent on advertising, sales will be $40 on average

    D    When advertising increases by $1, sales increase on average by $40/10 = $4

10    Five novels were reviewed by two different book critics, and the novels were ranked as follows.

| Novel | Critic 1 Rank | Critic 2 Rank |
|---|---|---|
| Sunshine love | 1 | 4 = |
| Oceanic war | 2 = | 1 |
| Liasing dangerously | 4 | 3 |
| Dark stranger | 5 | 2 |
| The road to Crockham Hill | 2 = | 4 = |

The rank correlation coefficient is

A  −0.425        B  +0.425        C  −0.368        D  +0.368

# 23 Inter-relationships between variables 2

1    The regression equation linking x and y is $y = 5x - 24$. Which of the following is correct?

    I    The slope of the equation if plotted on a graph is 5

    II    The line cuts the y-axis at −24 if plotted on a graph

    III    The slope of the equation if plotted on a graph is −24

    IV    The line cuts the y-axis at 4.8 if plotted on a graph

    A    I only

    B    I and II only

    C    I, II and III only

    D    I, II, III and IV

2    Using data from twelve European countries, it has been calculated that the correlation between the level of car ownership and the number of road deaths is 0.73. Which of the statements shown follow from this?

      I      High levels of car ownership cause high levels of road deaths

      II    There is a strong relationship between the level of car ownership and the number of road deaths

      III   53% of the variation in the level of road deaths from one country to the next can be explained by the corresponding variation in the level of car ownership

      IV   73% of the variation in the level of road deaths from one country to the next can be explained by the corresponding variation in the level of car ownership

      A    I and II only
      B    I and III only
      C    II and III only
      D    II and IV only

3    20 pairs of values of (X, Y) with X ranging from 15 to 45 were used to obtain the regression equation Y = 480 − 5X. The correlation coefficient is −0.95. It has been estimated that when X = 10, Y = 430.  Which of the following reduces the reliability of the estimate?

      A    Sample size
      B    The magnitude of the correlation coefficient
      C    X = 10 being outside the range of the sample data
      D    The correlation being negative

4    The relationship between expenditure in $ on advertising (X) in one time period and sales (in $) (Y) in the next period has been found to be Y = 50 + 7X. Which of the following interprets the value '7' correctly?

      A    For every $1 spent on advertising, sales increase by $7 on average
      B    For every $1 increase in sales, $7 must on average be spent on advertising
      C    For every $1 spent on advertising, sales increase by $8
      D    When advertising is zero, sales are $50/7

5    In calculating the regression equation linking two variables, the standard formulae for the regression coefficients are given in terms of X and Y. Which of the following is true?

      A    X must be the variable which will be forecast
      B    It does not matter which variable is which
      C    Y must be the dependent variable
      D    Y must be the variable shown on the vertical axis of a scattergram

6   The examination placings of seven students were as follows.

|         | Placings          |        |
|---------|-------------------|--------|
| Student | English literature | French |
| 1       | 2                 | 1      |
| 2       | 1                 | 3      |
| 3       | 4                 | 7      |
| 4       | 6                 | 5      |
| 5       | 5                 | 6      |
| 6       | 3                 | 2      |
| 7       | 7                 | 4      |

The rank correlation coefficient (to 3 decimal places) is

[                    ]

7   The linear relationship between advertising in thousands of dollars (X) and sales in tens of thousands of dollars (Y) is given by $Y = 5 + 2X$. Which of the following are correct?

I     For every $1,000 spent on advertising, sales revenue increases by $50,000 on average
II    When nothing is spent on advertising, the average level of sales is $50,000
III   For every extra $1,000 spent on advertising, sales revenue increases by $20,000 on average
IV    When nothing is spent on advertising, the average level of sales is $20,000

A    I and II only
B    II and III only
C    II and IV only
D    III and IV only

8   The regression equation $Y = 3 + 2X$ has been calculated from 6 pairs of values, with X ranging from 1 to 10. The correlation coefficient is 0.8. It is estimated that $Y = 43$ when $X = 20$. Which of the following are true?

I     The estimate is not reliable because X is outside the range of the data
II    The estimate is not reliable because the correlation is low
III   The estimate is reliable
IV    The estimate is not reliable because the sample is small

A    I and II only
B    I and III only
C    II and IV only
D    I and IV only

9   The coefficient of rank correlation ranges in value from

A  0 to 1            B  −1 to +1            C  0 to 10            D  −10 to +10

10    The regression equation linking sales revenue (Y) with advertising expenditure (X) has been found to be Y = 30 + 5X. Which of the following are correct?

      I       When nothing is spent on advertising, sales revenue will increase on average by $6
      II      When advertising expenditure increases by $1, sales revenue increases on average by $5
      III     When nothing is spent on advertising, sales revenue will on average be $5
      IV      When nothing is spent on advertising, sales revenue will be $30 on average

      A       I and II
      B       II and III
      C       I and IV
      D       II and IV

# 24 Inter-relationships between variables 3

1     Monthly sales of overcoats (Y in $'000s) are found to relate to the average monthly daytime temperature (X in degrees C) by the equation Y = 54 − 3X. Which of the following statements are true?

      I       Sales are zero when the temperature is 18°C
      II      Sales are positive when the temperature is below 54°C
      III     Sales are negative when the temperature is greater than 18°C
      IV      Sales are $54,000 when the temperature is 0°C

      A       I and II only
      B       I and III only
      C       I and IV only
      D       I, II and III only

2     If $\sum X = 100$, $\sum Y = 400$, $\sum X^2 = 2,040$, $\sum Y^2 = 32,278$, $\sum XY = 8,104$ and n = 5 the correlation coefficient (to 2 decimal places) is

      [            ]

3     If $\sum X = 100$, $\sum Y = 400$, $\sum X^2 = 2,040$, $\sum Y^2 = 32,278$, $\sum XY = 8,104$ and n = 5 which of the following values for a and b are correct in the formula Y = a + bX?

|     | a   | b    |
| --- | --- | ---- |
| A   | 28  | −2.6 |
| B   | 28  | +2.6 |
| C   | −28 | −2.6 |
| D   | −28 | +2.6 |

4     The coefficient of determination ($R^2$) explains the percentage variation in the independent variable which is explained by the dependent variable.

      True   [            ]
      False  [            ]

5     In a forecasting model based on Y = a + bX, the intercept is $248. If the value of Y is $523 and X is 25, then the value of the slope, to two decimal places, is [            ]

6     In a market research survey of a new dessert, respondents were asked to rank eight desserts in order of preference regarding taste, and then again rank them for looks, with a rank of 1 indicating nicest taste and best looks. The rank correlation coefficient was calculated and was 0.94. This means nothing at all, as the rank correlation cannot be used for this kind of test.

True [            ]

False [            ]

7     The following four data pairs have been obtained: (1, 5), (2, 6), (4, 9), (5, 11). Without carrying out any calculations, which of the following product moment correlation coefficients best describes the relationship between x and y?

A      −0.98

B      −0.25

C      +0.98

D      +0.25

## The following information is to be used for questions 8 and 9.

A scatter diagram shows the weekly total costs of production ($) in a certain factory plotted against the weekly outputs (units). A broadly linear pattern is evident, with r = 0.9. The regression equation is

Costs = 1,500 + (15 × output)

Fifty data points have been included in the analysis, with output ranging from 100 units to 1,000 units. Output next week is planned to be 500 units.

8     Which of the following statements about **estimates** is/are true, all other things being equal?

[        ] Weekly fixed costs are approximately $1,500.

[        ] Variable costs are approximately $15 per unit on average.

[        ] Next week's production costs are likely to be about $9,000.

9     Read the following statements:

(i)      There is very little correlation between weekly costs of production and production level.

(ii)     90% of the variation in weekly costs is attributable to the amount produced.

(iii)    Given the information, any forecast using the regression equation is likely to be very unreliable.

Which one of the following is justified?

[        ] (ii) only

[        ] (i) and (iii) only

[        ] (ii) and (iii) only

[        ] None of them

10      Which of the following could have a value of –2 (minus 2)?

| | Correlation coefficient |
| | Slope of a regression line |
| | Variance |

# 25 Inter-relationships between variables 4

1      The regression equation linking x and y is y = 4x – 15. Which of the following is correct?

| | The slope of the equation if plotted on a graph is –15 |
| | The line cuts the y-axis at 3.75 if plotted on a graph |
| | The slope of the equation if plotted on a graph is 4 |
| | The line cuts the y-axis at –15 if plotted on a graph |

2      For a set of six data pairs for the variable x (profit) and y (sales) the following values have been found.

$\sum x = 2$

$\sum y = 15$

$\sum x^2 = 30$

$\sum y^2 = 130$

$\sum xy = 14$

The correlation coefficient is [        ] to 2 decimal places.

3      What is the equation of the least-squares regression line of y on x for the following four data pairs?

| x | y |
|---|---|
| 1 | 4 |
| 2 | 6 |
| 3 | 10 |
| 4 | 10 |

y = [            ]

4      The following data give five astrologers' marks for technical merit and degree of accuracy.

| Astrologer | Technical merit | Degree of accuracy |
|---|---|---|
| Virgo | 5.9 | 5.5 |
| Libra | 5.7 | 5.6 |
| Scorpio | 5.4 | 5.4 |
| Sagittarius | 5.2 | 5.8 |
| Aquarius | 6.0 | 5.9 |

Spearman's rank correlation coefficient between the two sets of positions is [          ] (to 2 decimal places)

5   If the coefficient of determination is high, this proves that variations in one variable cause variations in the other.

True [            ]

False [            ]

6   What is the equation of the least-squares regression line of x on y for the following five data pairs?

| x | y |
|---|---|
| 9 | 2 |
| 10 | 3 |
| 9 | 1 |
| 8 | 1 |
| 9 | 2 |

X = [                    ]

State each value to 2 decimal places.

7   A company's weekly costs ($C) were plotted against production level (P) for the last 50 weeks and a regression line calculated to be C = 200 + 30P. Which statement about the breakdown of weekly costs is true?

[        ] Fixed costs are $200. Variable costs per unit are $30.

[        ] Fixed costs are $30. Variable costs per unit are $200.

[        ] Fixed costs are $30. Variable costs per unit are $6.67.

[        ] Fixed costs are $200. Variable costs per unit are $6.67.

8   The correlation coefficient between two variables, x and y, is +0.68. The proportion of variation in x that is explained by variation in y is [            ] (to 4 decimal places)

9   A company's market for computer supplies has trebled in value in exactly six years. The annual equivalent percentage growth rate in this market is (to 2 decimal places) closest to [            ] %

10   The calculation of a rank correlation coefficient shows that ten pairs of data are found to be perfectly negatively correlated.
The value of $\Sigma d^2$ (to the nearest whole number) equals [            ]

# 26 Inter-relationships between variables 5

1   If Y = a + bX, it is best to use the regression of Y upon X where X is the dependent variable and Y is the independent variable.

True [            ]

False [            ]

2    The coefficient of determination, $r^2$, must always fall within the range

Lowest value    = [          ]

Highest value    = [          ]

3    In the market research survey of a new drink, respondents were asked to rank eight drinks in order of preference regarding taste, and then again rank them for looks, with a rank of 1 indicating nicest taste and best looks. The rank correlation coefficient was calculated and was 0.95. This means that:

A    There appeared to be no correlation between taste and looks.

B    The nicest drinks looked the best.

C    The best-looking drinks did not taste very nice.

D    Nothing at all, as the rank correlation cannot be used for this kind of test.

4    An ice-cream supplier has recorded some sales data which he believes show a relationship between temperature and sales. The results shown below are for ten sample days in the summer.

| Temperature in degrees Celsius | Cartons sold |
|---|---|
| x | y |
| 13 | 10 |
| 16 | 11 |
| 17 | 14 |
| 19 | 15 |
| 20 | 16 |
| 21 | 19 |
| 23 | 24 |
| 26 | 25 |
| 27 | 26 |
| 28 | 27 |

Intermediate totals are as follows.

$\Sigma x$     = 210

$\Sigma y$     = 187

$\Sigma x^2$    = 4,634

$\Sigma y^2$    = 3,865

$\Sigma xy$    = 4,208

The correlation coefficient of temperature and sales is [          ] (to 2 decimal places).

5    A company has a fleet of vehicles and is trying to predict the annual maintenance costs per vehicle. The following data have been supplied for a sample of vehicles.

| Vehicle number | Age in years (x) | Maintenance cost per annum $ × 10 (y) |
|---|---|---|
| 1 | 2 | 60 |
| 2 | 8 | 132 |
| 3 | 6 | 100 |
| 4 | 8 | 120 |
| 5 | 10 | 150 |
| 6 | 4 | 84 |
| 7 | 4 | 90 |
| 8 | 2 | 68 |
| 9 | 6 | 104 |
| 10 | 10 | 140 |

Using linear regression analysis, calculate the values of a and b in the equation

$y = a + bx$

b = [          ]    (to 2 decimal places)

a = [          ]    (to 2 decimal places)

The equation to use for predicting the likely maintenance cost per vehicle per annum is [          ]

where    y = [          ]

         x = [          ]

6    A company operates ten factories. Its expenditure ($'000) on 'Training in accident prevention and safety' (TAPS) and the number of minor accidents there last quarter are shown in the table below. Any accidents were judged by nursing staff as either 'minor' and treated on site, or 'major' and referred to the local hospital.

Number of minor accidents and expenditure on TAPS ($'000)

| Site: | A | B | C | D | E | F | G | H | I | J |
|---|---|---|---|---|---|---|---|---|---|---|
| Minor accidents | 17 | 9 | 10 | 4 | 12 | 21 | 25 | 8 | 6 | 3 |
| TAPS ($'000) | 6 | 15 | 10 | 22 | 8 | 9 | 5 | 8 | 16 | 30 |

The Spearman's rank correlation coefficient is [          ] (to 4 decimal places).

7    If the correlation coefficient for two variables is −0.8, the coefficient of determination for the same two variables is [          ]

8    The value of b in the regression equation

A    Cannot be negative
B    Equals one when there is perfect correlation
C    Measures the scatter of points around the regression line
D    Measures the increase in the y variable for unit increase in x

9    The value of *a* in the regression equation

   A    Cannot be negative
   B    Measures the value of the independent variable
   C    Is the value of the dependant variable when the value of the independent variable is zero
   D    Must be positive

10   A correlation coefficient with a value of 0.9

   A    Indicates that *x* causes *y*
   B    Indicates that *y* causes *x*
   C    Indicates that the relationship between *x* and *y* is too strong to have been caused by chance
   D    Shows that *x* and *y* have something in common

## Forecasting

Questions 27 to 32 cover forecasting, the subject of Part E of the BPP Study Text for C3

# 27 Forecasting 1

1     In a time series analysis, the trend equation for a particular product is given by

Trend = $0.0004*YEAR^2 + 0.2*YEAR + 80.2$

Due to the cyclical factor, the forecast for 2006 is estimated at 1.87 times trend.

In whole units, the forecast for 2006 is

A   3,877            B   3,878            C   3,900            D   3,910

2     Over an 18-month period, sales have been found to have an underlying linear trend of y = 7.112 + 3.949x, where y is the number of items sold and x represents the month. Monthly deviations from trend have been calculated and month 19 is expected to be 1.12 times the trend value.

The forecast number of items to be sold in month 19 is approximately

A   91            B   92            C   93            D   94

3     Based on the last 15 periods the underlying trend of sales is y = 345.12 − 1.35x. If the 16th period has a seasonal factor of −23.62, assuming an additive forecasting model, then the forecast for that period, in whole units, is

A   300            B   301            C   324            D   325

4     Unemployment numbers actually recorded in a town for the second quarter of the year 2000 were 4,700. The underlying trend at this point was 4,300 people and the seasonal factor is 0.92. Using the multiplicative model for seasonal adjustment, the seasonally-adjusted figure (in whole numbers) for the quarter is

QUESTIONS

5    A forecasting model is based on the formula y = a + bx. Diagrammatically, this could be depicted as

A        −ve nos.

B    y    ↑ve nos

C    y    zero nos

D    Either A or B or C depending on the value of b. ✓

---

6    Monthly sales have been found to follow a linear trend of y = 9.82 + 4.372x, where y is the number of items sold and x is the number of the month. Monthly deviations from the trend have been calculated and follow an additive model. In month 24, the seasonal variation is estimated to be plus 8.5.

The forecast number of items to be sold in month 24 is approximately [          ] to the nearest whole number.

---

7    A company's management accountant is analysing the reject rates achieved by 100 factory operatives working in identical conditions. Reject rates, Y%, are found to be related to months of experience, X, by this regression equation: Y = 20 − 0.25X. (The correlation coefficient was r = −0.9.)

Using the equation, the predicted reject rate for an operative with 12 months' experience is closest to

A  17%              B  19%              C  20%              D  23%

---

8    A product has a constant (flat) trend in its sales, and is subject to quarterly seasonal variations as follows.

| Quarter | $Q_1$ | $Q_2$ | $Q_3$ | $Q_4$ |
| --- | --- | --- | --- | --- |
| Seasonality | +50% | +50% | −50% | −50% |

Sales last quarter, $Q_2$, were 240 units.

Assuming a multiplicative model for the time series, predicted unit sales for the next quarter, $Q_3$, will be closest to

A  80              B  120              C  160              D  320

---

9    Based on 20 past quarters, the underlying trend equation for forecasting is y = 28.37 + 4.2x.

If quarter 21 has a seasonal factor of times 1.055, using a multiplicative model, then the forecast for the quarter, in whole units, is [          ]

10 Which of the following are necessary if forecasts obtained from a time series analysis are to be reliable?

I       There must be no unforeseen events
II      The model used must fit the past data
III     The trend must be increasing
IV      There must be no seasonal variation

A  I only                B  I and II only         C  I, II and III only        D  I, II, III and IV

# 28 Forecasting 2

1 What is the purpose of seasonally adjusting the values in a time series?

A       To obtain an instant estimate of the degree of seasonal variation
B       To obtain an instant estimate of the trend
C       To ensure that seasonal components total zero
D       To take the first step in a time series analysis of the data

2 The results of an additive time series model analysing production are shown below.

|  | Daily production '000 units |
| --- | --- |
| Monday | −6 |
| Tuesday | +3 |
| Wednesday | +7 |
| Thursday | +4 |
| Friday | −8 |

Which of the following statements are true in relation to the data shown in the table above?

I       Production is on average 7,000 units above the trend on Wednesdays
II      Production is on average 4% above the trend on Thursdays
III     Production on Fridays is typically 8,000 units below the trend
IV      Production on Mondays is on average 6% below the trend

A  I only                B  I and II only         C  I and III only            D  I, II, III and IV

3 Using an additive time series model, the quarterly trend (Y) is given by Y = 65 + 7t, where t is the quarter (starting with t = 1 in the first quarter of 20X5). If the seasonal component in the fourth quarter is −30, forecast the actual value for the fourth quarter of 20X6, to the nearest whole number.

A  63                    B  546                   C  85                        D  91

4 The trend for monthly sales ($Y) is related to the month (t) by the equation Y = 1,500 − 3t where t = 1 in the first month of 20X8. The forecast sales (to the nearest pound) for the first month of 20X9 if the seasonal component for that month is 0.92 using a multiplicative model is

A  $1,377               B  $17,904               C  $1,344                    D  $1,462

5  In a time series analysis, the multiplicative model is used to forecast sales and the following seasonal variations apply:

| Quarter | 1 | 2 | 3 | 4 |
|---|---|---|---|---|
| Seasonal variation | 1.3 | 1.4 | 0.5 | ? |

The actual sales values for the first two quarters of the year 2000 were:

Quarter 1: $520,000
Quarter 2: $630,000

The seasonal variation for the fourth quarter is [          ] to one decimal place.

# The following data relate to questions 6 and 7

In a time series analysis, the multiplicative model is used to forecast sales and the following seasonal variations apply:

| Quarter | 1 | 2 | 3 | 4 |
|---|---|---|---|---|
| Seasonal variation | 1.3 | 1.4 | 0.5 | ? |

6  The actual sales values for the first two quarters of 1999 were:

Quarter 1: $520,000
Quarter 2: $630,000

Complete the following table.

| | Quarter | |
|---|---|---|
| | 1 | 2 |
| Seasonal component (S) | 1.3 | 1.4 |
| Actual series (Y) | $520,000 | $630,000 |
| Trend (T) | $ [          ] | $ [          ] |

7  The trend line for sales has therefore

[          ] increased between quarter 1 and quarter 2
[          ] decreased
[          ] remained constant

8  A time series was analysed using a multiplicative model. The seasonal ratios, given by actual value divided by trend, are adjusted so that they total 4. Carry out that calculation on the following unadjusted averages for quarters 1 to 4 respectively.

| | Quarter | | | |
|---|---|---|---|---|
| | 1 | 2 | 3 | 4 |
| Unadjusted average | 1.07 | 0.95 | 1.15 | 0.8 |

A  First quarter adjusted average = 1.10
B  Second quarter adjusted average = 0.92
C  Third quarter adjusted average = 1.1425
D  Fourth quarter adjusted average = 0.8075

9 A time series for weeks 1–12 has been analysed into a trend and seasonal variations, using the additive model. The trend value is 92 + 0.9W, where W is the week number. The actual value for week 7 is 77.8. The seasonal variation for week 7 is [          ] to 1 decimal place.

10 A regression equation Y = a + bX is used to forecast the value of Y for a given value of X. Which of the following increase the reliability of the forecast?

    I       A correlation coefficient numerically close to 1
    II     Working to a higher number of decimal places of accuracy
    III    Forecasting for values of X outside the range of those used in the sample
    IV    A large sample is used to calculate the regression equation— *the more observations the better!*

A  I only          B  I and II only         C  I and III only        (D) I and IV only

# 29 Forecasting 3

1 Complete the following table.

|  | | Season | | |
|---|---|---|---|---|
|  | Spring | Summer | Autumn | Winter |
| Year  1 |  |  | +5 | +6 |
| 2 | –6 | –4 | +4 | +7 |
| 3 | –5 | –5 |  |  |
| Average | [     ] | [     ] | [     ] | [     ] |
| Adjustment | [     ] | [     ] | [     ] | [     ] |
| Average seasonal adjustment | [     ] | [     ] | [     ] | [     ] |

2 Which of the following is/are not true of cylical variations?

[     ] Their period is longer than that of seasonal variations
[     ] Their magnitude is constant from one cycle to the next
[     ] They always reflect the trade cycle
[     ] They always repeat every five to ten years

3 The following data are to be analysed into a trend and seasonal variations, using the additive model, and assuming that the seasonal variations have a period of three months (ie follow a pattern of rises and falls which lasts three months).

| Month | Data |
|---|---|
| June | 16 |
| July | 26 |
| August | 32 |
| September | 22 |

Trend for April (to 2 decimal places) = [          ]
Seasonal variation (to 2 decimal places) for April = [          ]

4  A company analyses the time series of its quarterly sales figures using a multiplicative model. The seasonal adjustments for Autumn and Winter (based on data up to 20X0) are 97% and 108% respectively. Seasonally-adjusted figures for 20X1 (based on these adjustments) were $47,921 for autumn and $65,234 for winter. What were the actual sales for these two quarters?

Autumn
$

Winter
$

State your answer to the nearest whole number.

5  Which of the following is *not* one of the four components of a time series?

Random variations

Cyclical variations

Four-quarter totals

Seasonal variations

6  Which of the following components of a single time series would be identified as a cyclical variation?

A component increasing by the same amount each year over the last 50 years.

Occasional peaks which occur unpredictably but on average once every five years.

Regular cycles involving an increase in the first half of each year, followed by a corresponding decrease in the second half of the year.

A peak in the first three years of every decade, with a corresponding trough in the last five years of every decade.

7  In a time series analysis, which of the following is true of seasonal variations?

They always have a period of one year

They always repeat exactly year after year

They have a period shorter than that of any cyclical variations there may be

If you combine the trend and the seasonal variations, you always get back to the actual data

8  The following data are to be analysed into trend and seasonal variations.

| Day | Data | |
|---|---|---|
| | Week 1 | Week 2 |
| Monday | 71 | 21 |
| Tuesday | 82 | 65 |
| Wednesday | 61 | 71 |
| Thursday | 47 | 49 |
| Friday | 49 | 51 |
| Saturday | 42 | 45 |
| Sunday | 38 | 42 |

The seven-day total for Friday of week 1 = [          ] to the nearest whole number.

9    Shoe sales for a retail outlet for three weeks are as follows:

| | Sales units | | |
| --- | --- | --- | --- |
| | Week 1 | Week 2 | Week 3 |
| Monday | 102 | 103 | 107 |
| Tuesday | 78 | 79 | 80 |
| Wednesday | 119 | 129 | 130 |
| Thursday | 92 | 95 | 95 |
| Friday | 99 | 100 | 107 |

The manager of the outlet wishes to analyse this time series of sales data.

The most appropriate moving average trend figure for Wednesday of week 3 is [        ] to the nearest whole unit.

10    Under which of the following circumstances would a multiplicative model be preferred to an additive model in time series analysis?

A    When a model easily understood by non-accountants is required
B    When the trend is increasing or decreasing
C    When the trend is steady
D    When accurate forecasts are required

# 30 Forecasting 4

1    The quarterly sales (units) of a company are given in the table below.

| Year | $Q_1$ | $Q_2$ | $Q_3$ | $Q_4$ |
| --- | --- | --- | --- | --- |
| 1997 | 13 | 52 | 56 | 79 |
| 1998 | 29 | 43 | 48 | 80 |
| 1999 | 24 | 55 | 46 | 75 |

Which of the following statements is/are true?

[    ]    Annual sales are static.

[    ]    The fourth quarter, $Q_4$, has the highest quarterly sales in each of the three years.

[    ]    The mean sales for the second quarter ($Q_2$) equals the mean quarterly sales for the whole period, 1997-99.

2    The following data represent a time series for the last seven days:

2      6      10      6      10      14      10

Which ONE of the following moving averages would result in a straight-line graph?

A    2-point
B    3-point
C    4-point
D    None of these

3    In a time series analysis, the trend equation for a particular product is given by

TREND = $0.0002 \times YEAR^2 + 0.4 \times YEAR + 30.4$

Due to the cyclical factor, the forecast for the year 2000 is estimated at 1.6 times trend.

In whole units, the forecast for the year 2000 is

A  2,606                B  2,607                C  2,608                D  2,609

---

4    Profit is denoted by Y ($'000) and is given by the regression equation $Y = 0.5t - 12$, where t = 1 in the first month of 20X0. If there is no seasonal variability, in what month will the breakeven point (ie where profit = 0) be reached?

A      6th month of 20X0
B      12th month of 20X1
C      Midway between 12th month of 20X0 and 1st month of 20X1
D      12th month of 20X0

---

5    A multiplicative time series model is used to analyse annual data with a five-year cycle. If the annual components are 0.95, 1.12, 1.25, 0.82 and 0.6 for years 1 to 5 of the cycle respectively, which of the following are true?

I       In year 1 of the cycle, actual values are only 95% of the trend
II      In the fifth year of the cycle, actual values are 40% below the trend
III     In the fourth year of the cycle, actual values are 18% above the trend
IV      Actual values build up steadily and peak in the third year of the cycle

A  I only                B  I and II only                C  I, II and III only                D  I, II and IV only

---

6    A quarterly multiplicative time series model has seasonal components of +20%, −30%, −25% and +35% respectively. Seasonally adjust the following actual values for quarters 1 to 4 respectively, to the nearest pound: $500, $300, $330 and $610 and state which of the following are correct.

I       The first quarter seasonally-adjusted value is $600
II      The second quarter seasonally-adjusted value is $429
III     The third quarter seasonally-adjusted value is $413
IV      The fourth quarter seasonally adjusted value is $938

A  I only                B  I and II only                C  II only                D  II, III and IV only

7 Complete the following table using the data given in order to determine the three-month moving average for the period July-December.

| Month | No of ice creams sold | Moving total of 3 months ice creams sold | Moving average of 3 months ice creams sold |
|---|---|---|---|
| July | 2,000 | | |
| August | 2,500 | ☐ | ☐ |
| September | 1,800 | ☐ | ☐ |
| October | 1,400 | ☐ | ☐ |
| November | 900 | ☐ | ☐ |
| December | 1,000 | | |

8 Quarterly sales have a trend given by $Y = 5t - 1.5$, where Y is sales in $'000 and t is the time period with t = 1 in the first quarter of 20X8. Forecast sales (to the nearest pound) in the second quarter of 20X9 if the seasonal component using the multiplicative model is –7% in that quarter are

A $26,505  B $7,905  C $19,530  D $21,500

9 Number of moving averages to calculate when there are:

- Odd number of time periods = ☐
- Even number of time periods = ☐

10 Based on the last 9 periods, the underlying trend of profits is $p = 273.16 - 1.74C$. If the 10th period has a seasonal factor of 52.19, assuming an additive forecasting model, then the forecast profits for that period, in whole units is ☐

# 31 Forecasting 5

1 A company's annual profits have a trend line given by $Y = 20t - 10$, where Y is the trend in $'000 and t is the year with t = 0 in 20X0. Forecast profits for the year 20X9 using an additive model if the cyclical component for that year is –30 are

A $160,000  B $140,000  C $119,000  D $60,000

2    Which of the following are necessary if forecasts obtained from a time series analysis are to be reliable?

    I      The trend must not be increasing or decreasing
    II     The trend must continue as in the past
    III    Extrapolation must not be used
    IV     The same pattern of seasonal variation must continue as in the past

    A II only              B II and III only         C II and IV only          D I and IV only

3    The underlying trend equation for forecasting purposes based on the past 20 months is

    $y = 30.15 + 3.6x$  where x is the month number.

    If month 21 has a seasonal factor of $\times 1.02$, using the multiplicative model, then the forecast for this month (to the nearest whole unit) is

    A 104                  B 106                     C 107                     D 108

4    Unemployment numbers actually recorded in a town for the second quarter of the year 2006 were 4,000. The underlying trend at this point was 3,750 people and the seasonal factor is 0.95. Using the multiplicative model for seasonal adjustment, the seasonally-adjusted figure (in whole numbers) for the quarter is

    A 3,563                B 3,800                   C 3,947                   D 4,211

5    In a time series analysis, using the additive model, at a certain time, the following data is obtained.

    Actual value                              170
    Trend                                     182
    Seasonal value                            −12.8

    The residual value at this point is

    A −0.8                 B 0.8                     C −24.8                   D 24.8

## The following information is to be used for questions 6 and 7

In a time series analysis, the multiplicative model is used to forecast sales and the following seasonal variations apply:

| Quarter | 1 | 2 | 3 | 4 |
|---|---|---|---|---|
| Seasonal variation | 1.2 | 1.3 | 0.4 | ? |

The actual sales values for the first two quarters of 2006 were:

Quarter 1: $125,000
Quarter 2: $130,000

6    The seasonal variation for the fourth quarter is:

    A    −2.9
    B    0.9
    C    1.0
    D    1.1

BPP
PROFESSIONAL EDUCATION

7 The trend line for sales:

A Decreased between quarter 1 and quarter 2 .
B Increased between quarter 1 and quarter 2.
C Remained constant between quarter 1 and quarter 2.
D Cannot be determined from the information given.

8 In January, the unemployment in Ruritania is 567,800. If the seasonal factor using an additive time series model is +90,100, the seasonally-adjusted level of unemployment (to the nearest whole number) is

A 90,100          B 477,700          C 567,800          D 657,900

9 The trend in the quarterly costs of production is given by $Y = 300 - 2\sqrt{t}$ where Y is the trend in $'000 and t is the time period with t = 1 in the first quarter of 20X4. Using the additive model, forecast costs in the third quarter if the seasonal component for that quarter is +50 (give your answer to the nearest $'000) are

A $348,000          B $445,000          C $347,000          D $247,000

10 In a multiplicative time series analysis, the seasonal variations are calculated by averaging the Y/T values as follows.

| Quarter | Y/T value |
|---------|-----------|
| 1 | 1.04 |
| 2 | 1.15 |
| 3 | 0.94 |
| 4 | 0.90 |

What is the new value of the average for quarter 1?

A 0.965          B 1.0325          C 1.0475          D 1.1150

# 32 Forecasting 6

1 In an additive time series analysis, the seasonal variations given by averaging the (Y – T) values are as follows.

| Year | Y – T |
|------|-------|
| 1 | 18 |
| 2 | 30 |
| 3 | -16 |
| 4 | -36 |

The averages are subsequently adjusted so that their total is 0. What is the new value of the current average for Year 4?

A -32          B -35          C -37          D -40

2      The trend in the number of units sold is given by the equation: Trend = 850 + 27/x, where x is the year with 20X1 denoted by x = 1. Forecast the number of units to be sold in 20X9 if, due to cyclical factors, the forecast is expected to be 2% below the trend in that year.

     A   836                 B   97                C   870                D   853

3      Over a twenty-four month period, the underlying trend in the number of items sold (y) is related to the month (x) by the equation y = 4,320 + 5.2x, where x = 1 is the first month. If sales in the thirteenth month are known generally to be 15% above the trend, the sales forecast for month 13 to the nearest whole number is

     A   658                 B   3,729             C   5,046            D   4,388

4      Using an additive time series model, the underlying trend in sales in $'000 of product A is given by y = 250 − 1.57x, where x is the time period. If the seasonal component in time period 15 is expected to be −28, the forecast sales of product A for that quarter correct to the nearest $'000 is

     A   $163,000          B   $3,698,000        C   $226,000         D   $198,000

5      Which one of the following conditions does not need to be met if time series forecasts are to be reliable?

     A      The seasonal pattern should continue as it has done in the past
     B      The trend should continue as it has done in the past
     C      Extrapolation should always be avoided
     D      Residuals should be small

## The following information is to be used for questions 6 and 7 below.

In a time series analysis, the multiplicative model is used to forecast sales and the following seasonal variations apply.

| Quarter | 1 | 2 | 3 | 4 |
|---|---|---|---|---|
| Seasonal variation | 0.65 | 1.32 | 1.41 | ? |

The actual sales value for the first two quarters of 20X0 were:

Quarter 1:    $320,000
Quarter 2:    $500,000

6      The seasonal variation for quarter 4 is

     A   −3.38             B   0.62             C   1.00             D   1.38

7      The trend line for sales

     A      remained constant between quarter 1 and quarter 2
     B      increased between quarter 1 and quarter 2
     C      decreased between quarter 1 and quarter 2
     D      cannot be determined from the information given

8   Using an additive time series model, quarterly sales have been analysed and the quarterly seasonal components found to be +$200, +$400, −$300 and −$300 for quarters 1 to 4 respectively. If the actual sales for the four quarters are $1,300, $1,600, $1,050 and $1,100 respectively, the seasonally-adjusted sales are

   I     First quarter seasonally-adjusted sales are $1,100
   II    Second quarter seasonally-adjusted sales are $2,000
   III   Third quarter seasonally-adjusted sales are $570
   IV    Fourth quarter seasonally-adjusted sales are $1,400

   A  I only            B  I and II only            C  I and III only            D  I and IV only

9   The number of houses flooded in a town during the first quarter of 2000 was 750. The underlying trend at this point was 600 houses and the seasonal factor is 0.78. Using the multiplicative model for seasonal adjustment, the seasonally-adjusted figure (in whole numbers) for the quarter is

   A  468            B  585            C  769            D  962

10  A monthly multiplicative time series model for sales has seasonal components 0.54, 0.60, 0.73 and 1.09 for the months January to April. If the actual numbers sold in those months are 550, 650, 750 and 1,190 respectively, the seasonally-adjusted values to the nearest whole number are

   A    The January seasonally-adjusted sales are 297
   B    The February seasonally-adjusted sales are 1,083
   C    The March seasonally-adjusted sales are 606
   D    The April seasonally-adjusted sales are 1,297

## Financial mathematics

Questions 33 to 41 cover financial mathematics, the subject of Part F of the BPP Study Text for C3

# 33 Financial mathematics 1

*[handwritten]* $S_n = S_0(1+r)^n$
$= 1,000(1 + 0.0$

1    A building society adds interest monthly to investors' accounts even though interest rates are expressed in annual terms. The current rate of interest is 6% per annum.

An investor deposits $1,000 on 1 January. How much interest will have been earned by 30 June?

A $30.00          B $30.38          C $60.00          D $300

2    A one-year investment yields a return of 15%. The cash returned from the investment, including principal and interest, is $2,070. The interest is

3    It is estimated that, because of productivity improvements, costs will fall by 2½% per annum on a compound basis. If annual costs are now $160,000 then by the end of five years they will have fallen, to the nearest $, to

A  $137,450          B  $140,000          C  $140,975          D  $156,000

4    It is estimated that a particular cost will decline by 5% per annum on a compound basis.

If the cost now is $10,000, by the end of year 4 the cost will be approximately

A $7,738          B $8,000          C $8,145          D $8,574

5    If a single sum of $12,000 is invested at 8% per annum with interest compounded quarterly, the amount to which the principal will have grown by the end of year three is approximately

A $15,117          B $9,528          C $15,219          D $30,924

6    An annual percentage interest rate (APR) of 30% is equivalent to a monthly compound interest rate closest to:

A 2.02%          B 2.21%          C 2.50%          D 2.66%

*[handwritten]* $S_n = S_0(1+r)^n$
$= 12,000(1 + 0.08)^3$
$=$

7    The following formula is used in the calculation of the value of savings.

$Sr = R^N (Ar + P) - P$

where   A = amount saved at the start
        r = rate of interest
        N = number of periods
        P = payments added each period
        R = r + 1
        S = final sum

If r = 7%, A = 3,000, N = 20 and P = 500, then S equals (to the nearest $'000)

8    Rearranging the compound interest formula $S = \dfrac{A(R^2 - 1)}{(R - 1)}$, where $R \neq 1$, to make R the subject of the formula,

results in

A   $R = \dfrac{S}{A + 1}$          B   $R = \dfrac{S}{A}$          C   $R = \dfrac{S}{A} - 1$          D   $R = \dfrac{1 - S}{A}$

9    A bank offers depositors a nominal 4% pa, with interest payable quarterly. What is the effective annual rate
     of interest?          $4\%/123 = 0.33\% \cdot mthly \, rate.$                               $1 + R = (1 + r)^n$

     A 1%               B 4%               C 1.025%          D 4.06%     $1 + e = (1 + 0.33)^{12}$
                                                                        $R = (1 + 0.33)^{12} - 1$

10   $2,500 was invested exactly three years ago, at a guaranteed rate of compound interest of 8% per annum.
     Its value now (to the nearest $) is

     A $2,700           B $3,100           C $3,149          D $3,401

# 34 Financial mathematics 2

$S_n = S_0 (1 + r)^n \quad 1.259712$

$= 2,500 (1 + 0.08)^3$

1    Interest is stated as 12% per annum but is actually added monthly to accounts. Assuming the 12% to be a
     nominal rate, if a deposit of $500 is made on 1 January, how much interest will have been paid by 1 July of
     the same year?

     A $30.76           B $60.00           C $30.00          D $29.15

2    An asset which originally cost $100,000 depreciates at 20% per year. Its value after 5 years (to the nearest
     pound) is

     A $40,200          B $20,000          C $32            D $32,768

3    It is estimated that a particular cost will decline by 7% per annum on a compound basis. If the cost is now
     $20,000, by the end of year 5 the cost will be approximately

     A $12,940          B $13,000          C $13,914         D $14,961

4    House prices rise at 2% per calendar month. The annual rate of increase correct to one decimal place is

     A 24%          B 26.8%          C 12.7%          D 12.2%

5    A car costing $17,000 depreciates at 15% in its first year, then 10% per year for five years and thereafter at 2% per year. What is its value after eight years, correct to the nearest pound?

     [        ]

6    If a house was valued at $80,000 during a period when prices were rising at 21% per year, what would its price be 8 months later, to the nearest pound?

     A $90,840          B $91,200          C $86,453          D $89,084

7    Mary invests $6,500 now at 8% compound interest per year, but at the end of year 4 the interest rate changes to 10%. How much will there be invested after 6 years to the nearest $100?

     [        ]

8    The value of a car declined by 25% last year. What was the monthly rate at which the value declined, correct to 2 decimal places?

     A 2.08%          B 9.76%          C 6.25%          D 2.37%

9    If a bond rises in price from $50 to $75 over five years, what is the annual rate of increase, to one decimal place?

     A 10%          B 8.4%          C 5%          D 10.8%

10   A house was valued at $90,000 at the end of a six-month period during which prices had been rising at 21% per annum. What was its value at the beginning of the six-month period, to the nearest pound?

     A $80,550          B $81,000          C $81,818          D $81,448

# 35 Financial mathematics 3

1    The annual rent of a building is $1,200 payable in advance at the beginning of each year. At an interest rate of 14%, the present value of the rental payments is $5,319.60.

    The length of the lease is

     A 3 years          B 4 years          C 5 years          D 6 years

2    The present value of a five-year annuity receivable which begins in one year's time at 5% per annum compound is $60,000. The annual amount of the annuity, to the nearest $, is

     A $12,000          B $11,259          C $13,860          D $76,577

3   A farmer is to lease a field for six years at an annual rent of $500, the rentals being paid at the beginning of each year.

What is the present value of the lease at 7%?

A  $1,998          B  $2,383          C  $2,550          D  $2,883

---

4   A firm has arranged a ten-year lease, at an annual rent of $8,000. The first rental payment has to be paid immediately, and the others are to be paid at the end of each year.

What is the present value of the lease at 12%?

A  $50,624          B  $42,624          C  $45,200          D  $53,200

---

5   A financial adviser leases an office for 5 years, the rentals being paid at the beginning of each year. At 10% the present value of the rentals is $32,800. To the nearest $, the annual rental is

A  $3,280          B  $6,560          C  $7,866          D  $8,652

---

6   Which is worth most, at present values, assuming an annual rate of interest of 8%?

A     $1,200 in exactly one year from now     96 .
B     $1,400 in exactly two years from now     112 × 2 = 224
C     $1,600 in exactly three years from now   128 × 3 = 384
D     $1,800 in exactly four years from now   144 × 4 = 376

$PV = AC_i + COF_{i-4})$

$32800 = A(113 · 170) = 7561·7$

---

7   An annual rent of $1,000 is to be received for ten successive years. The first payment is due tomorrow.

Assuming the relevant interest rate to be 8%, the present value of this stream of cash flows is closest to

A  $6,247          B  $6,710          C  $7,247          D  $7,710

---

8   A project requires an investment of $10,000 and will generate returns of $7,000 in the first year and $5,000 in the second year. Which of the following equations would enable you to calculate the IRR given that x = (1 + r)?

I       $10,000 = \dfrac{7,000}{x} + \dfrac{5,000}{x^2}$

II      $10x^2 - 7x - 5 = 0$
III     $-10x^2 + 7x + 5 = 0$
IV      $5x^2 + 7x - 10 = 0$

A  I only          B  I and II only          C  I, II and III only          D  I, II, III and IV

---

9   A project requiring an investment of $1,200 is expected to generate returns of $400 in years 1 and 2 and $350 in years 3 and 4. If the NPV = $22 at 9% and the NPV = –$4 at 10%, what is the IRR for the project?

A  9.15%          B  9.85%          C  10.15%          D  10.85%

$IRR = a + \dfrac{NPV_a}{NPV_a - NPV_b} (b-a) = 9 + \dfrac{22}{22+4}(10-9) = 9.85\%$

0.846

10  Which of the following mutually exclusive projects would you advise your client to undertake if only one could be undertaken, given *only* the following information.

|  | IRR | NPV |
|---|---|---|
| Project 1 | 18.5% | 1,000 |
| Project 2 | 17.6% | 1,200 |
| Project 3 | 16.7% | 1,400 |
| Project 4 | 15.6% | 1,600 |

A  Project 1      B  Project 2      C  Project 3      D  Project 4

# 36 Financial mathematics 4

1  A sum of money was invested for 10 years at 7% per annum and is now worth $2,000. The original amount invested (to the nearest pound) was

A  $1,026      B  $1,016      C  $3,937      D  $14,048

2  Which of the following are problems in using net present value to appraise an investment?

I      The difficulty of estimating future cash flows
II    The difficulty of selecting an appropriate discount rate
III   It does not take account of inflation
IV   The concept of net present value is difficult for non-accountants to understand

A  I and II only      B  I, II and III only      C  I, II and IV only      D  I, II, III and IV

3  A company requires a sinking fund of $500,000 in four years' time. They can invest $X at the start of each of the four years at 4%. The value of X (to the nearest $'000) using tables is

A  $125,000      B  $118,000      C  $154,000      D  $113,000

4  A mortgage of $30,000 is to be repaid by 15 equal year-end payments. If interest is charged at 9%, the value of the annual payment (using tables) correct to the nearest $10 is

A  $1,020      B  $3,720      C  $2,000      D  $3,410

5  $1,000 is invested at the end of each year for 12 years at 7%. Using tables, the value of the investment immediately after the final payment, to the nearest $10, is

A  $17,890      B  $12,000      C  $19,140      D  $19,139.76

6    Which of the following statements about the IRR/NPV methods of investment appraisal are correct?

    I     The graph of the net present value against discount rate has a negative slope

    II    If the net present value of an investment at r% is positive, the NPV will be negative at a rate of s% if s% is less than r%

    III   The internal rate of return can be obtained exactly using algebra whereas the graphical method provides only an approximate rate for the IRR

    IV   An estimate of the internal rate of return requires the calculation of the net present value at two different discount rates

    A  I only          B  I and III only          C  II and IV only          D  I and IV only

7    A mortgage of $40,000 is to be repaid at the rate of $5,000 at the end of each year. If interest is to be charged at 7%, how many years will it take to repay the mortgage?

    A  8          B  10          C  13          D  7

8    What is the 'internal rate of return' of an investment?

    A    The discount rate at which the investment should be appraised
    B    The rate charged on loans used to finance the investment
    C    The probability of making a profit on the investment
    D    The discount rate at which the net present value of the investment is zero

9    A mortgage of $30,000 for 15 years at 7% has been repaid at the rate of $3,290 at the end of each year. If the mortgage is to be closed immediately after the eighth annual payment, use discount factor tables to find the amount still outstanding, giving your answer to the nearest pound.

    A  $19,036          B  $21,083          C  $3,680          D  $17,792

10   At a discount rate of 7%, Project A has a net present value of $3,000 whilst that of Project B is only $2,000. Which of the following statements are correct?

    I     At present prices, A costs $3,000 and B costs $2,000

    II    All other things being equal, A is preferable to B

    III   At present prices, A's profit is $3,000 and B's is $2,000

    IV   The cash flows of A are equivalent to investing a net amount of $3,000 now whilst those of B are equivalent to investing only $2,000

    A  I and II only          B  II only          C  II, III and IV only          D  II and IV only

# 37 Financial mathematics 5

1   Fred invested 6 annual payments of $100 into an investment fund earning compound interest of 4% per year. If the first payment was at time zero, calculate the value of the fund at time 5.

    A $663          B $541          C $437          D $545

2   Find the present value of ten annual payments of $700, the first paid immediately and discounted at 8%, giving your answer to the nearest pound.

    A $4,697         B $1,050         C $4,435         D $5,073

3   When the discount rate is 8%, an investment has a net present value of $18,000. At 9% its net present value is –$11,000 (*minus* eleven thousand dollars). The internal rate of return of this investment (to two decimal places) is

    A 8.62%         B 8.38%         C 8.50%         D 10.57%

4   A fund of $55,000 will be required in 15 years' time. $2,000 will be invested at 8% pa at the end of each year for 14 years. Use tables to find the further payment which will be required at time 15, to 3 significant figures.

    A $2,660         B $27,000         C $837         D $657

5   What is the present value of an annuity of $3,000 per annum discounted at 6% per annum if it starts at the end of the third year and finishes at the end of the 10th year. Use tables and give your answer to the nearest pound.

    A $22,080         B $16,581         C $996         D $14,061

6   The NPV of an investment is $230 when the discount rate is 5% and $160 when it is 12%. Estimate the internal rate of return to 2 decimal places.

    A    It is not possible to estimate the IRR unless one of the NPVs is negative
    B    28%
    C    9.13%
    D    8.5%

7   If $5,000 is invested at 6% per annum, what is its value after three years to the nearest pound?

    A $5,955         B $5,900         C $5,098         D $4,198

8   Over a period of 12 months, the present value of the payments made on a credit card is $10,500 at a discount rate of 3% per month. What is the equivalent constant monthly amount, to the nearest pound?

    A $875         B $4,371         C $1,055         D $7,361

9     Which of the following statements about Net Present Value are correct.

     I     An investment with a positive NPV is financially viable
     II    Net Present Value is a superior method to Internal Rate of Return
     III   The graph of Net Present Value against discount rate has a negative slope
     IV   Net Present Value is the present value of expected future net cash receipts less the cost of the investment

     A    I only
     B    I and II only
     C    I, II and III only
     D    I, II, III and IV

10   A single sum of $9,000 is invested at an interest rate of 1% per quarter. The amount to which the principal will have grown by the end of year 2 is approximately

     A  $9,746            B  $8,311           C  $9,720           D  $9,181

# 38 Financial mathematics 6

1     An investor has funds to invest now to produce an annuity of $1,494.87 per year for ten years commencing in one year.

     The present value of the annuity to the nearest $ is $10,500.

     The prevailing interest rate is [          ] %

2     A firm buys a material on a long-term contract which stipulates a price increase per annum of 6% compound. If the current price is $200 per kg, the price in 5 years, to the nearest cent, will be $ [         ]

3     Joe is to receive a ten-year annuity of $X per year, received at the end of each year. At an interest rate of 8% this annuity has a present value of $33,550.

     The value of $X = $ [         ]

     State your answer to the nearest $.

4     A leasing agreement is for five years. $20,000 must be paid at the beginning of the first year, to be followed by four equal payments at the beginning of years two, three, four and five. At a discount rate of 8%, the present value of the four equal payments is $52,992. The total amount to be paid during the lease period is $ [         ]

5     The difference between the total present value of a stream of cash flows at a given rate of discount, and the initial capital outlay is known as the internal rate of return.

     True  [         ]
     False [         ]

6      An investor is to receive an annuity of $19,260 for six years commencing at the end of year 1. It has a present value of $86,400.

The rate of interest (to the nearest whole percent) is [          ] %

7      Isabelle is to receive an annuity of $6,529.97 at the end of each of the next 7 years. The present value of the annuity is $33,995.18 at 8%, the relevant annuity factor (from tables) is [        ]

8      A company charges depreciation at the rate of 25% per annum on the reducing balance method on an asset which cost $40,000.

At the end of year 4 the written down value will be $ [          ]

State your answer to the nearest cent.

9      An individual placed a sum of money in the bank and left it there for 12 years at 8% per annum. The sum is now worth $2,728.90.

Using the compound interest formula, the original principal was found (to the nearest whole $) to be

$ [          ]

10     Jacob invested $10,000 on 1 January 20X1, earning interest of 4% per annum. The value of his investment on 31 December 20X5 will be (to the nearest $) $ [        ]

# 39 Financial mathematics 7

1      How much should be invested now (to the nearest $) to receive $24,000 per annum in perpetuity if the annual rate of interest is 5%?

Answer = $ [         ]

2      In the formula:

$$PV = \frac{1}{r} - \frac{1}{r(1+r)^n}$$

$r = 0.04$; $n = 16$; then PV equals [        ] to 2 decimal places.

3      A company is considering purchasing a new machine for $45,000. This would increase the annual cash flow of the company by $12,400 in each of the next six years. If the cost of capital is 9% per annum, the net present value of this investment is $ [        ]

State your answer to the nearest $.

4      The net present value of an investment at 12% is $24,000, and at 20% is −$8,000. The internal rate of return of this investment is [        ] %

State your answer to the nearest whole percent.

5    A building society adds interest to investors' accounts monthly even though interest rates are expressed in annual terms. The current rate of interest is 3% per annum.

An investor deposits $2,000 on 1 July. How much interest will have been earned by 31 December?

Answer = $ [          ] to the nearest cent.

---

6    An asset which originally cost $400,000 depreciates at 15% per year. Its value after 5 years (to the nearest $) is $177,482.13.

True  [          ]

False  [          ]

---

7    A single sum of $10,000 is invested at an interest rate of 1% per quarter. The amount to which the principal will have grown by the end of year 3 is approximately (to the nearest $) $ [          ]

---

8    It is estimated that, because of productivity improvements, costs will fall by 8% per annum on a compound basis. If annual costs are now $420,000 then by the end of four years they will have fallen, to the nearest $, to $ [          ]

---

9    Friendly Bank Ltd offers depositors a nominal interest rate of 12% per annum, with interest added to their accounts quarterly. The effective annual percentage rate, to 2 decimal places is [          ]

---

10   $400,000 was invested on 1 January 2001, earning interest of 5% pa. The value of this investment on 31 December 2005 will be (to the nearest $)

| | |
|---|---|
| [    ] | $1,061,319 |
| [    ] | $536,038 |
| [    ] | $510,513 |
| [    ] | $486,203 |

# 40 Financial mathematics 8

1    A fund of $180,000 will be required in 15 years' time. $5,000 will be invested at 8% pa at the end of each year for 14 years. Use tables to complete the following.

Present value of final fund = $ [          ] to the nearest $

Present value of annuity = $ [          ] to the nearest $

Payment required at time 15 = $ [          ] to the nearest $

---

2    $8,000 was invested exactly four years ago, at a guaranteed rate of compound interest of 6% per annum. Its value now (to the nearest $) is $ [          ]

3   A sum of money invested at compound interest of 7% has grown to $84,848 after 10 years. The original sum invested, to the nearest $, was $ [                    ]

State your answer to 2 decimal places.

4   After 15 years an investment of $2,400 has grown to $54,600. The annual rate of compound interest applied is [                ] % (to 2 decimal places).

5   A company is currently evaluating a project which requires investments of $5,000 now, and $2,000 at the end of year 1. The cash inflow from the project will be $7,000 at the end of year 2 and $6,000 at the end of year 3. The discount rate is 16%. Complete the following table. Use tables to calculate the present values.

| Year | Cashflow $ | Discount factor | Present value $ |
|------|-----------|-----------------|-----------------|
| 0 | [          ] | [          ] | [          ] |
| 1 | [          ] | [          ] | [          ] |
| 2 | [          ] | [          ] | [          ] |
| 3 | [          ] | [          ] | [          ] |
| | | Net present value = | [          ] |

6   A company is considering a project which would cost $26,000 now and would yield $4,200 per annum in perpetuity, starting one year from now. The cost of capital is 12%.

Present value of perpetuity   = $ [                ]   to the nearest $
Net present value of project   = $ [                ]   to the nearest $

7   An investment will generate cashflows of $3,100 each year in years 3 to 7 (ie first amount to be received 3 years from now). The discount rate is 15% per annum. The present value of the cash flows is $ [                    ]

Use tables to calculate your answer to the nearest $.

8   An investment has a net present value of $8,000 at 10% and one of −$2,000 at 17%. The approximate IRR (to 1 decimal place) is [                ] %.

9   Mr Norton wishes to invest a lump sum at 9% interest per annum. How much should he invest now in order to have $40,000 at the end of the next three years?

[          ]   $40,000 − (3 × 0.09 × $40,000)

[          ]   $40,000 $\left(\dfrac{1}{1.09} + \dfrac{1}{1.09^2} + \dfrac{1}{1.09^3}\right)$

[          ]   $\dfrac{\$40,000}{3 \times 1.09}$

[          ]   $\dfrac{\$40,000}{(1.09)^3}$

10    A mortgage of $90,000 for 15 years at 7% has been repaid at the rate of $8,000 at the end of each year. If the mortgage is to be closed immediately after the eighth annual payment the amount still outstanding (giving your answer to the nearest $ and using discount factor tables) is $ [        ]

# 41 Financial mathematics 9

1    Which of the following statements about the IRR/NPV methods of investment appraisal is/are **NOT** correct?

[        ]    If the NPV of an investment at r% is positive, the NPV will be negative at a rate of s% if s% is less than r%

[        ]    The IRR can be obtained exactly using algebra whereas the graphical method provides only an approximate rate for the IRR

[        ]    The graph of the NPV against the discount rate has a negative slope

[        ]    An estimate of the IRR requires the calculation of the NPV at two different discount rates

2    In the formula

$$PV = \frac{1}{r} - \frac{1}{r(1+r)^n}$$

If r = 0.25 and n = 10, then PV equals [                    ] to 6 decimal places.

3    An investment would involve spending $10,000 now, and getting cash returns of $8,000 one year from now and $6,000 four years from now. The NPV of this investment at a discount rate of 10% (use your calculator and not tables) is [            ] to the nearest whole number.

4    A company requires a sinking fund of $800,000 in four years' time. They can invest $X at the start of each of the four years at 4%. The value of X (to the nearest $'000) using tables is $ [            ]

5    A machine was purchased for $100,000. Depreciation is calculated using the 'reducing balance method' (that is, a constant percentage is applied each year to the written down value). In the last balance sheet, the net book value of the machine, exactly four years old, was shown as $50,000.

In the **next** balance sheet the machine should be shown to have a net book value, rounded to the nearest $100, closest to $ [            ]

6    A $100,000 mortgage, with interest compounded at 11% each year, is to be repaid by 10 equal year-end payments of $X, the first being due one year after the mortgage was contracted.

$X is closest to $ [            ]

State your answer to the nearest $.

7 Lynn invests $55,000 now. To what value would this sum have grown after the following periods using the given interest rates. Complete the following table, stating your answers to 2 decimal places.

| Value now $ | Investment period Years | Interest rate % | Final value $ |
|---|---|---|---|
| 55,000 | 4 | 7 | |
| 55,000 | 5 | 14 | |
| 55,000 | 4 | 21 | |

8 A perpetuity is an annuity which lasts for at least 25 years.

True 

False 

9 Terry has just bought a van which has a life of eight years. At the end of eight years a replacement van will cost $27,000 and Terry would like to provide for this future commitment by setting up a sinking fund into which equal annual investments will be made, starting **now**. The fund will earn interest at 4% per annum.

The equal annual investments to be made = $ 

State your answer to 2 decimal places.

10 Owen plc is considering whether to make an investment costing $56,000 which would earn $18,000 cash per annum for four years. The company expects to make a return of at least 12% per annum.

Complete the following table and state whether the project is viable or not.

| Year | Cashflow $ | Discount factor 12% | Present value $ |
|---|---|---|---|
| 0 | | | |
| 1 | | | |
| 2 | | | |
| 3 | | | |
| 4 | | | |
| | | NPV = | |

Project viable   Yes 

No

## Spreadsheets

Questions 42 to 45 cover spreadsheets, the subject of Part G of the BPP Study Text for C3

# 42 Spreadsheets 1

1    A chart wizard can be used to generate graphs. Which type of chart would be best used to track a trend over time?

    A    A pie chart
    B    A line graph
    C    A multiple bar chart
    D    A radar chart

2    A **macro** is used for occasional complicated tasks in spreadsheets.

True
False

3    The following statements relate to spreadsheet formulae

    I    Absolute cell references (B3) change when you copy formulae to other locations
    II    The F4 key is used to change cell references from absolute to relative
    III    Relative cell references ($B$3) stay the same when you copy formulae to other locations

Which statements are correct?

    A    I and II only
    B    I and III only
    C    II and III only
    D    II only

## Questions 4 to 6 refer to the spreadsheet shown below.

|    | A | B | C | D |
|----|---|---|---|---|
| 1 | Unit selling price | $65 | Annual volume | 10,000 |
| 2 | | | | |
| 3 | Seasonal variations | | | |
| 4 | Quarter 1 | -20% | | |
| 5 | Quarter 2 | -35% | | |
| 6 | Quarter 3 | 10% | | |
| 7 | Quarter 4 | 45% | | |
| 8 | | | | |
| 9 | **Sales budgets** | Seasonal variations (units) | Quarterly volume | Quarterly turnover |
| 10 | Quarter 1 | | | |
| 11 | Quarter 2 | | | |
| 12 | Quarter 3 | | | |
| 13 | Quarter 4 | | | |
| 14 | | | | |

4    The cell B10 shows the seasonal variation in units for quarter 1. Which of the following would be a suitable formula for this cell?

    A     =$D$1/4*B4
    B     =(D1/4)*B4
    C     =$D$1/4*B1
    D     =D1/4*$B$4

5    The cell C10 shows the sales volume in units for quarter 1. Which of the following would be a suitable formula for this cell?

    A     =$D$1/4+B10
    B     =D1/4+$B$10
    C     =D1+B10
    D     =($D$1/4)+B10

6    The cell D10 shows the turnover in Quarter 1 Which of the following would be a suitable formula for this cell?

    A     =D1*$B$1
    B     =C10-B10
    C     =C10*$B$1
    D     =(C10+B10)*$B$1

7    The following spreadsheet can be used to investigate the inter-relationship between advertising expenditure and sales.

|   | A | B | C | D | E |
|---|---|---|---|---|---|
| 1 | Monthly advertising | Sales | | | |
| 2 | Expenditure | | | | |
| 3 | X | Y | X² | Y² | XY |
| 4 | 1.2 | 132.5 | 1.44 | 17556.25 | 159 |
| 5 | 0.9 | 98.5 | 0.81 | 9702.25 | 88.65 |
| 6 | 1.6 | 154.3 | 2.56 | 23808.49 | 246.88 |
| 7 | 2.1 | 201.4 | 4.41 | 40561.96 | 422.94 |
| 8 | 1.6 | 161.0 | 2.56 | 25921.00 | 257.6 |
| 9 | 7.4 | 747.7 | 11.78 | 117549.95 | 1175.07 |

The cell E9 shows the total of the XY values. Which of the following would be a correct entry for this cell?

A    =A9*B9
B    =SUM(E4:E8)
C    =SUM(A9:D9)
D    =C9*D9

8    The following spreadsheet is used to forecast sales volumes in each quarter.  It involves the use of the linear regression formula $y = a + bx$, where x is the quarter number. Enter the formulae for the trend and sales volume forecasts for the first two quarters of 20X5 in cells **B7** and **C7** in the spreadsheet template below.

|   | A | B |
|---|---|---|
| 1 | a | 10000 |
| 2 | b | 400 |
| 3 | x at 31 December 20X4 | 36 |
| 4 | Period | 3 months to 31 March 20X5 |
| 5 | Quarter | 1 |
| 6 | Seasonal variation | +500 |
| 7 | Trend = y | |
| 8 | Forecast | |

9       For which of the following tasks would a spreadsheet be used?

                                              Tick box

Cashflow forecasting

Monthly sales analysis by market

Writing a memo

Calculation of depreciation

10      The formula bar displays

        A       The formula in the active cell and no other information
        B       The location of the active cell and the formula in the active cell
        C       The formula in the active cell and the result of the formula
        D       The location of the active cell, the formula in the active cell and the result of the formula

# 43 Spreadsheets 2

1       The following statements relate to spreadsheet formulae

        I       The formula =C4*5 multiplies the value in C4 by 5

        II      The formula =C4*117.5% reduces the value in C4 by 17.5%

        III     The formula =C4*B10-D1 multiplies the value in C4 by that in B10 and then subtracts the value in D1
                from the result

        Which statements are correct?

        A       I and II only
        B       I and III only
        C       II and III only
        D       I, II and III

2       Which of the following formulae gives an answer of 16?

        A       =11-3*2
        B       =32^(1/2)
        C       =4^4
        D       =4^2

## Questions 3 to 5 refer to the spreadsheet shown below

The list prices of the products, net of sales tax, have been obtained from a catalogue.

| | A | B | C | D |
|---|---|---|---|---|
| 1 | Product | List price (net) | Sales tax | Gross |
| 2 | line | $ | $ | $ |
| 3 | | | | |
| 4 | Buster | 294.00 | 51.45 | 345.45 |
| 5 | Crusty | 362.50 | 63.44 | 425.94 |
| 6 | Dibble | 88.20 | 15.44 | 103.64 |
| 7 | | | | |

3    What formula in cell C4 would calculate sales tax on the product Buster at 17.5%?

4    What is the formula in cell D5?

5

| | A | B | C | D |
|---|---|---|---|---|
| 1 | Product | List price | Sales tax | Gross |
| 2 | line | $ | $ | $ |
| 3 | | | | |
| 4 | Buster | 294.00 | 51.45 | 345.45 |
| 5 | Crusty | 362.50 | 63.44 | 425.94 |
| 6 | Dibble | 88.20 | 15.44 | 103.64 |
| 7 | | | | |
| 8 | | | | |
| 9 | Sales tax | 17.50% | | |
| 10 | | | | |

The current sales tax rate has now been entered in cell B9. What formula in cell C4 would calculate sales tax on the product line Buster, using the value in this cell?

6    Use of the keys Ctrl + " enables you to view the formulae in each cell on the spreadsheet itself.

|  | Tick box |
|---|---|
| True | |
| False | |

## Questions 7 and 8 refer to the spreadsheet shown below

|    | A | B | C |
|----|---|---|---|
| 1  | **Monthly production** | | |
| 2  | | | |
| 3  | Month | Units | |
| 4  | Jan | 149 | |
| 5  | Feb | 247 | |
| 6  | Mar | 382 | |
| 7  | Apr | 451 | |
| 8  | May | 300 | |
| 9  | Jun | 298 | |
| 10 | Jul | 187 | |
| 11 | Aug | 361 | |
| 12 | Sep | 85 | |
| 13 | Oct | 394 | |
| 14 | Nov | 322 | |
| 15 | Dec | 400 | |
| 16 | | | |
| 17 | Total | 3576 | |
| 18 | | | |
| 19 | Average | 298 | |

7    Which of the following would achieve the total in cell B17?

A     Autosum
B     Ctrl + s
C     Ctrl + t
D     F2

8    What is the formula in cell  B19?

[                                        ]

# Questions 9 and 10 refer to the spreadsheet and chart shown below

| | A | B | C | D | E |
|---|---|---|---|---|---|
| 1 | **Projected Results for 20X7: New products** | | | | |
| 2 | | | | | |
| 3 | | Flipp | Bopp | Mapp | Total |
| 4 | | | | | |
| 5 | Sales units | 280 | 640 | 320 | |
| 6 | | | | | |
| 7 | | $ | $ | $ | $ |
| 9 | Sales | 7000 | 20480 | 5120 | 32600 |
| 10 | Cost of Sales | 3360 | 8960 | 1600 | 13920 |
| 11 | Profit | 3640 | 11520 | 3520 | 18680 |
| 12 | | | | | |
| 13 | | | | | |
| 14 | | | | | |
| 15 | | | | | |
| 16 | | | | | |
| 17 | Selling price | 25 | 32.00 | 16.00 | |
| 18 | Unit cost | 12 | 14.00 | 5.00 | |
| 19 | | | | | |

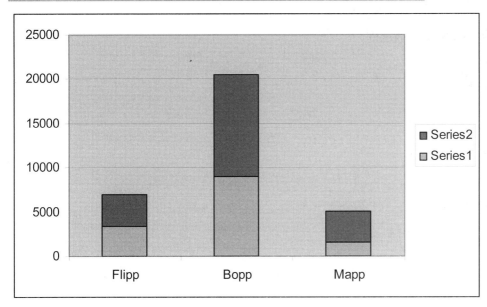

9    Which option in chart wizard was selected?

    A    Clustered bar
    B    Stacked bar
    C    Clustered column
    D    Stacked column

10    The data from which cells were used by chart wizard to prepare the chart?

A    B3:D3  B9:D9  and  B10:D10
B    B9:D9  B10:D10  and  B11:D11
C    B3:D3  B10:D10  and  B11:D11
D    B3:D3  B9:D9  B10:D10  and  B11:D11

# 44 Spreadsheets 3

1    The following statements relate to spreadsheet formulae

I      The formula =C4*B10 multiplies the value in C4 by the value in B10
II     The formula =C4*117.5% adds 17.5% to the value in C4
III    The formula =C4+C5+C6/3 adds C4, C5 and C6 together and divides the result by 3

Which statements are correct?

A    I and II only
B    I and III only
C    II and III only
D    I, II and III

## Questions 2 to 4 refer to the spreadsheet shown below

|     | A | B | C | D | E |
|-----|---|---|---|---|---|
| 1   | Trading account | | | | |
| 2   | | | 2008 | | 2007 |
| 3   | | $ | $ | $ | $ |
| 4   | | | | | |
| 5   | Sales | | 6402 | | 5747 |
| 6   | Less: cost of sales | | | | |
| 7   | opening stock | 341 | | 299 | |
| 8   | purchases | 3972 | | 3652 | |
| 9   | | 4313 | | 3951 | |
| 10  | less closing stock | (480) | | (341) | |
| 11  | | | 3833 | | 3610 |
| 12  | Gross profit | | 2569 | | 2137 |
| 13  | | | | | |
| 14  | Gross profit margin | | 40.13% | | 37.18% |

2    The format of cell B7 is

A    General
B    Number to 2 decimal places
C    Currency
D    Accounting

3    The format of cell D10 is

    A     General
    B     Number to 2 decimal places
    C     Custom
    D     Accounting

4    The formula in cell C14 is =C12/C5. The format of the cell is

    A     Fraction
    B     Number to 2 decimal places
    C     General
    D     Percentage to 2 decimal places

## Questions 5 to 8 refer to the spreadsheet shown below

The cost card below shows how the cost of producing each unit of the component 214X is built up. Each individual cost in the total column is found by multiplying the quantity (kg or hours) by the cost per kg or hour.

|    | A | B | C | D |
|----|---|---|---|---|
| 1 | Cost Card : Component 214X | | | |
| 2 | | | | |
| 3 | | | | Total |
| 4 | Material | kg | $ | $ |
| 5 | | | | |
| 6 | mat A | 2 | 2.80 | 5.60 |
| 7 | mat S | 3 | 3.60 | 10.80 |
| 8 | | | | |
| 9 | Labour | hours | $ | |
| 10 | | | | |
| 11 | skilled | 2.4 | 9.40 | 22.56 |
| 12 | unskilled | 5.3 | 6.35 | 33.66 |
| 13 | | | | |
| 14 | Overheads | 2.4 | 12.40 | 29.76 |
| 15 | | | | |
| 16 | Total cost per unit of component 214X | | | 102.38 |
| 17 | | | | |
| 18 | | | | |
| 19 | Rates per hour: | | $ | |
| 20 | -skilled labour | | 9.40 | |
| 21 | -unskilled labour | | 6.35 | |
| 22 | -overhead | | 12.40 | |
| 23 | absorption | | | |

5    The formula in cell D6 is =B6*C6. This has been replicated to cells D7, D11, D12 and D14. What is the formula in D11?

89

6   If the skilled labour rate were to change from $9.40 to $9.50 per hour, the values in which cells would change?

    A     C20 only
    B     C20 and C11
    C     C20, C11 and D11
    D     C20, C11, D11 and D16

7   Overheads are absorbed into product costs by charging $12.50 for each skilled labour hour worked on the component. If the skilled labour hours needed for each unit increased to 2.5 hours, the values in which cells would change?

    A     B11 and B14 only
    B     B11, C11 and D16
    C     B11, B14, D11, D14 and D16
    D     B11, B14, C11, C14, D11, D14 and D16

8   The text in cells A22 and A23 currently occupies two lines. Which of the following options would keep the text on one line within cell A22?

    I     Use a smaller font size
    II    Increase the row height
    III   Increase the column width

    A     I only
    B     I and II
    C     I and III
    D     I, II and III

9   Which of the following statements is true regarding the automatic positioning of items within a cell, before any editing?

    A     Text is right aligned
    B     Numbers are right aligned
    C     Text is centred
    D     Numbers are centred

10  If a cell contains ####, this means

    A     There is not enough room to display the required number in the cell
    B     There is not enough room to display the required text in the cell
    C     There is not enough room to display either the required number or text in the cell
    D     The result of the formula cannot be displayed as the formula is nonsensical

# 45 Spreadsheets 4

## Questions 1 to 3 refer to the spreadsheet shown below

|  | A | B | C | D | E | F |
|---|---|---|---|---|---|---|
| 1 | **Materials budgets: 50mm x 20mm pine** | | | | | |
| 2 | | | | | | |
| 3 | | September | October | November | Total | |
| 4 | | | | | | |
| 5 | **Usage budget** | *units* | *units* | *units* | *units* | |
| 6 | | | | | | |
| 7 | Production of tables | 250 | 280 | 290 | 820 | |
| 8 | | | | | | |
| 9 | | *metres* | *metres* | *metres* | *metres* | |
| 10 | **Raw material usage** | 625 | 700 | 725 | ? | |
| 11 | | | | | | |
| 12 | | | | | | |
| 13 | **Purchases budget** | *metres* | *metres* | *metres* | *metres* | |
| 14 | Production usage | 625 | 700 | 725 | ? | |
| 15 | Add: closing stock | 28 | 29 | 30 | ? | |
| 16 | Less: opening stock | (25) | (28) | (29) | ? | |
| 17 | Purchases | 628 | 701 | 726 | 2055 | |
| 18 | | | | | | |
| 19 | | $ | $ | $ | $ | |
| 20 | | | | | | |
| 21 | **Raw material purchases** | 5903.20 | 6589.40 | 6824.40 | 19317.00 | |
| 22 | | | | | | |
| 23 | | | | | | |
| 24 | **Raw materials data** | | | | | |
| 25 | Usage per unit of production (metres) | 2.5 | | | | |
| 26 | Purchase price per metre ($) | 9.40 | | | | |
| 27 | | | | | | |
| 28 | **Assumptions** | | | | | |
| 29 | 1 The closing stock in one month is 4% of the following month's production requirement | | | | | |
| 30 | 2 From December onwards production of tables will plateau at 290 | | | | | |

1     Which of the following cells require the input of an actual value rather than a formula relating to another cell on the spreadsheet?

|  | Tick box |
|---|---|
| B15 | |
| B16 | |
| C7 | |
| C10 | |

2    Suggest formulae for the following cells:

| | |
|---|---|
| D14 | |
| C16 | |
| D17 | |
| C21 | |

3    The total column has yet to be completed. Match up the cells below with the appropriate formulae in order to complete this column.

| E10 |
|---|

| E14 |
|---|

| E15 |
|---|

| E16 |
|---|

| =E10 |
|---|
| =SUM(B16:D16) |
| =D15 |
| =B15 |
| =SUM(B10:D10) |
| =D16 |
| =B16 |
| =SUM(B10:E10) |
| =SUM(B15:D15) |

## Questions 4 and 5 refer to the spreadsheet shown below

The spreadsheet below calculates the value of orders to be placed for raw materials by comparing the quantity in stock on a particular date with the level at which an order is needed.

| | A | B | C | D | E | F | G |
|---|---|---|---|---|---|---|---|
| 1 | Raw material orders:28 January | | | | | | |
| 2 | | | | | | | |
| 3 | Product code | Reorder | Reorder | Purchase | Stock | Place | Order |
| 4 | | level | quantity | price | level | order? | value |
| 5 | | | | $ | | | $ |
| 6 | | | | | | | |
| 7 | PY33 | 500 | 4000 | 0.24 | 600 | NO | 0 |
| 8 | BC78 | 350 | 2000 | 1.30 | 350 | YES | 2600 |
| 9 | FLO2 | 1000 | 5000 | 0.10 | 800 | YES | 500 |
| 10 | CJ54 | 200 | 1200 | 0.85 | 300 | NO | 0 |
| 11 | | | | | | | |
| 12 | | Total value of orders required | | | | | 3100 |

4    Suggest a conditional formula for cell F7 that can be replicated to cells F8 to F10.

| |
|---|

5    Suggest a conditional formula for cell G7 that can be replicated to cells G8 to G10.

| |
|---|

# Questions 6 to 8 refer to the spreadsheet shown below

A supplier offers a 5% discount on orders of 1000 units or more of material P.

| | A | B | C | D |
|---|---|---|---|---|
| 1 | Sales of material P | | | |
| 2 | | | | |
| 3 | Customer | Order | Price | Sales |
| 4 | | quantity | $ | $ |
| 5 | | | | |
| 6 | Smith | 500 | 245.00 | 1225.00 |
| 7 | Brown | 1200 | 232.75 | 2793.00 |
| 8 | Jones | 1000 | 232.75 | 2327.50 |
| 9 | Hamdy | 2000 | 232.75 | 4655.00 |
| 10 | Campbell | 400 | 245.00 | 980.00 |
| 11 | | | | 11980.50 |
| 12 | | | | |
| 13 | Price per hundred units | $245.00 | | |
| 14 | Bulk discount% | 5 | | |
| 15 | | | | |

6  The formula in cell C6 is

   A  =IF(B6>=1000,$B$13,$B$13*0.05)

   B  =IF(B6<1000,$B$13,$B$13*0.05)

   C  =IF(B6>=1000,$B$13,$B$13*(100-$B$14)/100)

   D  =IF(B6<1000,$B$13,$B$13*(100-$B$14)/100)

7  The formula in cell D8 is

   A  =B8/100*B13

   B  =B8*245

   C  =C8/100*B8

   D  =C8*B8

8  If, instead of 5, the value 5% were entered in cell B14, the spreadsheet would still calculate the discount correctly.

   Tick box

   True  [ ]

   False [ ]

9  How often should you save your spreadsheet whilst working on it?

   A  Every 10 minutes

   B  Every hour

   C  Every 2 hours

   D  At the end of the day, or before moving to work on another file

10    Passwords can be set to protect

       A      An individual cell on a spreadsheet
       B      A worksheet
       C      A workbook
       D      A cell, a worksheet or a workbook

Answers

# 1 Basic mathematics 1

1 | 9 |

Let length of box = L cm

Let side of square end = s cm

$\therefore$ 2s = L                                                                                               (equation (1))

Volume of box = $(s^2 \times L)cm^3$ = 1,458 $cm^3$

$\therefore$ L = $\dfrac{1,458}{s^2}$                                                                              (equation (2))

Sub (2) into (1)                2s  = $\dfrac{1,458}{s^2}$

Multiply both sides by $s^2$       $2s^3$  = 1,458
                                    $s^3$  = 729
                                    s  = 9

2   C    $\dfrac{(x^2)^3}{x^5}$ = $x^{(2\times3)-5}$ = $x^1$ = x

You should have been able to eliminate Options A and B immediately since your basic mathematical skills should enable you to see that the correct answer is x or x to the power of something.

Option D is incorrect since $x^6 \div x^5$ is x and not $x^2$. Note that if the question had been $\dfrac{(x^2)^3}{x^4}$ instead, the correct answer would have been $x^2$.

3 | 7.90% |

% reduction    = $\dfrac{56.99 - 52.49}{56.99}$ × 100%

                = 7.90%

4   B    $(x^3)^4 = x^{3\times4} = x^{12}$

Option A is incorrect because this is the answer to $x^3 \times x^4 = x^{3+4} = x^7$. Remember that when $x^3$ is raised to the power of 4, the powers are simply multiplied together.

Option C is incorrect because $(x^3)^4 \neq x^{3+4} \neq 7x$.

Option D is incorrect because $(x^3)^4 \neq x^{3+4} \neq x/7$.

5   A   **Total cost**   $30,151   =   $(100 \times \$50) + \$8,250 + \$11,200 + 100x$

$30,151   =   $24,450 + 100x$

100x   =   $\$30,151 - \$24,450 = \$5,701$

$x$   =   $\dfrac{£5,701}{100} = \$57.01$

If you selected option B, then you forgot to include the 100 units at $50 each.

$30,151   =   $\$8,250 + \$11,200 + 100x$

$30,151   =   $19,450 + 100x$

100x   =   $\$30,151 - \$19,450$

$x$   =   $\dfrac{£10,701}{100}$

$x$   =   $107.01$

Option C is incorrect because it does not take account of the batch costing $8,250.

$30,151   =   $(100 \times \$50) + \$11,200 + 100x$

$30,151   =   $5,000 + \$11,200 + 100x$

100x   =   $\$30,151 - \$5,000 - \$11,200$

$x$   =   $\dfrac{£13,951}{100}$

=   $139.51$

Option D is incorrect because it does not take account of the batch costing $11,200.

$30,151   =   $\$5,000 + \$8,250 + 100x$

$30,151   =   $13,250 + 100x$

100x   =   $\$30,151 - \$13,250$

100x   =   $16,901$

$x$   =   $\dfrac{£16,901}{100}$

=   $169.01$

6   B   The term $x^{-1}$ equals $1/x$ by definition.

7   17.395%

% increase   =   $\dfrac{\$53.99 - \$45.99}{\$45.99} \times 100\%$

=   17.395%

8   B   $(y^2)^3 = y^{2 \times 3} = y^6$

Remember that when $y^2$ is raised to the power of 3, the powers are simply multiplied together.

9 | 10 |

Let selling price = 100%

Profit = 20% of selling price

∴ cost = 80% of selling price

Cost = $40 = 80%

∴ 1% = $40/80

∴ 20% = profit = ($40/80) × 20 = $10.

It is very important that you understand how to do this question. If you had trouble understanding the correct answer, go back to your BPP Study Text for Business Mathematics and study Chapter 1 Section 3 again.

10   A   $x^{-3/4} = 1/x^{3/4}$

Remember that the negative sign represents a reciprocal.

$x^{3/4}$ can also be written as $(x^3)^{1/4}$

$1/4$ represents the fourth root of $x^3 = \sqrt[4]{x^3}$

∴ $x^{-3/4} = 1/\sqrt[4]{x^3}$

# 2 Basic mathematics 2

1   C   $\dfrac{x^8}{x^7} = x^{8-7} = x^1 = x$

Revise the material on roots and powers in Chapter 1 of the BPP Study Text if you got this question wrong. Understanding basic mathematical techniques is of fundamental importance to your **Business Mathematics** studies.

2   A   Price = $4 for 2 kgs
Price per kg = $2
Original price per kg = $2.60
Absolute reduction per kg = $(2.60 − 2.00) = $0.60
Percentage reduction per kg = $0.60/$2.60 × 100% = 23%

Option B is incorrect since the percentage reduction has been calculated by comparing the change in price ($2) with the final price ($2) ie, $\dfrac{\$2.60 - \$2.00}{\$2.00} \times 100\% = 30\%$ which is not correct.

Options C and D are incorrect because they do not account for the new price of $2 per kg but interpreted the new price as $4 per kg (and not per 2 kg).

3   B   If x = 0, y = 0
If x = 2, y = 2 × 2 = 4
∴ The line goes through (0,0) and (2,4)
∴ It is line B.

4      $(x^4)^{-4} = x^{(4 \times -4)} = x^{-16} = \dfrac{1}{x^{16}}$

| ✓ | $\dfrac{1}{x^{16}}$ |
|---|---|

5   C    $Q = \sqrt{\dfrac{2CoD}{Ch}}$

         $400 = \sqrt{\dfrac{2 \times 20 \times 24{,}000}{Ch}}$

Square both sides

         $400^2 = \dfrac{2 \times 20 \times 24{,}000}{Ch}$

         $Ch = \dfrac{2 \times 20 \times 24{,}000}{400 \times 400}$

         $Ch = \$6$

If you selected one of the other options A, B or D then work through the solution again remembering that if you do anything to one side of an equation, you must make sure you do the same to the other side of the equation as well!

6   C    22kg costs $7.00

     $\therefore$ 1kg costs $7.00/22 = $0.3182

     $\therefore$ Percentage saving $= \dfrac{0.39 - 0.3182}{0.39} \times 100\% = 18.4\%$

Option A is incorrect since it represents the saving in pence, ie 39.0c − 31.8c = 7.2c and not a **percentage saving**.

Option B is also incorrect since it has been calculated using a cost per kg of $0.32 instead of $0.3182, ie a percentage saving of $\dfrac{0.39 - 0.32}{0.39} \times 100\% = 17.9\%$.

Option D is wrong because the incorrect denominator has been used in the calculation.

Percentage saving   $\neq \dfrac{0.39 - 0.3182}{0.3182} \times 100\%$

                 $\neq 22.6\%$

7 $\boxed{644}$

$$\frac{286+192+4y+307+185+y+94}{7}=267$$

$$\therefore \frac{1,064+5y}{7}=267$$

$$1,064+5y = 1,869$$
$$5y = 1,869-1,064$$
$$5y = 805$$
$$y = \underline{161}$$

If $x = 4y$
$$x = (4 \times 161)$$
$$x = 644$$

8 C Number of defects per 10 hinges $= (6 \times 0.05) + (3 \times 0.2) + (1 \times 0.1)$
$$= 0.3 + 0.6 + 0.1$$
$$= 1$$

1 defect in 10 is equivalent to 10% $(1/10 \times 100\% = 10\%)$.

9 D $x\%$ of 200 $= \dfrac{x}{100} \times 200$

$$= \frac{200x}{100}$$

$$= 2x$$

Percentages represent one of the basic mathematical techniques that you will need to be able to master fully for your **Business Mathematics** studies. Revisit Chapter 1 if you struggled with this question.

10 $\boxed{23\%}$

If gross earnings $= \$18,435$

Tax $= \$18,435 - \$15,000$
$= \$3,435$

Taxable income $= \$18,435 - \$3,500$
$= \$14,935$

$\therefore$ Sylvia's taxable income is taxed at $\dfrac{£3,435}{£14,935} \times 100\% = 23\%$

# 3 Basic mathematics 3

1     A     If profit    = revenue − cost

              profit     $= 410P - 22P^2 - (3{,}800 - 24P)$
                          $= 410P - 22P^2 - 3{,}800 + 24P$
                          $= 434P - 22P^2 - 3{,}800$

Option B is incorrect – you have got the sign of 3,800 wrong (it should be negative, not positive).

Option C is incorrect – you have calculated profit as cost – revenue (instead of revenue – cost).

Option D is incorrect since you have not changed the −24P units to +24P when subtracting costs of 3,800 − 24P.

2     B     If    D        $= 60 - 5P$
               $D - 60$    $= -5P$
              $5P$       $= 60 - D$
              $P$        $= \dfrac{60}{5} - \dfrac{D}{5}$
              $P$        $= 12 - D/5$

Option A is incorrect since you have divided the 60 by 5 but not the D.

Option C is incorrect since you have forgotten to change the sign of the D from positive to negative when you took it to the other side of the equation. $5P = 60 - D$, $5P \neq 60 + D$.

Option D is also incorrect since you have incorrectly calculated that $D = 60 - 5P$ is $D = 55P$. This would only be the case if there were brackets as such $(D = (60 - 5)P)$.

3     | 5 |

           $y^2$          $= x^2 - 3x + 25$
           If x = 3,   $y^2$   $= 3^2 - (3 \times 3) + 25$
                    $y^2$   $= 9 - 9 + 25$
                    $y^2$   $= 25$
         ∴         $y$    $= \sqrt{25}$
                          $= 5$

Make sure that you substitute the value of x into the equation to evaluate $y^2$ and then take the square root of this value.

4 D If  P  = $250 - D/1.2$

      $P - 250$ = $-D/1.2$

      $\dfrac{D}{1.2}$ = $250 - P$

      D  = $1.2(250 - P)$

      D  = $300 - 1.2P$

If you incorrectly selected Option A, you have got the incorrect sign for 1.2P (it should be negative, not positive).

Option B is wrong because you forgot to multiply –P by 1.2.

Option C is also incorrect. You have forgotten to change the signs so that P – 250 becomes –P + 250 (or 250 – P) when changing –D/1.2 to D/1.2.

5 &boxed{8}

  When x = 4

     $y^{1/3}$ = $4^3 - (3 \times 4^2) + (22 \times 4) - 102$

     $y^{1/3}$ = $64 - 48 + 88 - 102$

     $y^{1/3}$ = 2

     y = $2^3$

     y = 8

6 &boxed{15.59}

  If      x = 3

      $(3)^{-0.5}$ = 0.57735026919

  $(0.57735026919)^{-5}$ = 15.59 (to two decimal places)

If you selected option B, you only performed the first part of the calculation, ie $(3)^{-0.5} = 0.58$ (to two decimal places). Option C represents $(3^{-0.5})^5$ instead of $(3^{-0.5})^{-5}$ as required by the question. Do make sure that you read the question properly.

7 D $(x^{-3})^{-4} = x^{(-3 \times -4)} = x^{12}$

8 &boxed{106.38}

  $\$125 = \dfrac{117.5}{100} \times$ price excluding sales tax

  $\dfrac{\$125}{117.5} \times 100 =$ price excluding sales tax

  $\therefore$ Price excluding sales tax = $106.38 (to the nearest cent)

9    | 7% |

Selling price at end of year 2    $= \$30 \times 1.05 \times 1.06$
                                   $= \$33.39$

Change in selling price in year 3 is $(35.73 - 33.39)$    $= \$2.34$

Percentage change in year 3 was $\dfrac{£2.34}{£33.39} \times 100\%$    $= 7\%$

Work through the numbers again if you selected an incorrect option.

10    B    $\dfrac{x^3}{x^4} = \dfrac{1}{x} = x^{-1}$

Revise the material on roots and powers in Chapter 1 of the BPP Study Text if you got this question wrong. Understanding basic mathematical techniques is of fundamental importance to your **Business Mathematics** studies.

# 4 Basic mathematics 4

1    | 319.81 |

If $x = 3$

Value $= (3^{-0.75})^{-7}$
      $= 319.81$

2    False | ✓ |

Selling price $= \$90.68 = 118\%$

∴ Selling price excluding tax    $= \dfrac{100}{118} \times \$90.68 = \$76.85$

∴ New price after 20% reduction    $= (100\% - 20\%) \times \$76.85$

                                    $= \$61.48$

$61.50 is the new price to 1 decimal place.

3    | 1 | to | 2 |

Company A : Company B
$350,000 : $700,000
      $1 : $2
       1 : 2

4    $ $\boxed{245.96}$

1.175 × cost of article = $289

Cost of article = $\dfrac{£289}{1.175}$ = $245.96

5    $\dfrac{\left(x^3\right)^4}{x^7} = \dfrac{x^{12}}{x^7} = x^5$

If x = 3, value is $3^5$ = $\boxed{243}$

If x = 4, value is $4^5$ = $\boxed{1,024}$

6    $\boxed{-2}$ %

Selling price at end of year 2    = $27.50 × 1.08 × 1.04
                                   = $30.89

Change in selling price in year 3 is therefore $(30.27 − 30.89) = −$0.62

Percentage change in year 3 was therefore $\dfrac{-0.62}{30.27}$ = −0.02 = −2%

7    A    The new selling price to the nearest cent is 50c

*Workings*

Let x = cost of article

1.125x    = 48c

X    = $\dfrac{48c}{1.125}$

= 42.67c

New selling price = 1.175 × 42.67c = 50c (to the nearest cent)

8    $\boxed{384}$

80    = $\sqrt{\dfrac{2 \times D \times 10}{6 \times 0.2}}$ = $\sqrt{\dfrac{20D}{1.2}}$

$80^2$    = $\dfrac{20D}{1.2}$

6,400    = $\dfrac{20D}{1.2}$

7,680    = 20D

D    = $\dfrac{7,680}{20}$ = 384

9      B

$$x^7 \div x^8 = x^{7-8} = x^{-1}$$

$$x^{-1} = 1/x$$

10

| x | y |
|---|---|
| 3.5 | −1.5 |

$$5x + 3y = 13 \quad (1)$$
$$3x - y = 12 \quad (2)$$
$$9x - 3y = 36 \quad (3) \quad (2) \times 3$$
$$14x = 49 \quad (4) \quad (1) + (3)$$
$$x = \frac{49}{14}$$
$$x = 3.5$$

$$3(3.5) - y = \quad 12 \text{ Substitute into (2)}$$
$$10.5 - y = \quad 12$$
$$y = 10.5 - 12$$
$$y = -1.5$$

# 5 Basic mathematics 5

1      $ [ 425.53 ]

$$\$500 = \frac{117.5}{100} \times \text{price excluding sales tax}$$

$$\frac{£500}{117.5} \times 100 = \text{price excluding sales tax}$$

∴ price excluding sales tax = \$425.53

2      C

25 kg costs \$7.00

∴ 1 kg costs $\frac{£7.00}{25}$ = \$0.28

∴ Percentage saving = $\frac{0.35 - 0.28}{0.35} \times 100\% = 20\%$

3    y is $\boxed{6}$

$y^2 = x^2 - 4x + 36$
If $x = 4$, $y^2 = 4^2 - (4 \times 4) + 36$
$y^2 = 16 - 16 + 36$
$y^2 = 36$
$y = \sqrt{36}$
$y = 6$

4    $ $\boxed{66.67}$

Let selling price = 100%

Profit = 25% of selling price

∴ Cost = 75% of selling price

Cost = $200 = 75%

∴ 1% = $\dfrac{\$200}{75}$

∴ 25% = profit = $\dfrac{\$200}{75} \times 25 = \$66.67$

5    $ $\boxed{1,021}$

Let x = telephone costs of company **excluding** sales tax

∴ $x \times 1.175 = \$10,000$

$x = \dfrac{\$10,000}{1.175}$

$= \$8,510.63$

Central administration share   = 60% × $8,510.63
                                = $5,106.38

∴ Remainder   = $8,510.63 − $5,106.38
                 = $3,404.25
30% of remainder to finance   = 30% × $3,404.25
                                    = $1,021 (to the nearest $)

6    A    $Q = \sqrt{\dfrac{2CD}{H}}$

            $Q^2 = \dfrac{2CD}{H}$ (square both sides)

            $H = \dfrac{2CD}{Q^2}$

7

| X | Y |
|---|---|
| −1 | 6 |

$$y = 7 + X$$
$$y = 9 + 3X$$
$$0 = 2 + 2X$$
$$2X = −2$$
$$X = \frac{−2}{2}$$
$$= −1$$

If $X = −1$, $Y = 7 + (−1)$
$$= 7 − 1$$
$$= 6$$

8    $\boxed{24}$

*Workings*

Katie's share = $9 = 3 parts.
Therefore one part is worth $9 ÷ 3 = $3.
Total of 8 parts shared out originally
Therefore total was 8 × $3 = $24

$\boxed{14.40}$

*Workings*
Katie's share = $9 = 5 parts.
Therefore one part is worth $9 ÷ 5 = $1.80
Therefore original total was 8 × $1.80 = $14.40

9    A    *Workings*

Proportion with dark hair = 24/45

Proportion who do not have dark hair $= \dfrac{45 − 24}{45} = \dfrac{21}{45}$
$$= 0.4667$$

10    $x = \boxed{21.13}$ or $\boxed{−17.13}$

$y = \boxed{−17.13}$ or $\boxed{21.13}$

Let the two numbers be x and y

| | |
|---|---|
| $x^2 + y^2 = 740$ | (1) |
| $x − y = 4$ | (2) |
| $y = x − 4$ | (3) (from (2)) |

Substituting in (1), we get

$x^2 + (x-4)^2 = 740$
$x^2 + (x^2 - 8x + 16) = 740$
$2x^2 - 8x + 16 - 740 = 0$
$2x^2 - 8x - 724 = 0$
$x^2 - 4x - 362 = 0$

Solve the quadratic equation

$$x = \frac{-(-4) \pm \sqrt{16 - (4 \times 1 \times (-362))}}{2 \times 1} = \frac{4 \pm \sqrt{1,464}}{2}$$

$$= \frac{4 + 38.26}{2} \text{ or } \frac{4 - 38.26}{2}$$

$$= 21.13 \text{ or } -17.13$$

If x = 21.13
   y = 4 − 21.13
      = −17.13
If x = −17.13
   y = 4 − (−17.13)
      = 21.13

# 6 Probability 1

1    D    P(male) = 40% = 0.4

P(female) = 1 − 0.4 = 0.6

P(CIMA candidate) = 80% = 0.8

We need to use the general rule of addition (to avoid double counting)

∴ P(female *or* CIMA candidate)

= P(female) + P(CIMA candidate) − P(female *and* CIMA candidate)

= 0.6 + 0.8 − (0.6 × 0.8) = 0.92

If you incorrectly selected option A you calculated the probability of a student being female *and* a CIMA candidate instead of the probability of a student being female *or* a CIMA candidate.

Option B represents 1 − P(female *and* CIMA candidate) = 1 − (0.6 × 0.8) = 1 − 0.48 = 0.52. This option is also incorrect.

You should have been able to eliminate option C immediately since it is simply the probability that a candidate is female.

2    A

|  | Large | Small | Total |
|---|---|---|---|
| Fast payers | 20* | 10** | 30 |
| Slow payers | 40 | 30**** | 70*** |
|  | 60 | 40 | 100 |

\* 60 – 40   ** 30 – 20   *** 100 – 30   **** 70 – 40

P(fast paying small company) = 10/100 = 0.1

3    D    Probability of A or B occurring = P(A) + P(B), provided A and B cannot both be true, so P(sales remaining the same or falling) = P(same) + P(falling) = 0.21 + 0.23 = 0.44.

You must make sure that you understand the laws of probability so that you can apply them correctly to objective test questions such as this.

4    B    Number of female students        = 100 – 30 = 70

P(not studying for Certificate Level) $= \dfrac{100 - 55}{100} = \dfrac{45}{100}$

P(female and not studying for Certificate Level) $= \dfrac{45 - 6}{70} = \dfrac{39}{70}$

$= 0.56$

Option A is incorrect since it is the probability that a student is female.

Option C is not correct because it represents the probability that a student is male and is not studying for Certificate Level (6/30 = 0.20).

Option D is incorrect because it represents the probability that a student is **not** studying for the Certificate Level.

5    D    Pr(household has either a satellite or a video)

= Pr(satellite) + Pr(video) – Pr(both satellite and video)
= 0.3 + 0.8 – (0.3 × 0.8)
= 0.3 + 0.8 – 0.24
= 0.86

Option A is incorrect because it is the probability that a household has both satellite *and* video instead of satellite *or* video.

Option B is the probability that a household has just satellite television.

Option C is the probability that a household has just a video recorder.

6    0.92

We need to use the general rule of addition.

Pr (digital camera or DVD player) = Pr (digital camera) + Pr (DVD player) – Pr (digital camera *and* DVD player)

= 0.6 + 0.8 – (0.6 × 0.8)
= 1.4 – 0.48
= 0.92

7    0.26

Pr (only one is defective)  =  Pr (defective) × Pr (not defective) = 0.15 × 0.85 =    0.13,  or
    =  Pr (not defective) × Pr (defective) = 0.85 × 0.15 =    $\dfrac{0.13}{0.26}$

8    3    %

Pr(sale) = 0.8

Pr(no sale) = 0.2

∴ Pr(sale on third call)    = Pr(no sale, no sale, sale)
    = 0.2 × 0.2 × 0.8
    = 0.032
    = 3%

9    0.42

|  | *Independent firm* | |
|---|---|---|
|  | L | W |
| P(sale) | 0.3 | 0.4 |
| P(no sale) | 0.7 | 0.6 |

Pr(no sale at L and W) = 0.7 × 0.6 = 0.42

10   B    Pr(serious error or a minor error)    = Pr(serious error) + Pr(minor error)
    = 0.06 + 0.12
    = 0.18

# 7 Probability 2

1    **75**

Expected value = probability × profit

| Contract | | Expected value |
| --- | --- | --- |
| | | $ |
| X | 1/2 × $50,000 | 25,000 |
| Y | 1/3 × $90,000 | 30,000 |
| Z | 1/5 × $100,000 | 20,000 |
| | | 75,000 |

∴ Expected value is closest to $75,000.

2    C    Assume all people are exposed to the virus and that there are 1,000 employees.

| | | Vaccinated | | Non-vaccinated | Total |
| --- | --- | --- | --- | --- | --- |
| Get flu | (10% × 500) | 50 | (30% × 500) | 150 | 200 |
| No flu | (90% × 500) | 450 | (70% × 500) | 350 | 800 |
| | | 500 | | 500 | 1,000 |

Probability employee was vaccinated given that she caught influenza = $\dfrac{50}{200}$ = 0.25.

Option A represents the probability that an employee catches influenza *and* was vaccinated (as opposed to catching influenza *given* that she was vaccinated). Option A is therefore incorrect.

There is a 10% chance (probability of 0.1) that the vaccine is not effective, ie option B, which is incorrect.

3    **0.48**

| Pr (10 on day 1 and 16 on day 2) | = | 0.4 × 0.6 | = | 0.24 |
| --- | --- | --- | --- | --- |
| Pr (16 on day 1 and 10 on day 2) | = | 0.6 × 0.4 | = | 0.24 |
| | | | | 0.48 |

4    D    The expected sales are given by

J:  10,000 × 0.3 + 20,000 × 0.5 + 30,000 × 0.2 = 19,000
K:  10,000 × 0.3 + 20,000 × 0.4 + 30,000 × 0.3 = 20,000
L:  10,000 × 0.2 + 20,000 × 0.6 + 30,000 × 0.2 = 20,000

The correct answer is therefore D since K and L have the highest expected sales.

5    D    P(King)                 = 4/52 = 1/13
          P(Heart)                = 13/52 = 1/4
          P(King of hearts)       = 1/52

          P(King or heart)        = P(King) + P(heart) − P(King of hearts)
                                  = 4/52 + 13/52 − 1/52
                                  = 16/52 = 4/13

Option A is the probability of selecting the King of hearts only.

Option B is the probability of selecting a heart only.

Option C is the probability of selecting a King only.

Note that you need to use the **general rule of addition** in order to calculate the answer to this question. This is because the events are **not mutually exclusive**, ie you can select a king and a heart at the same time.

6    D    The probability of throwing a 3 on a die = 1/6

The probability of a tossed coin coming up tails = 1/2

The probability of throwing a 3 and getting tails on a coin is $1/2 \times 1/4 = 1/12$

Option A represents the probability of getting tails on the coin only.

Option C represents the probability of getting a 3 when throwing a die.

Note that throwing a die and tossing a coin are **independent events** (the occurrence of one event does not affect the outcome of the other event). Such a situation calls for the use of the **simple multiplication law**.

7    A    Suppose there were 100 volunteers, we could show the results of the test on the 100 volunteers as follows.

|                | New shampoo | Normal shampoo | Total |
|----------------|-------------|----------------|-------|
| Improvement    | 50***       | 10****         | 60    |
| No improvement | 20**        | 20             | 40    |
|                | 70*         | 30***          | 100   |

*       70% × 100 = 70
**      2/7 × 70 = 20
***     Balancing figure
****    1/3 × 30 = 10

If we know that the volunteer shows some improvement we can rewrite the question as P(volunteer used normal shampoo given that he shows some improvement) or P(volunteer used normal shampoo/shows some improvement)

= 10/60

Option B(10/100) is the probability that a volunteer used normal shampoo and there was some improvement.

If you selected option C, you calculated the probability that the volunteer used the new shampoo given that there was some improvement.

If you selected option D, you calculated the probability that there was some improvement given that the volunteer used normal shampoo.

8    B    Look back at the contingency table in the answer to question 7 above.

P(volunteer used new shampoo/shows no improvement) = 20/40.

If you selected option A, you calculated the probability that there was no improvement given that the volunteer used the new shampoo.

If you selected option C, you calculated the probability that the volunteer used the new shampoo and showed no improvement.

If you selected option D, you calculated the probability that there was no improvement, given that the volunteer used normal shampoo.

9    A    Look back at the contingency table in the answer to question 7 above.

We need to rephrase the question first.

P(volunteer showed some improvement/used new shampoo) = 50/70.

Option B is the probability that a volunteer used the new shampoo and showed some improvement.

Option C is the probability that a volunteer used the new shampoo given that there was some improvement.

Option D is the probability that a volunteer showed some improvement.

10    C    P(female) = 70% = 0.7
P(CIMA candidate) = 60% = 0.6

We need to use the general rule of addition to avoid double counting.

P(female or CIMA candidate) = P(female) + P(CIMA candidate) − P(female *and* CIMA candidate)

= 0.7 + 0.6 − (0.7 × 0.6)
= 1.3 − 0.42
= 0.88

You should have been able to eliminate options B and D immediately. 0.7 is the probability that a candidate is female and 1.00 is the probability that something will definitely happen – neither of these options are likely to correspond to the probability that the candidate is both female or a CIMA candidate.

Option A is the probability that a candidate is both female **and** a CIMA candidate.

# 8 Probability 3

1   C   The expected value for each project is as follows.

**Project A**   $(0.45 \times \$4,000) + (0.55 \times \$2,000)$    $= \$1,800 + \$1,100$
                                                                 $= \$2,900$

**Project B**   $(0.64 \times \$8,000) + (0.36 \times (\$1,000))$    $= \$5,120 - \$360$
                                                                     $= \$4,760$

Project B has a higher expected value of profit which means that it could offer a better return than A, so Project B should be chosen (with an expected profit of \$4,760).

Options A and B are incorrect because project A does not have the highest expected value.

If you selected option D, you forgot to take account of the expected loss of \$1,000 and treated it as a profit instead.

2   B   Suppose there were 1,000 volunteers, we could show the results of the test on these volunteers as follows.

|  | New tablet | Placebo | Total |
|---|---|---|---|
| Less headaches | 600 | 20 | 620 |
| No improvement | 200 | 180 | 380 |
|  | 800 | 200 | 1,000 |

P(used placebo/shows no improvement) = 180/380 = 0.47.

If you selected option A, you calculated the probability that a volunteer took the placebo and showed no improvement (180/1,000 = 0.18).

If you selected option C, you calculated the probability that a volunteer showed no improvement **given that** he took the placebo (180/200 = 0.9).

Option D represents the probability that a volunteer used the new tablet given that he showed no improvement = 200/380 = 0.53. You have answered the wrong question!

3   C   Look back at the contingency table in the answer to question 2 above.

This question can be rewritten as 'What is the probability that a volunteer used the new tablets given that he has less headaches'.

P(used new tablets/had less headaches) = 600/620 = 0.97.

Option A is incorrect since you have calculated the probability that a volunteer used the new tablets and had less headaches (600/1,000 = 0.6).

Option B is incorrect since you have calculated P(had less headaches/used new tablets) = 600/800 = 0.75.

You should have been able to eliminate option D immediately since it represents absolute certainty.

## ANSWERS

4    C    Look back at the contingency table in the answer to question 2 above.

P(had less headaches/used the placebo) = 20/200 = 0.1.

If you selected option A, you calculated the probability that a volunteer used the placebo and had less headaches (20/1,000 = 0.02).

If you selected option B, you calculated the probability that a volunteer used the placebo **given that** he had less headaches (20/620 = 0.03).

If you selected option D, you incorrectly calculated 20/1,000 = 0.2 (which is the calculation of the wrong probability also).

5        | 0.49 |

The best way to approach a question such as this is to draw a diagram.

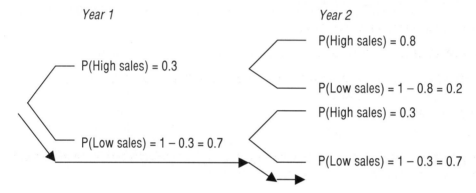

Therefore, the probability of low sales in both years is shown along the path with the arrows above and is P(low sales year 1) × P(low sales year 2)

= 0.7 × 0.7
= 0.49

6

| Type | Expected profit $'000 |
|------|------------------------|
| I | 20 |
| II | 15 |
| III | 26 |
| IV | 23 |

*Workings*

**Type I**
(0.5 × 20) + (0.3 × 20) + (0.2 × 20) = 10 + 6 + 4 = 20

**Type II**
(0.5 × 50) + (0.3 × 0) + (0.2 × (50)) = 25 + 0 − 10 = 15

BPP
PROFESSIONAL EDUCATION

**Type III**

$(0.5 \times 40) + (0.3 \times 20) + (0.2 \times 0) = 20 + 6 + 0 = 26$

**Type IV**

$(0.5 \times 30) + (0.3 \times 20) + (0.2 \times 10) = 15 + 6 + 2 = 23$

If the company wants to maximise profit it should launch Type [ III ]

7    C    If A and B are mutually exclusive outcomes then the occurrence of A excludes the possibility of B happening. It is therefore impossible to have both A and B occurring at the same time.

8    A    The general rule of multiplication is $P(A \text{ and } B) = P(A) \times P(B/A)$.

If you selected option B, you incorrectly chose the simple multiplication law.

Option C is the general rule of addition.

Option D represents the simple addition law.

9    C    Pr(resident went abroad and bought a new car)

= Pr(went abroad) + Pr(bought a new car) – Pr(went abroad and bought a new car)
= 0.4 + 0.55 – (0.4 × 0.55)
= 0.95 – 0.22
= 0.73

If you selected option A you calculated the probability that a resident went abroad *and* bought a new car.

You should have been able to reject option B straightaway since it represents the probability that a resident bought a new car *only*.

If you selected option D, you forgot to take account of the probability that a resident went abroad *and* bought a new car.

10    D    We need to use the simple addition law because we are dealing with mutually exclusive events, ie sales cannot both remain the same *and* rise.

Pr(sales remain same or rise)    = Pr(sales remain same) + Pr(sales rise)
= 0.44 + 0.18
= 0.62

If you selected option A, you multiplied the probabilities together instead of adding them (0.44 × 0.18 = 0.08).

If you selected option B you did not treat the events as mutually exclusive, ie 0.44 + 0.18 – (0.44 × 0.18) = 0.54 (you cannot have sales rising and remaining at the same level at the same time).

Option C represents the probability that sales fell or remained the same (0.38 + 0.18 = 0.56).

# 9 Probability 4

1    0.25

| | Age of customer | | |
|---|---|---|---|
| | Under 21 | 21 and over | Total |
| Expenditure | | | |
| Under $25 | 55 | 205 | 260 |
| $25 to $50 | 125 | 80 | 205 |
| Over $50 | 10 | 25 | 35 |
| | 190 | 310 | 500 |

Number of customers under 21 spending between $25 and $50 is 125. Therefore, the probability that a customer is under 21 *and* spent between $25 and $50 is

$$\frac{125}{500} = 0.25$$

2    0.66

We can rephrase this question to 'given that a customer is aged under 21, what is the probability that he spent between $25 and $50?'

Instead of being concerned with the whole sample (500) we are only concerned with those who are under 21 (190).

The table shows that 125 under 21 year olds spent between $25 and $50.

$\therefore$ Pr (Customer under 21 spent $25- $50) = $\dfrac{125}{190}$ = 0.66

3    0.61

We can rephrase this question to 'given that a customer spent between $25 and $50, what is the probability that they are aged under 21?'

Number of customers spending between $25 and $50 = 205, of which 125 are under 21 years.

$\therefore$ Pr (Customer spending between $25 and $50 is under 21) = $\dfrac{125}{205}$ = 0.61

4    C    Since the probability of an error is 0.2, 0.4 and 0.6 in each section, the probability of no error in each section must be 0.8, 0.6 and 0.4 respectively.

|              | Section 1 | Section 2 | Section 3 |
|--------------|-----------|-----------|-----------|
| Error? (0.2) | Y         | N         | N         |
| Error? (0.4) | N         | Y         | N         |
| Error? (0.6) | N         | N         | Y         |

|                                                        | Probabilities |
|--------------------------------------------------------|---------------|
| Pr(Section 1 has error) = $0.2 \times 0.6 \times 0.4$ = | 0.048         |
| Pr(Section 2 has error) = $0.8 \times 0.4 \times 0.4$ = | 0.128         |
| Pr(Section 3 has error) = $0.8 \times 0.6 \times 0.6$ = | 0.288         |
|                                                        | 0.464         |

The probability of only one error is 0.464.

Option A is incorrect since it represents the probability of no errors ($0.8 \times 0.6 \times 0.4 = 0.192$).

Option B is incorrect because it represents the arithmetic mean of the probabilities of getting an error in each department, ie $\dfrac{0.2 + 0.4 + 0.6}{3} = 0.4$.

Option D is incorrect because it represents the probability of getting at least one error ($1 - 0.192 = 0.808$).

5    D    
| Pr(dry tomorrow)                     | $= 1 - 0.3 = 0.7$ |
|--------------------------------------|-------------------|
| Pr(rain day after/rain tomorrow)     | $= 0.6$           |
| $\therefore$ Pr(dry day after/rain tomorrow) | $= 1 - 0.6 = 0.4$ |
| Pr(rain day after/dry tomorrow)      | $= 0.2$           |
| $\therefore$ Pr(dry day after/dry tomorrow)  | $= 1 - 0.2 = 0.8$ |

P(dry day after tomorrow) =

P(dry tomorrow) × (dry day after tomorrow/dry tomorrow) + P(rain tomorrow) × (dry day after tomorrow/rain tomorrow)

$= (0.7 \times 0.8) + (0.3 \times 0.4)$

$= 0.56 + 0.12$

$= 0.68$

If you didn't select option D, work through the correct answer again until you fully understand the steps involved.

ANSWERS

6    C    P(T) = 1/4

            P(V) = 1/4

            P(W) = 1/4

            P(X) = 1/4

            P(Y) = 1/3

            P(Z) = 2/3 (twice as likely to go through Z)

            P(T or Y)  = P(T) + P(Y) − P(T and Y)

                      = 1/4 + 1/3 − (1/4 × 1/3)

                      = 7/12 − 1/12

                      = 6/12

            = ½

7    B    **Expected value of Project Alpha**

                (0.5 × $50,000) + (0.5 × $20,000)

        =    $25,000 + $10,000 = $35,000

            **Expected value of Project Beta**

                (0.6 × $60,000) + (0.4 × $10,000)

        =    $36,000 + $4,000 = $40,000

            Project Beta should therefore be chosen since it generates the highest expected profits of $40,000.

8       0.44

            P(male) = 1 − P(female) = 1 − 0.8 = 0.2

            P(Shops every Saturday) = 30% = 0.3

            We need to use the general rule of addition to avoid double counting.

            P(male or shops every Saturday)  =  P(Male) + P(shops every Saturday) − P(male *and* shops every Saturday)

                                    =  0.2 + 0.3 − (0.2 × 0.3)

                                      =  0.5 − 0.06

                                      =  0.44

9    B    Expected value = probability × profit

| Contract | Probability | Estimated profits $ | Expected value $ |
|---|---|---|---|
| A | 1/2 | 500,000 | 250,000 |
| B | 1/5 | 800,000 | 160,000 |
| C | 1/3 | 900,000 | 300,000 |
| | | 2,200,000 | 710,000 |

            Option A is incorrect because it is just the highest expected value (from Contract C).

            Option C is the arithmetic mean of the estimated profits ($2,200,000 ÷ 3 = $733,000).

            Option D is the maximum expected profit from any one contract, ie $900,000 from Contract C.

10    | 35 | %

We need to use the general rule of addition to avoid double counting.

P(woman) = 55% = 0.55

P(mathematician) = 10% = 0.10

P(woman or mathematician)   = P(woman) + P(mathematician) − P(woman **and** mathematician)
                                   = 0.55 + 0.10 − (0.55 × 0.10)
                                   = 0.65 − (0.055)
                                   = 0.595

However, the probability that **both** students are women and mathematicians

= $0.595^2$
= 0.354025 = 35%

# 10 Probability 5

1    A    The options are mutually exclusive (they cannot all happen at the same time) so we need to use the simple addition law.

P(production remaining the same or falling) = P(remaining the same) + P(falling) = 0.3 + 0.15 = 0.45.

If you selected option B you have calculated the probability that production will stay the same *or* fall (which is impossible) = 0.3 × 0.15 = 0.045.

If you selected option C you have calculated the probability of production staying the same or falling as if the events were *not* mutually exclusive, ie 0.3 + 0.15 − (0.3 × 0.15) = 0.405.

Option D represents the probability that production has increased (the opposite of what is actually required), ie 0.55.

2    C    You will miss the train if it leaves on time or is one minute late.

∴ Pr(miss the train) = Pr(leaves on time) + Pr(one minute late)

      = 0.30 + 0.25
      = 0.55

If you selected option A, this is incorrect because it represents the probability that the train will be two minutes late (0.2).

Option B is the incorrect answer since this represents the probability that you will catch the train, not miss it.

3    A    At least one of them is impossible

Mutual exclusivity means that for two outcomes X and Y
P(X and Y) = 0
Independence of the two events of which X and Y are outcomes means that
P(X and Y) = P(X) × P(Y).
So P(X) × P(Y) = 0
Therefore at least one of P(X) and P(Y) must be zero, representing an impossible outcome.

4    D    The expected value = $(1,000 \times 0.3) + (4,000 \times 0.5) + (8,000 \times 0.2) = 3,900$

Option A represents the most likely sales level, you forgot to calculate the expected value.

Option B represents the arithmetic mean, you forgot to calculate the expected value.

Option C is the total of estimated sales at different levels of probability, you forgot to calculate the expected level of sales.

5    D    Expected value = $\sum px$

where    x = the value
         p = probability of the value

Expected probability
$$= \frac{(2 \times 0.35) + (1 \times 0.15) + (1 \times 0.12)}{4}$$
$$= \frac{0.7 + 0.15 + 0.12}{4}$$
$$= \frac{0.97}{4} = 0.2425$$

If you selected option A, you forgot to take into account how frequently each area is visited.

If you selected option B, you have averaged the probabilities without referring to how frequently each area is visited.

Option C is simply the result of all probabilities being added together, you have used the wrong method and should have calculated the expected probability as $\sum px$.

6    C    Pr(at least one sale) = 1 – Pr(no sales)

Pr(no sales) = $(0.6 \times 0.55 \times 0.5) = 0.165$

$$\begin{aligned}\text{Pr(at least one sale)} &= 1 - 0.165 \\ &= 0.835\end{aligned}$$

If you selected answer A, you calculated the probability that each person makes one sale (giving a total of three sales), ie $0.4 \times 0.45 \times 0.5 = 0.09$. The question did not ask this.

If you selected answer B, you calculated the probability of no sale being made which was not the requirement of the question.

Option D represents the probability that the most successful member of the sales team will make a sale, ie 0.5. This was not the requirement of the question.

7    | 0.25 |

The ways of getting three heads are:

|      | Probability |   |        |
|------|-------------|---|--------|
| HHHT | $0.5 \times 0.5 \times 0.5 \times 0.5$ | = | 0.0625 |
| HHTH | $0.5 \times 0.5 \times 0.5 \times 0.5$ | = | 0.0625 |
| HTHH | $0.5 \times 0.5 \times 0.5 \times 0.5$ | = | 0.0625 |
| THHH | $0.5 \times 0.5 \times 0.5 \times 0.5$ | = | 0.0625 |
|      |             |   | 0.2500 |

8    C    **Current expected value**

$(0.6 \times \$3,000) + (0.4 \times \$1,500)$    $= \$1,800 + \$600$
                                           $= \$2,400$

**Revised expected value**

$(0.55 \times \$3,000) + (0.45 \times \$1,500)$    $= \$1,650 + \$675$
                                             $= \$2,325$

|                          | $     |
|--------------------------|-------|
| Current expected value   | 2,400 |
| Revised expected value   | 2,325 |
|                          | 75    |

There is therefore a fall of $75.

If you selected A, you correctly calculated a change of $75 but it was a fall, not a gain.

If you selected option B, you only accounted for the drop in expected value of the $3,000 profit. You forgot to take into account the fact that this is partly offset by the $75 from the increase in expected value of the $1,500 profit.

If you selected option D, you treated the $1,500 as if it were a loss instead of a profit.

9    A    Expected daily sales    $= (100 \times 0.23) + (200 \times 0.29) + (300 \times 0.42) + (400 \times 0.06)$
                                                    $= 23 + 58 + 126 + 24$
                                                    $= 231$

If you selected option B, you have calculated the arithmetic mean of the four sales levels, without referring to their associated probabilities.

Option C represents the most likely sales value multiplied by its probability ($300 \times 0.42 = 126$).

Option D is the most likely sales level and is not what was required by the question.

10    | 38.8 | %

P(worker 1 does not make error) $= 1 - 0.15 = 0.85$

P(worker 2 does not make error) $= 1 - 0.20 = 0.80$

P(worker 3 does not make error) $= 1 - 0.25 = 0.75$

Let   Y   = error made (yes)
      N   = no error made (no)

| *Error made by worker* | | | *Probabilities* | |
|---|---|---|---|---|
| 1 | 2 | 3 | | |
| Y | N | N | $0.15 \times 0.80 \times 0.75 =$ | 0.0900 |
| N | Y | N | $0.85 \times 0.20 \times 0.75 =$ | 0.1275 |
| N | N | Y | $0.85 \times 0.80 \times 0.25 =$ | 0.1700 |
| | | | | 0.3875 |

$0.3875 = 38.8\%$

# 11 Probability 6

1     ☐ ✓    Both W and Y

EV(Expert W)    = (0.2 × $1m) + (0.3 × $0.5m) + (0.5 × $0.25m)
                  = $(0.2 + 0.15 + 0.125)m = $0.475m

EV(Expert X)     = (0.1 × $1m) + (0.4 × $0.5m) + (0.5 × $0.25m)
                  = $(0.1 + 0.2 + 0.125)m = $0.425m

EV(Expert Y)     = (0.1 × $1m) + (0.6 × $0.5m) + (0.3 × $0.25m)
                  = $(0.1 + 0.3 + 0.075)m = $0.475m

The highest expected value for the company's estimated annual sales is given by Expert W and Expert Y.

2    0.976

P(at least one error found) = 1 – P(0 errors)

P(0 errors) = 0.2 × 0.3 × 0.4

∴ P(at least one error found)   = 1 – (0.2 × 0.3 × 0.4)
                               = 1 – 0.024
                               = 0.976

3   Pr(queen or heart) = 4/52 + 13/52 – 1/52 = 4/13

Probability

| Queen | Heart | Queen of hearts | Queen or heart |
|-------|-------|-----------------|----------------|
| 4/52  | 13/52 | 1/52            | 4/13           |

4   EV of demand = 6,500 units

*Workings*

| Demand | Probability | Expected value |
|--------|-------------|----------------|
| Units  |             | Units          |
| 5,000  | 0.1         | 500            |
| 6,000  | 0.6         | 3,600          |
| 8,000  | 0.3         | 2,400          |
|        |             | 6,500          |

5   EV of unit variable costs = $ 3.70 (to 2 decimal places)

*Workings*

| Variable costs | Probability | Expected value |
|----------------|-------------|----------------|
| $              |             | $              |
| 3.00           | 0.1         | 0.30           |
| 3.50           | 0.5         | 1.75           |
| 4.00           | 0.3         | 1.20           |
| 4.50           | 0.1         | 0.45           |
|                |             | 3.70           |

6    EV of profit = $ 10,950

*Workings*

|  |  | $ |
|---|---|---|
| Sales 6,500 × $10 |  | 65,000 |
| Less variable costs 6,500 × $3.70 |  | 24,050 |
| Contribution |  | 40,950 |
| Less fixed costs |  | 30,000 |
|  |  | 10,950 |

7    19.0 %

A demand of 520 units occurred on 19 days out of a total of 100.
Pr(demand = 520 units) = 19/100 × 100% = 19%

8    0.45 (to 2 decimal places). See question 10 for workings

9    0.40 (to 2 decimal places). See question 10 for workings

10    0.56 (to 2 decimal places).

*Workings for questions 8,9 and 10*

|  | Given low-fat food | Given normal food | Total |
|---|---|---|---|
| Lost weight | 200 | 250 | 450 |
| No weight loss | 300 | 250 | 550 |
|  | 500 | 500 | 1,000 |

Pr(dog has lost weight) = $\frac{450}{1,000}$ = 0.45

Pr(dog has lost weight given that it received low-fat food) = $\frac{200}{500}$ = 0.40

Pr(dog was given normal food given that it lost weight) = $\frac{250}{450}$ = 0.56

# 12 Probability 7

1

| Assembly line | Number of plates sampled |
|---|---|
| X | 40 |
| Y | 80 |
| Z | 120 |

*Workings*

The inspector samples finished plates from the assembly lines X, Y and Z in the ratio 1:2:3, and he will therefore examine the following quantities.

**Assembly X** $= \dfrac{1}{(1+2+3)} \times 240 = 40$ plates

**Assembly Y** $= \dfrac{2}{(1+2+3)} \times 240 = 80$ plates

**Assembly Z** $= \dfrac{3}{(1+2+3)} \times 240 = 120$ plates

2 The probability that a plate sampled is defective is $\boxed{0.192}$ (to 3 decimal places).

**Contingency table**

|  | Assembly Line | | | |
|---|---|---|---|---|
|  | X | Y | Z | Total |
| Defective | 2 (W1) | 8 (W2) | 36 (W3) | 46 |
| Not defective | 38 (W4) | 72 (W5) | 84 (W6) | 194 |
|  | 40 | 80 | 120 | 240 |

*Workings*

- (1) $= 5\% \times 40 = 2$
- (2) $= 10\% \times 80 = 8$
- (3) $= 30\% \times 120 = 36$
- (4) $= 40 - 2 = 38$
- (5) $= 80 - 8 = 72$
- (6) $= 120 - 36 = 84$

$$\frac{\text{Total number of defective plates}}{\text{Total number of plates}} = \frac{46}{240} = 0.192 \text{ (to 3 decimal places)}$$

3 $\boxed{0.725}$ (to 3 decimal places)

*Working*

$$\text{Pr(some improvement)} = \frac{725}{1{,}000} = 0.725$$

4 $\boxed{0.545}$ (to 3 decimal places)

*Working*

$$\text{Pr(treatment received/no improvement observed)} = \frac{150}{275} = 0.545$$

5 The probability that an African brochure is **not** selected is $\boxed{97\%}$ (see workings below).

6     The probability that neither an American nor an Asian brochure is selected is ⟨ 60% ⟩

*Workings for questions 5 and 6*

The best way to approach these types of question is to draw up a table as follows, which shows the individual probabilities of the different types of brochure being selected.

| Brochure | European | American | Asian | African | Total |
|---|---|---|---|---|---|
| Number | 285 | 90 | 110 | 15 | 500 |
| Proportion/ Probability | 0.57 | 0.18 | 0.22 | 0.03 | 1.00 |

Pr (African brochure not selected)    = 1 − Pr (African brochure selected)
$$= 1 - (15/500) = 1 - 0.03$$
$$= 0.97 = 97\%$$

Pr (Neither American nor Asian brochure selected) =

1 − Pr (American or Asian brochure selected)    = 1 − (90/500 + 110/500) =
1 − (0.18 + 0.22)                            = 1 − 0.4
                                                = 0.6 = 60%

7    ⟨ 0.25 ⟩

We can calculate the required probability by using the values calculated in the following contingency table.

| | Pay | Default | Total |
|---|---|---|---|
| Check | 36 | 4 | 40 |
| No check | 48 | 12 | 60 |
| Total | 84 | 16 | 100 |

*Workings*

No check = 60% of 100 = 60
Check = 100 − 60 = 40
No check but pay = 80% of 60 = 48
Check, pay = 90% of 40 = 36

The other figures are balancing figures.

Pr(customer checked/defaults) = 4/16 = 0.25

8    B    The best way to approach a question such as this is to draw a diagram.

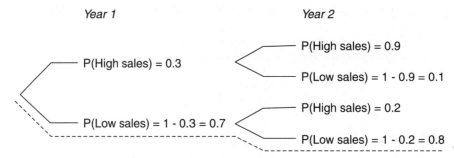

Therefore, the probability of low sales in both years is shown along the path with the dotted line above and is P(low sales year 1) × P(low sales year 2).

$$= 0.7 \times 0.8$$
$$= 0.56$$

The correct answer is therefore B.

Option A is incorrect because this is simply the probability of low sales in year 2 *only*.

Option C is incorrect because this is the probability of high sales in year 2 *only*.

Option D is incorrect because the probabilities 0.7 and 0.8 have been added (0.7 + 0.8 = 1.5) instead of multiplied together. This option could have been eliminated straightaway since you cannot have a probability of more than 1.

9    C    Firstly, we need to calculate the expected profit that each product might generate.

**Type W**
$(0.5 \times 20) + (0.3 \times 20) + (0.2 \times 20)$    $= 10 + 6 + 4$
    $= 20$

**Type X**
$(0.5 \times 50) + (0.3 \times 0) + (0.2 \times (50))$    $= 25 + 0 - 10$
    $= 15$

**Type Y**
$(0.5 \times 40) + (0.3 \times 20) + (0.2 \times 0)$    $= 20 + 6 + 0$
    $= 26$

**Type Z**
$(0.5 \times 30) + (0.3 \times 20) + (0.2 \times 10)$    $= 15 + 6 + 2$
    $= 23$

Since the question states that the company wishes to maximise the expected profit, it should launch Type Y (which has the highest expected profit, $26,000).

10    C    The diagram is a Venn diagram illustrating two mutually exclusive outcomes.

Complementary outcomes would be illustrated using the following diagram.

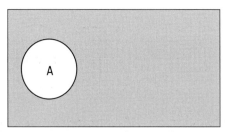

# 13 Summarising and analysing data 1

1    | 20.48 |

Let midpoint of estimate = X.

$21.50 = 100% + 5% of midpoint of estimate = 1.05X

∴ $21.50 = 1.05X

∴ $\frac{\$21.50}{1.05}$ = X = $20.48

Midpoint of estimate = $20.48

2    D

|              | 1980 | 1994 | 1996 |
|--------------|------|------|------|
| 1980 = 100   | 100  | 126  |      |
| 1994 = 100   |      | 100  | 109  |

Between 1994 and 1996 prices increased by 9% ( $\frac{109 - 100}{100}$ × 100%)

∴ The price index for 1996 with 1980 as the base year should also show a 9% increase on the 1994 index of 126.

∴ 1996 index with 1980 as base year = 126 × 109% = 126 × 1.09 = 137.34

You should have been able to eliminate options A and B straightaway since the new index cannot be less than or equal to 100.

Option C is incorrect since the 9% has just been added to the 126 points to give 135.

3 | 41 |

$100 \times P_1/P_0 = 135$

$P_1 = \$55.35$

$\therefore \dfrac{100 \times \$55.35}{P_0} = 135$

$\therefore \dfrac{100 \times \$55.35}{135} = P_0 = \$41$

4 | 11.39 |

| x | fx | | f |
|---|---|---|---|
| $ | $ | | |
| 10.00 | 400 | 400 ÷ 10.00 = | 40 |
| 12.50 | 500 | 500 ÷ 12.50 = | 40 |
| 11.00 | 550 | 550 ÷ 11.00 = | 50 |
| 12.00 | 600 | 600 ÷ 12.00 = | 50 |
| | 2,050 | | 180 |

$\therefore \bar{x} = \dfrac{\sum fx}{\sum f} = \dfrac{\$2,050}{180} = \$11.39$

5    C    In order of magnitude scores are

8        9        11        12        14        15        17        21        24        34

Position of median is $\dfrac{10+1}{2}$ = 5½ and therefore the median is the average of 5th and 6th items, that is of 14 and 15. The median is therefore 14.5.

You should also have been able to eliminate option D immediately since it does not represent an actual score, and if it were the average of two scores, they would be 16 and 17. The scores do not include a 16 and therefore this option does not appear to be valid.

6    B    Total sales for first five months        = $8,200 × 5 = $41,000
Total sales for last four months        = $8,500 × 4 = $34,000

So total sales for remaining 3 months    = $(102,000 − 41,000 − 34,000)
= $27,000,

giving an average of $\dfrac{\$27,000}{3}$ = $9,000

7    C    The median is the middle value in order of magnitude.

| 9 | 12 | 23 | 24 | 28 | 34 | 43 | 56 | 78 | 87 |

In this case there are two middle values, 28 and 34, and so the median is their average = (28 + 34)/2 = 31.

Options B and D represent the two middle values and are therefore incorrect. The average of the two middle values must be calculated when establishing the median of a set of scores.

Option A is incorrect since it represents the average between the 4th and 5th items (24 and 28) which is 26.

8    
> 28

If the width of an interval is n times the width of the remaining intervals, then the height of the corresponding histogram rectangle is given by that interval's frequency divided by n. In this case, n is 3/4, so the height is $21 \div 3/4 = 21 \times 4/3 = 28$.

This was a popular type of objective test question in the old syllabus CQM examinations – do make sure you understand it!

9    A    Frequency is indicated by the area covered by the block on a histogram, rather than by the block's height. If the width of the block is one and a half the standard width, we must divide the frequency by one and a half, ie multiply by 0.67 ($1/1.5 = 1^3/_2 = 2/3 = 0.67$).

10    D    $80 = \dfrac{(10 \times 50) + (10 \times 70) + (20 \times X)}{10 + 10 + 20}$

$80 \times 40 = 500 + 700 + 20X$

$3{,}200 - 1{,}200 = 20X$

$2{,}000 = 20X$

$100 = X$

You would need to do a full calculation before you would be able to select the correct option since none of the distracters are obviously wrong. Remember in a question such as this, however, that you must calculate a **weighted** average.

# 14 Summarising and analysing data 2

1    D    When a distribution has unequal class intervals, the heights of the bars have to be adjusted for the fact that the bars do not have the same width.

Adjustment = 0.8 (100 × 0.8 = 80)

∴ The width of the non-standard bar must be $\dfrac{\$20}{0.8} = \$25$

If the common class width is $20, then a class with a non-standard class width will not also be $20. Option C can therefore be eliminated.

If the frequency of one bar is 80% (80/100) of the standard frequency, we must divide the common class width by 80%, not multiply it by 80% (80% × $20 = $16). Option B is therefore also incorrect.

ANSWERS

2    False

An ogive is a graph of a cumulative frequency distribution.

3    B    A histogram is a chart that looks like a bar chart except that the bars are joined together. On a histogram, frequencies are represented by the area covered by the bars (compare this with a bar chart where the frequencies are represented by the heights of the bars).

4    40

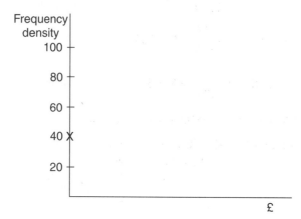

The common class width = $10

The width in question = $12.50

The height of the bar must be adjusted by $\dfrac{10}{12.50}$ = 0.8

∴ The frequency which must be plotted = 0.8 × 50 = 40

5    D    The best diagram to draw to highlight the differences between areas is a simple bar chart .

A simple bar chart is a chart consisting of one or more bars, in which the length of each bar indicates the magnitude of the corresponding data items. This is the best diagram to draw to highlight the differences of typical salaries in different areas.

We are not interested in showing the breakdown of the total salary, therefore a pie diagram and a percentage component bar chart are not really appropriate.

A multiple bar chart is a bar chart in which two or more separate bars are used to present sub-divisions of data. The data available relating to salaries is not subdivided and this type of chart is therefore not appropriate in this situation.

6　　B　　The annual pension payable from 1 January 2000 is

$$\$10,000 \times \frac{142.0}{135.6} = \$10,472$$

Options A, C and D are all incorrect since they have been calculated using the incorrect numerators/denominators as follows.

Option A　　$= \$10,000 \times \dfrac{142.0}{137.9} = \$10,297$

Option C　　$= \$10,000 \times \dfrac{142.0}{130.2} = \$10,906$

Option D　　$= \$10,000 \times \dfrac{135.6}{100} = \$13,560$

7　　C　　Total of invoices　　$=$　　average $\times 10 = 20 \times 10$

$$
\begin{aligned}
15 + 22 + 14 + 21 + 15 + 20 + 18 + 27 &= 152 \\
2X + 152 &= 200 \\
2X &= 200 - 152 = 48 \\
X &= \$24
\end{aligned}
$$

Option B is incorrect because it represents the arithmetic mean of the values (excluding the Xs), ie $152 \div 8 = 19$. It also represents the median of the values shown.

If you selected option D then this indicates that you only accounted for one $X instead of two.

Option A ($15) represents the mode and is therefore incorrect.

8　　B　　To calculate a mean factory wage we need to determine total wages and total number of employees.

| Department | Mean wage $ | Number of employees | | Total wage $ |
|---|---|---|---|---|
| W | 50 | × | 20 | = 1,000 |
| X | 100 | × | 5 | = 500 |
| Y | 70 | × | 10 | = 700 |
| Z | 80 | × | 5 | = 400 |
| | | | 40 | 2,600 |

Mean factory wage = $2,600/40 = $65

Option A represents the most frequently occurring wage ($50) or the mode and is therefore incorrect.

Option C represents the second most frequently occurring wage ($70) and is also incorrect.

Option D is simply the average of the mean wages (an unweighted average), ie 50 + 100 + 70 + 80 = 300 ÷ 4 = 75. This option is also incorrect.

9    A    To calculate a mean speed we need to know the distance and the time of the journey.

Time = 20/30 hr + 10/60 hr = 5/6 hr
∴ Mean speed = 30 miles ÷ 5/6 hr = 36 mph

Option B is incorrectly calculated as follows.

(20 miles × 30 mph) + (10 miles × 60 mph) = 600 + 600 = 1,200

Total distance travelled = 30 miles
∴ Mean speed = 1,200 ÷ 30 = 40 mph (incorrect)

Remember that you need to know the length of time that it took to travel the 30 mile distance.

Option D, 45 mph represents an average of 30 mph and 60 mph (30 + 60 = 90 ÷ 2 = 45). This is also incorrect.

10   C    Arithmetic mean $= \dfrac{\text{Sum of value of items}}{\text{Number of items}}$

For 10 units,    $1 = \dfrac{\text{Sum of value of items}}{10}$

$10 = \text{Sum of value of items}$

For 20 units,    $2 = \dfrac{\text{Sum of value of items}}{20}$

$40 = \text{Sum of value of items}$

For 30 units,    $3 = \dfrac{\text{Sum of value of items}}{30}$

$90 = \text{Sum of value of items}$

Arithmetic mean of all items $= \dfrac{\text{Sum of value of all items}}{\text{Number of items}}$

$= \dfrac{10 + 40 + 90}{10 + 20 + 30} = \dfrac{140}{60}$

$= \$2.33$

Option A is incorrect because it simply represents the **unweighted average**, ie $1 + $2 + $3 = $6 ÷ 3 = $2.

# 15 Summarising and analysing data 3

1    A

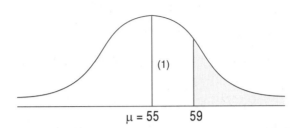

Standard deviation ($\sigma$)  $= \sqrt{\text{variance}}$
$= \sqrt{14.44}$
$= 3.8$

We are therefore looking for the probability corresponding to the shaded area on the graph above.

Using normal distribution tables we can calculate the area (1) above.

$$z = \frac{x - \mu}{\sigma}$$

$$= \frac{59 - 55}{3.8}$$

$$= 1.05$$

A z value of 1.05 corresponds to a probability of 0.3531.

∴ Area (1) = 0.3531 and therefore the shaded area that we are interested in = 0.5 − 0.3531 = 0.1469 = 0.15.

If you incorrectly selected option B, you forgot to deduct the probability of area (1) from 0.5.

You could have eliminated option C immediately. The probability of a score of 55 or more (not 59) is exactly 0.5.

Option D is also incorrect and represents the probability of a score of 59 or **less**, ie 0.5 + 0.3531 = 0.8531 or 0.85.

2    C    25% of normal frequencies will occur between the mean and the upper quartile. From normal distribution tables, 25% of frequencies lie between the mean and a point 0.67 standard deviations above the mean.

The standard deviation is the square root of the variance and is $\sqrt{25}$ = 5 in this case.

The upper quartile is therefore 0.67 × 5 = 3.35 above the mean

∴ The upper quartile = 3.35 + 75 = 78.35

You should have been able to eliminate options A and B straightaway since 58.25 and 71.65 are **below** the mean. The upper quartile of any distribution will be **above** the mean. Option B represents the **lower quartile** (75 − 3.35).

If you had forgotten to take the square root of the variance in order to obtain the standard deviation, you would have calculated the upper quartile as being 0.67 × 25 = 16.75 above the mean, ie 75 + 16.75 = 91.75. Option D is therefore also incorrect for this reason.

3    D    It is always best to sketch a rough diagram first when tackling a normal distribution question such as this.

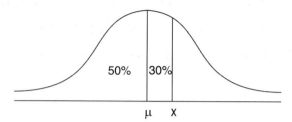

μ = 150
σ = 20

We need to find the point X such that 30% of the distribution falls between the mean and x.

From normal distribution tables, we can see that 30% of the distribution lies between the mean and 0.84 standard deviations above the mean.

If $z = \dfrac{x - \mu}{\sigma}$

$$0.84 \quad = \quad \dfrac{x - 150}{20}$$

$$x - 150 \quad = \quad 0.84 \times 20$$

$$x - 150 \quad = \quad 16.8$$

$$x \quad = \quad 16.8 + 150$$

$$= \quad 166.8$$

Therefore 80% of the distribution lies below the point 167 (approximately).

You must make sure that you are confident with reading normal distribution tables in OT questions – you are unlikely to gain any marks at all in such questions if you read them incorrectly.

4    D    Total area under normal curve = 1

Therefore each of four areas = 0.25

The table shows the area between 0 and the specified value of Z so we must find the value 0.25 in the table and the Z value that corresponds most closely to it.

Z = 0.67

Sketch a normal distribution curve and divide it into four areas if you are not convinced about the answer to this question!

5    A    μ = 50 cm
σ = 5 cm

57 cm is 7 cm above the mean = 1.4 standard deviations above the mean.

Using normal distribution tables, the proportion between the mean and 1.4 standard deviations above the mean = 0.4192

∴ The percentage of tubes at least 57 cm long is (0.5 – 0.4192) = 0.0808 = 8.08%

The percentage is closest to 8%.

Option B, 42% represents the proportion of tubes between 50 and 57 cm long.

Option C, 58% represents the proportion of tubes below the mean and above 57cm.

Option D represents the proportion of tubes below 57 cm.

6    $\boxed{0.0082}$

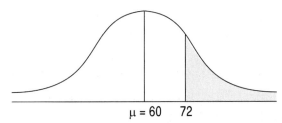

We are interested in the shaded area shown in the graph above. We can calculate z score using the following formula.

$$z = \frac{x - \mu}{\sigma}$$

$$= \frac{72 - 60}{\sqrt{25}}$$

$$= \frac{12}{5}$$

$$= 2.4$$

Using normal distribution tables, we can calculate that the probability of a score between 60 and 72 is 0.4918 (where z = 2.4). The probability of a score greater than 72 is 0.5 − 0.4918 = 0.0082.

7    D

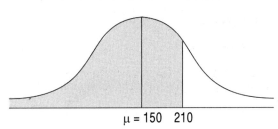

We are interested in the shaded area shown in the graph above. We can calculate the z score using the following formula.

$$z = \frac{x - \mu}{\sigma}$$

$$= \frac{210 - 150}{\sqrt{6,944}}$$

$$= \frac{60}{83.33} = 0.72$$

From normal distribution tables, the probability of a value between 150 and 210 is 0.2642. Therefore the probability of a value less than 210 = 0.5 + 0.2642 = 0.7642 or 76.42%.

If you selected option A, you incorrectly subtracted 0.2642 from 0.5 instead of adding it.

If you selected option B, you forgot to add your answer to 0.5.

If you selected option C, you forgot to convert your z score into a probability using normal distribution tables.

8    B

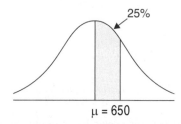

$\mu = 650$

25% of normal frequencies will occur between the mean and the upper quartile. From normal distribution tables, 25% of frequencies lie between the mean and a point 0.67 standard deviations above the mean (ie our z score is 0.67).

Let x = upper quartile

If $z = \dfrac{x - \mu}{\sigma}$

and $\sigma = \sqrt{100} = 10$

$$
\begin{aligned}
0.67 &= \frac{x - 650}{10} \\
(0.67 \times 10) &= x - 650 \\
6.7 &= x - 650 \\
x &= 650 + 6.7 \\
&= 656.7
\end{aligned}
$$

Therefore the upper quartile = 656.7 and the correct answer is therefore B.

If you selected option A, you calculated the lower quartile of the distribution (the question required you to calculate the upper quartile).

If you chose option C, you forgot to calculate the standard deviation (and used the value given for the variance, ie 100).

If you chose option D, you simply took 25% of the mean ($650 \times 25\% = 162.5$) and added it to the mean ($162.5 + 650 = 812.5$) which is not the correct way to calculate the upper quartile.

9    C    Total area under normal curve = 1.

Therefore each of eight areas = 0.125 (0.125 × 8 = 1).

Normal distribution tables show the area between 0 and the specified value of z so we must find the value of 0.125 in the tables and the z value that corresponds most closely to it.

z = 0.32

Sketch a normal distribution curve and divide it into eight areas if you are not convinced about the answer to this question!

10   A

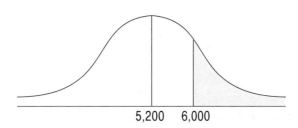

5,200    6,000

We are interested in calculating the area of the shaded part of the graph above.

We can find the area of the graph that lies between 5,200kg and 6,000kg as follows.

Using    $z = \dfrac{X - \mu}{\sigma}$

$z = \dfrac{6,000 - 5,200}{430}$

$z = 1.86$

z = 1.86 corresponds to an area of 0.4686. However, we are interested in the shaded area = 0.5 − 0.4686 = 0.0314.

If you selected option B, you divided the probability obtained (0.4686) by 2 instead of subtracting it from 0.5.

If you selected option C, you forgot to subtract 0.4686 from 0.5.

If you selected option D, you added 0.4686 to 0.5 instead of subtracting it.

# 16 Summarising and analysing data 4

1    | 97 |

To change the base date, divide each index by the index corresponding to the new base time point and multiply the result by 100.

Rebased 20 × 2 index    $= \dfrac{107}{110} \times 100$

$= 97$

2    B    Pie charts illustrate the way in which one or more totals are broken down into their components.

3    A    The coefficient of variation = $\dfrac{\text{Standard deviation}}{\text{Mean}}$

The coefficients of variation are calculated as follows:

W:    $\dfrac{10}{100} \times 100$    = 10%

X:    $\dfrac{5}{40} \times 100$    = 12½%

Y:    $\dfrac{8}{80} \times 100$    = 10%

Z:    $\dfrac{12}{150} \times 100$    = 8%

The correct answer is therefore A, X only, since X has the largest coefficient of variation.

4    A    Every fifth item is selected, therefore the sampling interval is 5.

5    | 40 |

If a distribution has unequal class intervals, the heights of the bars have to be adjusted for the fact that the bars do not have the same width.

$\dfrac{\$7.50}{\$5.00} = 1.5$

$7.50 is one and a half times the standard width so we must therefore divide the frequency of 60 by 1.5, ie 60 ÷ 1.5 = 40.

6    | 92 |

The individual weights (in kg) arranged in order are as follows.

53, 59, 69, 84, 94, 97, 105

$$\text{Median} = \dfrac{84 + x}{2}$$

$$88 = \dfrac{84 + x}{2}$$

$$x = (88 \times 2) - 84$$
$$= 176 - 84$$
$$= 92$$

7    D    An ogive shows a **cumulative frequency distribution**, ie it shows the cumulative number of items with a value less than or equal to, or alternatively greater than or equal to, a certain amount.

8 B Since the class intervals are different, adjusted frequencies need to be calculated. The adjusted frequencies are calculated as follows. (Standard class width is taken as 2.)

| Class interval | Size of interval | Frequency | Adjustment | Height of bar |
|---|---|---|---|---|
| 0-6 | 6 | 18 | $\times 2/6$ | 6 |
| 6-8 | 2 | 30 | $\times 2/2$ | 30 |
| 8-10 | 2 | 18 | $\times 2/2$ | 18 |
| 10-14 | 4 | 12 | $\times 2/4$ | 6 |

The histogram which represents the above bar heights correctly is Graph 2. The correct answer is therefore B.

Options A, C and D are incorrect because the class intervals need to be adjusted to take account of unequal class widths (as shown above).

9 | 45 |

The arithmetic mean $= \dfrac{\sum x}{n}$

$\therefore \quad 5 \quad = \quad \dfrac{\sum x}{19}$

$\sum x \quad = \quad 19 \times 5$

$\quad\quad = \quad 95$

Let x = twentieth number

Sum of twenty numbers = 95 + x

Arithmetic mean = 7

$\therefore \quad \dfrac{\sum x}{n} \quad = \quad 7$

$\dfrac{95 + x}{20} \quad = \quad 7$

$95 + x \quad = \quad 7 \times 20$

$95 + x \quad = \quad 140$

$x \quad = \quad 140 - 95$

$x \quad = \quad 45$

10 | 30 |

The median is the value of the middle item of a distribution once all of the items have been arranged in order of magnitude.

$$10, 10, 15, 20, 30, 35, 35, 35, 35$$

↑
middle item

The median is the 5th item in the array (the $\frac{9+1}{2}$ = 5th item).

The median is therefore 30.

# 17 Summarising and analysing data 5

1 | 2 |

The median is the middle member in the distribution, ie the $\frac{55+1}{2}$ = 28th member which is 2.

2    A    Properties of a positively skewed distribution.

- Its mean, mode and median all have different values
- The mode has a lower value than the median
- The mean has a higher value than the median
- It does not have two halves which are mirror images of each other

3 | 0.60 |

Frequency is indicated by the area covered by the block on a histogram, rather than by the block's height. If the width of the block is $1\,^2/_3$ times the standard width, we must divide the frequency by $1^2/_3$ (1.67) ie multiply by $\frac{1}{1.67}$ = 0.60.

4    A    An ogive is a graph of a cumulative frequency distribution.

5 | 230 |

If y = 2.5x

$$\frac{286 + 192 + x + 307 + 185 + 2.5x + 94}{7} \quad = \quad 267$$

$$\frac{1,064 + 3.5x}{7} \quad = \quad 267$$

$$3.5x \quad = \quad (267 \times 7) - 1,064$$

$$3.5x \quad = \quad 1,869 - 1,064$$

$$3.5x \quad = \quad 805$$

$$x \quad = \quad \frac{805}{3.5}$$

$$= \quad 230$$

6 B The quartile deviation is also known as the semi-interquartile range.

7 A Properties of a positively skewed distribution

- Its mean, mode and median all have different values
- The mode will have a lower value than the median
- Its mean will have a higher value than the median
- It does not have two halves which are mirror images of each other

8 ┌─────────┐
  │   360   │
  └─────────┘

Let x = the number of cases of Product D purchased.

$(40 \times \$7.84) + (20 \times \$8.20) + (24 \times \$8.50) + (\$8.60 \times x) = \$939.60$

$$\begin{aligned}
\$(313.6 + 164 + 204) + 8.6x &= \$939.60 \\
\$681.6 + 8.6x &= \$939.60 \\
8.6x &= \$(939.60 - 681.6) \\
8.6x &= \$258 \\
x &= 30
\end{aligned}$$

If there are 12 items in each case of Product D, the buyer purchases $30 \times 12$ items = 360 items.

9 C

| | 1984 | 1998 | 2000 |
|---|---|---|---|
| 1984 = 100 | 100 | 129 | |
| 1998 = 100 | | 100 | 110 |

Between 1998 and 2000 prices increased by 10%

$$\left( \frac{110 - 100}{100} \times 100\% \right)$$

∴ The price index for 2000 with 1984 as the base year should also show a 10% increase on the 1998 index of 129.

∴ 2000 index with 1984 as base year = $129 \times 110\% = 129 \times 1.1 = 141.90$

You should have been able to eliminate options A and B straightaway since the new index will not be less than or equal to 100.

Option D is incorrect because you have added the 10 points (110 – 100) to the 129 points. It should be 129 plus 10%.

10 C If a distribution has unequal class intervals, remember that the heights of the bars must be adjusted for the fact that the bars do not have the same width. Thus, if one class is two thirds the standard width, you need to **divide** the frequency by 2/3, ie $25 \div 2/3 = 37.5$.

If you selected option A then you multiplied the frequency by 2/3 instead of dividing it by 2/3.

Option B represents the unadjusted frequency of the class under consideration, which is incorrect; an adjustment needs to be made.

If you selected option D you incorrectly took 2/3 of 25 (= 16.67) and added this to the unadjusted class frequency of 25. 25 + 16.67 = 41.67.

# 18 Summarising and analysing data 6

1    C    If an interval is 1¼ times as wide as other classes, the frequency of that class must be divided by 1¼, which is the same as multiplying it by 0.8 since $\dfrac{1}{1\frac{1}{4}} = 0.8$.

2    | 160 |

Number of employees in department 2 = 100 − 54 − 24 = 22. For all employees, mean output per month = 139.

Let x = the mean output per employee per month for department 2.

$$139 \quad = \quad \frac{(54 \times 130) + (22 \times x) + (24 \times 140)}{100}$$

$$139 \times 100 \quad = \quad 7{,}020 + 22x + 3{,}360$$

$$13{,}900 \quad = \quad 10{,}380 + 22x$$

$$22x \quad = \quad 13{,}900 - 10{,}380$$

$$x \quad = \quad \frac{3{,}520}{22}$$

$$x \quad = \quad 160$$

3    | 112 |

$$\frac{(20 \times 50) + (10 \times 60) + (25 \times x)}{20 + 10 + 25} \quad = \quad 80$$

$$\frac{1{,}000 + 600 + 25x}{55} \quad = \quad 80$$

$$1{,}600 + 25x \quad = \quad 4{,}400$$

$$25x \quad = \quad 4{,}400 - 1{,}600$$

$$25x \quad = \quad 2{,}800$$

$$x \quad = \quad 112$$

Remember, in a question like this, you **must** calculate a **weighted** average.

4    D    $\bar{x} \quad = \quad \dfrac{\Sigma x}{n}$

$$= \quad \frac{2 + 4 + 6 + 8 + 10}{5}$$

$$= \quad 30/5$$

$$= \quad 6$$

Variance $= \dfrac{\Sigma (x - \bar{x})^2}{n}$

| $x$ | 2 | 4 | 6 | 8 | 10 |
|---|---|---|---|---|---|
| $(x - \bar{x})$ | −4 | −2 | 0 | 2 | 4 |
| $(x - \bar{x})^2$ | 16 | 4 | 0 | 4 | 16 |

$$\text{Variance} = \frac{16 + 4 + 0 + 4 + 16}{5}$$

$$= \frac{40}{5}$$

$$= 8$$

If you selected option A, you calculated the coefficient of variation (standard deviation ÷ mean = 8 ÷ 6 = 1.33).

Option B is the standard deviation of the data. The question asked you to calculate the **variance**.

If you selected option C, you calculated the arithmetic mean (and also the median).

5  A

|                            | A     | B     | C     | D     |
|----------------------------|-------|-------|-------|-------|
| Mean                       | 150   | 175   | 200   | 250   |
| Standard deviation         | 25    | 20    | 25    | 30    |
| Coefficient of variation*  | 0.167 | 0.114 | 0.125 | 0.120 |

$$\text{*Coefficient of variation} = \frac{\text{Standard deviation}}{\text{Mean}}$$

The bigger the coefficient of variation, the wider the spread. The largest coefficient of variation is for that of data set A. The correct answer is therefore A.

The formula for calculating the coefficient of variation is not provided in your examination – you must therefore know it by heart so that you can answer questions such as this easily.

6  B  $\text{Semi-interquartile range} = \dfrac{\text{Upper quartile - Lower quartile}}{2}$

$$= \frac{621 - 438}{2}$$

$$= \frac{183}{2}$$

$$= 91.5$$

Option A is the difference between the upper quartile and the median (which is not the semi-interquartile range).

Option C is the difference between the median and the lower quartile (which is not the semi-interquartile range).

Option D represents the inter-quartile range (upper quartile – lower quartile). You must divide this range by 2 to calculate the semi-interquartile range.

7    C

| Commodity | Price $(P_1/P_0)$ | Weight (W) | Relative weight $(W \times P_1/P_0)$ |
|---|---|---|---|
| A | 20/16 = 1.25 | 20 | 25.0 |
| B | 50/40 = 1.25 | 2 | 2.5 |
| C | 105/100 = 1.05 | 10 | 10.5 |
| | | 32 | 38.0 |

$$\text{Index} = \frac{\Sigma W \times P_1/P_0}{\Sigma W}$$

$$= \frac{38}{32} \times 100 = 118.75 = 119$$

This question is very similar to one of the OT questions in the Pilot paper for **Business Mathematics**. Make sure you understand how to arrive at the correct answer.

8    If a distribution has unequal class intervals, the heights of the bars have to be adjusted for the fact that the bars do not have the same width.

$$\frac{\$18}{\$12} = 1.5$$

$18 is one and a half times the standard width so we must therefore divide the frequency of 180 by 1.5, ie $180 \div 1.5 = 120$.

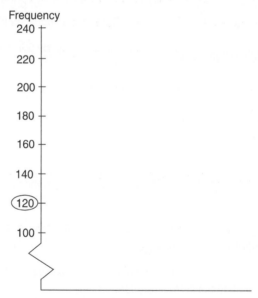

9    B    Negatively-skewed distribution.

Properties of a negatively-skewed distribution:

- Its mean, median and mode all have different values
- The mode will be higher than the median
- The mean will have a lower value than the median (and than most of the distribution)

10 B The coefficient of variation = $\dfrac{\text{Standard deviation}}{\text{Mean}}$

The coefficients of variation are calculated as follows:

W: $\dfrac{10}{100} \times 100 = 10\%$

X: $\dfrac{5}{40} \times 100 = 12\frac{1}{2}\%$

Y: $\dfrac{8}{80} \times 100 = 10\%$

Z: $\dfrac{12}{150} \times 100 = 8\%$

The correct answer is therefore B, since Z has the smallest coefficient of variation.

Note that the formula for the coefficient of variation (coefficient of relative spread) is **not** provided in your examination.

# 19 Summarising and analysing data 7

1 | 7.000 |

Firstly, we need to calculate the cumulative frequency of earnings.

| Annual earnings $ | Frequency | Cumulative frequency |
|---|---|---|
| 6,000 | 3 | 3 |
| 7,000 | 5 | 8 |
| 10,000 | 3 | 11 |
| 11,000 | 1 | 12 |
| 12,000 | 2 | 14 |
| 15,000 | 1 | 15 |

The median is the $\dfrac{(15+1)}{2}$ = 8th item which has a value of $7,000.

2 | 116 |

| Year | Index (Base year = 1980) | Index (Base year = 1990) |
|---|---|---|
| 1980 | 100 | |
| 1990 | x | 100 |
| 1998 | 130* | 112 |

* Total price movement between 1980 and 1998 was 30% ∴ 100 × 1.3 = 130.

$\dfrac{130}{x} = \dfrac{112}{100}$

$x = \dfrac{130 \times 100}{112} = 116$

3

Low        High

245.2   to   554.8

99% of sales each week lie in the range mean $\pm$ 2.58 standard deviations

$= 400 \pm (2.58 \times 60)$
$= 400 \pm 154.8$
$= 245.2 - 554.8$

4       ✓   The mean is smaller than the median

Properties of a negatively-skewed distribution:

- Its mean, median and mode all have different values
- The mode will be higher than the median
- The mean will have a lower value than the median (and than most of the distribution)

5   C   Mean of A + B + C = (120 + 100 + 80)kg = 300 kg

Variance of A + B + C = ($20^2 + 20^2 + 10^2$) = 900kg

(However, don't forget to calculate the square root of 900 in order to calculate the standard deviation as required by the question.)

Standard deviation   =   $\sqrt{\text{variance}}$

                     =   $\sqrt{900}$ = 30kg

Packets of one of each of A, B and C have a mean weight of 300kg and a standard deviation of 30kg.

If you selected option A, you forgot that the overall means should have been added together.

If you selected option B you forgot to add the means together, and you also forgot to take the square root of the variance in order to calculate the standard deviation.

If you selected option D, you forgot to take the square root of the variance in order to calculate the standard deviation.

6   C   The heights of lampposts is an example of **quantitative** data as they can be measured. Since the lampposts can take on any height, the data is said to be **continuous**.

You should have been able to eliminate options B and D immediately since **qualitative data** are data that cannot be measured but which reflect some quality of what is being observed.

7      4

The mode is the most frequently occurring number of loaves required by a shopper, ie 4 loaves.

**Remember, the mode is the most frequently occurring item.**

8    A

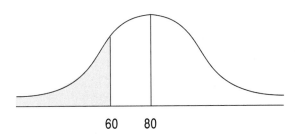

60    80

We are interested in the shaded area shown on the graph. Firstly, we must calculate a z value corresponding to the area between 60 and 80.

$$z = \frac{X - \mu}{\sigma}$$

$$z = \frac{60 - 80}{15.75}$$

$$z = 1.27$$

From normal distribution tables, z = 1.27 corresponds to an area of 0.3980 (or 39.8%).

However, we are interested in the shaded area on the graph which corresponds to an area of 0.5 − 0.3980 = 0.102 (or 10.2%).

If you selected option B, you divided the probability obtained from normal distribution tables by 2 (0.3980 ÷ 2 = 0.199 = 19.9%) instead of subtracting it from 0.5.

If you selected option C, you forgot to subtract 0.3980 from 0.5.

If you selected option D, you added 0.3980 to 0.5 instead of subtracting it.

9    D    It is always best to draw a sketch of the area you are interested in, ie the area between 470cm and 550cm (ie the shaded area below).

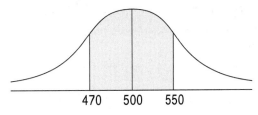

470    500    550

Standard deviation = $\sqrt{\text{variance}}$ = $\sqrt{484}$ = 22

**Area between 470cm and 500cm**

Using $z = \frac{X - \mu}{\sigma}$

$$z = \frac{470 - 500}{22}$$

$$= 1.36$$

A z value of 1.36 corresponds to an area of 0.4131 (from normal distribution tables).

**Area between 500cm and 550cm**

$$z = \frac{550 - 50}{22}$$
$$= 2.27$$

A z value of 2.27 corresponds to an area of 0.4884.

The percentage of pipes between 470cm and 550cm is therefore $(0.4131 + 0.4884) \times 100\% = 0.9015 \times 100\% = 90.15\%$.

If you selected option A, you used the variance instead of the standard deviation when calculating the z score.

Option B is the percentage of pipes between 470cm and 500cm only.

Option C is the percentage of pipes between 500cm and 550cm only.

10　　C　　A histogram is a chart that looks like a bar chart except that the bars are joined together. On a histogram, frequencies are represented by the **area** covered by the bars. The correct answer is therefore C.

# 20 Summarising and analysing data 8

1 　　| 28 |

$13 + 42 + 7 + 51 + 69 + 28 + 33 + 14 + 8 + 15 = 280$

$280 \div 10 = 28$

2 　　| 24.5 |

17, 19, 21, 21, 24, 25, 27, 31, 32, 42

Middle item is between 24 and 25, ie 24.5

3 　　| 19 | kgs

$$\text{Mean} = \frac{15 + x + 22 + 14 + 21 + 15 + 20 + x + 28 + 27}{10}$$

$$20 = \frac{162 + 2x}{10}$$

$$200 = 162 + 2x$$

$$38 = 2x$$

$$x = 19$$

**4**  $\boxed{240}$

Let x = the number of cases of Delta purchased

∴ $512.80 = (20 × $7.84) + (10 × $8.20) + (12 × $8.50) + (X × $8.60)

$512.80 = $156.80 + $82 + $102 + $8.60X

∴ $(512.80 − 156.80 − 82 − 102) = $8.60X

∴ $172 = $8.60X

∴ $172/$8.60 = X = 20

If there are 12 items in each case of Delta, the buyer purchases 20 × 12 = 240 items.

**5**  $\boxed{8}$

$$\text{Variance} = \frac{\sum (x - \bar{x})^2}{n}$$

$$\bar{x} = \frac{\sum x}{n} = \frac{30}{5} = 6$$

We therefore need to calculate $\sum(x - \bar{x})^2$ as follows.

| x | $(x - \bar{x})$ | $(x - \bar{x})^2$ |
|---|---|---|
| 2 | 4 | 16 |
| 4 | 2 | 4 |
| 6 | 0 | 0 |
| 8 | 2 | 4 |
| 10 | 4 | 16 |
| | $\sum(x - \bar{x})^2 =$ | 40 |

n = 5

$$\text{Variance} = \frac{40}{5} = 8$$

**6**  $\boxed{65}$

The mode is an average which means the 'most frequently occurring value'. 65 is the only mark which appears more than once. It is the most frequently occurring item. Therefore the mode = 65.

**7**  $\boxed{59}$

The median is the value of the middle item of a distribution once all of the items have been arranged in order of magnitude.

37, 45, 55, 55, 59, 64, 70, 72, 86

There are an odd number of items, so the middle item of an odd number of items is calculated as the

$$\frac{(n+1)^{th}}{2} \text{ item} = \frac{9+1}{2} = 5^{th} \text{ item.}$$

The 5th item in this array is 59. Therefore the median = 59.

8   ☑ Relative dispersion

The spreads of two distributions can be compared by using the coefficient of variation (or the coefficient of relative dispersion).

9

| Commodity | Price relative | Weight | Relative weight |
|-----------|---------------|--------|-----------------|
| A | 1.10 | 10.00 | 11.00 |
| B | 1.20 | 1.00 | 1.20 |
| C | 1.04 | 5.00 | 5.20 |
| D | 1.05 | 4.00 | 4.20 |
| | | 20.00 | 21.60 |

Price index for year 2 based on year 1 (using weighted average of relatives method) = 108

10   $ 239

Price index in 2006 = 148

Price index in 2002 = 124

Therefore $200 $\times \dfrac{148}{124}$ = $239

# 21 Summarising and analysing data 9

1   3

| Number of meals eaten out | Frequency (number of people) | Cumulative frequency |
|---------------------------|------------------------------|----------------------|
| 0 | 10 | 10 |
| 1 | 110 | 120 |
| 2 | 10 | 130 |
| 3 | 160 | 290 |
| 4 | 170 | 460 |
| 5 | 30 | 490 |
| 6 | 9 | 499 |
| | 499 | |

The median is the middle member in the distribution, ie the $\dfrac{499+1}{2}$ = 250th member which is 3 meals (ie where cumulative frequency = 290).

2    $ | 100,000 |

Firstly, we need to calculate the cumulative frequency of earnings.

| Annual earnings $ | Frequency | Cumulative frequency |
|---|---|---|
| 60,000 | 3 | 3 |
| 70,000 | 3 | 6 |
| 100,000 | 5 | 11 |
| 110,000 | 1 | 12 |
| 120,000 | 2 | 14 |
| 150,000 | 1 | 15 |

The median is the $\frac{(15+1)}{2}$ = 8th item which has a value of $100,000.

3    | 25.45 |

| Value of delivery ($) | | Frequency | Cumulative frequency |
|---|---|---|---|
| at least | less than | | |
| 1 | 10 | 3 | 3 |
| 10 | 20 | 6 | 9 |
| 20 | 30 | 11 | 20 |
| 30 | 40 | 15 | 35 |
| 40 | 50 | 12 | 47 |
| 50 | 60 | 7 | 54 |
| 60 | 70 | 6 | 60 |

The lower quartile is the value below which 25% of the population fall, ie the ¼ × 60 = 15th item.

The 15th item lies in the class at least 20 but less than 30. There are 11 items in this class and the 15th item in the whole distribution is the 6th item in this class = 6/11 × (30 − 20) = 6/11 × 10 = 5.45.

We must however add 5.45 to 20 in order to find the value of the 15th item in the distribution which is 25.45 (to 2 decimal places).

4    | 48 |

| Value of delivery ($) | | Frequency | Cumulative frequency |
|---|---|---|---|
| at least | less than | | |
| 1 | 10 | 3 | 3 |
| 10 | 20 | 6 | 9 |
| 20 | 30 | 11 | 20 |
| 30 | 40 | 15 | 35 |
| 40 | 50 | 12 | 47 |
| 50 | 60 | 7 | 54 |
| 60 | 70 | 6 | 60 |

The upper quartile is the value below which 75% of the population fall, ie the ¾ × 60 = 45th item.

The cumulative frequency table above shows that the 45th item is in the class interval $40 to $50. There are 12 items in this class and the 45th item in the whole distribution is the 10th item in this class. The value of the 45th item is therefore $40 + (10/12 × $10) = $40 + $8.33 = $48.33 = $48 to the nearest $.

## ANSWERS

**5**    ☑ The standard deviation will increase by 14%

☑ The coefficient of variation will be unaltered

If everybody's salary rises by 14%, the mean salary will also rise by 14%. In computing the standard deviation, we work out $(x - \bar{x})^2$ for each employee, add up the results, divide by n and then take the square root. If each employee's salary and the mean salary are all increased by 14%, each $(x - \bar{x})$ will rise by 14%. Because the squaring is followed by square rooting, the overall effect will be to increase the standard deviation by 14%.

Since both the standard deviation and the mean increase by 14%, the coefficient of variation, which is the one divided by the other, will be unchanged.

**6**    $\boxed{128}$

$$100 \times \frac{P_1}{P_0} = 140$$

$$P_1 = 160$$

$$\therefore P_0 = \frac{100 \times 160}{125}$$

$$= 128$$

**7**    $\boxed{151.56}$

| Commodity | Price relative* | Weight | Relative weight** |
|---|---|---|---|
| Brighton | 1.25 | 40.00 | 50.00 |
| Eastbourne | 1.25 | 4.00 | 5.00 |
| Worthing | 2.10 | 20.00 | 42.00 |
| | | 64.00 | 97.00 |

\* Price relative = $\dfrac{P_1}{P_0}$

\*\* Relative weight = Price relative × weight

$$\text{Index} = \frac{\Sigma W \times P_1 / P_0}{\Sigma W}$$

$$= \frac{97}{64} \times 100 = 151.56 \text{ (to 2 decimal places)}$$

PROFESSIONAL EDUCATION

8    (a)    Growing steadily

           False   ☑

    (b)    Keeping up with inflation

           True   ☑

The sales index for a particular quarter multiplied by the inflation index for a particular quarter is approximately equal to the sales index of the following quarter.

Real sales are therefore approximately constant and keeping up with inflation.

9      &boxed{2.2}

Arithmetic mean $= \dfrac{\sum fx}{\sum f}$

$$\sum fx = (5 \times 0) + (10 \times 1) + (10 \times 2) + (20 \times 3) + (5 \times 4) + (0 \times 5)$$
$$= 0 + 10 + 20 + 60 + 20 + 0$$
$$= 110$$

$$\sum f = 5 + 10 + 10 + 20 + 5 + 0$$
$$= 50$$

Arithmetic mean $= \dfrac{110}{50}$

$$= 2.2$$

10    &boxed{125}

Price relative $= 100 \times \dfrac{P_1}{P_0}$

Where    $P_1 = \$1.75$
            $P_0 = \$1.40$

$\therefore$ Price relative $= 100 \times \dfrac{\$1.75}{\$1.40} = 125$

# 22 Inter-relationships between variables 1

1    | 0.63 |

$$r = \frac{n\sum XY - \sum X \sum Y}{\sqrt{(n\sum X^2 - (\sum X)^2)(n\sum Y^2 - (\sum Y)^2)}}$$

$$= \frac{(11 \times 13{,}467) - (440 \times 330)}{\sqrt{((11 \times 17{,}986) - (440^2))((11 \times 10{,}366) - (330^2))}}$$

$$= \frac{2{,}937}{\sqrt{(4{,}246 \times 5{,}126)}} = 0.63$$

The above formula is provided in your exam. If you failed to get the correct answer, rework the calculations carefully. Questions such as this are an easy source of marks as all of the information required to answer it correctly are given to you in the question – you just need to plug the numbers into the formula provided.

2    D    $$R = 1 - \frac{6\sum d^2}{n(n^2 - 1)}$$

$$R = 1 - \frac{6 \times 50}{10 \times 99} = 0.70$$

If you selected option A, you omitted the '1' from the equation above.

If you selected option B, you didn't state your answer to two decimal places.

If you selected option C, you forgot to deduct your answer from 1. Make sure you perform the entire calculation using the complete formula (which is provided in your exam) next time!

3    D    If C = 1,000 + 250P, then fixed costs are $1,000 and variable costs are $250 per unit.

4    C    From the data given, it is clear that the correlation is **positive** and **strong**. The correlation coefficient describing a positive strong relationship is 0.98.

5    B    If temperatures increase by one degree, X is replaced by (X + 1)

If X = X + 1

Y = 32 – 1.6 (X + 1)
Y = 32 – 1.6X – 1.6
Y = 30.4 – 1.6X

ie sales have now fallen by $32,000 – $30,400 = $1,600

If you selected option C, you have forgotten that sales are given in $'000s.

If you selected option D, you have forgotten that a negative sign in the regression equation means that as X increases, Y decreases.

6    D    The correlation coefficient of 0.9 is very close to 1 and so there is a very strong relationship between x and y.

7    C    Correlation coefficient, r = 0.85

Coefficient of determination, $r^2 = 0.85^2 = 0.72$

The coefficient of determination tells us that 72% of the variation in sales revenue can be explained by the corresponding variation in advertising expenditure.

8    ┌──────┐
     │ 0.98 │
     └──────┘

The formula for the correlation coefficient is provided in your exam. There are no excuses for getting this question wrong.

$$\text{Correlation coefficient, } r = \frac{n\sum XY - \sum X \sum Y}{\sqrt{[n\sum X^2 - (\sum X)^2][n\sum Y^2 - (\sum Y)^2]}}$$

$$= \frac{(4 \times 157) - (12 \times 42)}{\sqrt{[4 \times 46 - 12^2][4 \times 542 - 42^2]}}$$

$$= \frac{628 - 504}{\sqrt{(184 - 144) \times (2,168 - 1,764)}}$$

$$= \frac{124}{\sqrt{40 \times 404}}$$

$$= \frac{124}{127.12}$$

= 0.98 (to 2 decimal places)

9    B    X = advertising expenditure

If    X = 0
      Y = 40 + 10X
      Y = 40 + (10 × 0)
      Y = 40

Therefore if nothing is spent on advertising, sales revenue will be $40 on average.

10   A

|                           | Critic 1 | Critic 2 | d   | $d^2$ |
|---------------------------|----------|----------|-----|-------|
| Sunshine love             | 1.0      | 4.5      | 3.5 | 12.25 |
| Oceanic war               | 2.5      | 1.0      | 1.5 | 2.25  |
| Liaising dangerously      | 4.0      | 3.0      | 1.0 | 1.00  |
| Dark stranger             | 5.0      | 2.0      | 3.0 | 9.00  |
| The road to Crockham Hill | 2.5      | 4.5      | 2.0 | 4.00  |
|                           |          |          |     | 28.50 |

$$R = 1 - \frac{6 \times 28.5}{5 \times (25 - 1)}$$

$$= -0.425$$

If you selected option B you subtracted 1 from 1.425 instead of the other way around.

If you selected option C, you forgot to subtract 1 from $n^2$ on the denominator of the equation thereby having a denominator of $5 \times 25$ instead of $5 \times (25 - 1)$.

If you selected option D, you forgot to subtract the 1 from $n^2$ on the denominator of the equation and you stated the final result as a positive number rather than a negative number, ie

$$R = 1 - \frac{6 \times 28.5}{5 \times 25}$$

$$= 1 - 1.368$$

$$= -0.368 \text{ (C) or } + 3.68 \text{ (D)}$$

Both workings are incorrect.

# 23 Inter-relationships between variables 2

1   B   I   When an equation has the form $y = a + bx$, b gives the slope which is 5 in the equation $y = 5x - 24$.

    II   When an equation has the form $y = a + bx$, a gives the intersection on the y axis which is $-24$ in the equation $y = 5x - 24$.

    III   The slope of the equation is 5. The intercept on the y axis is 24.

    IV   The line cuts the y axis at $-24$. The line cuts the x axis at 4.8.

    I and II are correct and the answer is therefore B.

2   C   I   High levels of correlation do not prove that there is cause and effect.

    II   A correlation coefficient of 0.73 would generally be regarded as indicating a strong linear relationship between the variables.

    III   The coefficient of determination provides this information and is given by squaring the correlation coefficient, resulting in 53% in this case.

    IV   The coefficient of determination provides this information and not the correlation coefficient. Remember that you must square the correlation coefficient in order to obtain the coefficient of determination.

    Statements II and III are relevant and the correct answer is therefore C.

3   C   The value X = 10 does not lie between 15 and 45 so we do not know whether or not the relationship between the variables still holds for this value of X. We therefore cannot rely upon the estimate.

    The sample size is quite large for this type of analysis and will provide reliable estimates. Option A will not therefore reduce the reliability of the estimate.

    The correlation coefficient is very close to $-1$, indicating a very strong relationship between the variables which will provide reliable estimates. Option B will not therefore reduce the reliability of the estimate.

    The fact that the correlation coefficient is negative tells us that Y decreases as X increases but it says nothing about the strength of the relationship between the variables nor the reliability of the estimates. Option D is therefore an incorrect answer.

4    A    $Y = 50 + 7X$

If we increase expenditure on advertising by \$1, we replace X with (X + 1)

$Y = 50 + 7(X + 1)$
$Y = 50 + 7X + 7$
$Y = 57 + 7X$

Therefore, sales are now \$57 on average, compared with \$50 previously. Sales increase by \$7 on average.

**If advertising costs are increased by \$7**

$Y = 50 + 7(X + 7)$
$Y = 50 + 7X + 49$
$Y = 99 + 7X$

Sales are increased by \$49 on average.

Option B is therefore incorrect.

If $Y = 50 + 7X$

when advertising is zero, X = 0

$\therefore$    $Y = 50 + (7 \times 0)$
      $Y = 50 + 0$
      $Y = 50$

Therefore option D is incorrect.

5    C    The independent variable is denoted by X and the dependent one by Y.

The variable to be forecast must always be Y. Option A is therefore incorrect.

In calculating the correlation coefficient, it does not matter which variable is X and which is Y, and a totally different regression line equation will result if X and Y are interchanged. Option B is therefore incorrect.

The scatter diagram is used to show whether or not there is a relationship between X and Y and it does not matter which variable is associated with a particular axis. Option D is therefore incorrect.

6    | 0.536 |

| Student | Rank English literature | Rank French | d | $d^2$ |
|---|---|---|---|---|
| 1 | 2 | 1 | 1 | 1 |
| 2 | 1 | 3 | 2 | 4 |
| 3 | 4 | 7 | 3 | 9 |
| 4 | 6 | 5 | 1 | 1 |
| 5 | 5 | 6 | 1 | 1 |
| 6 | 3 | 2 | 1 | 1 |
| 7 | 7 | 4 | 3 | 9 |
| | | | $\sum d^2 =$ | 26 |

Using the formula for Spearman's rank correlation coefficient, R

$$R = 1 - \frac{6\sum d^2}{n(n^2 - 1)}$$

$$= 1 - \frac{6 \times 26}{7 \times (49 - 1)}$$

$$= 1 - \frac{156}{336}$$

$$= 0.536$$

Note that the formula for the coefficient of rank correlation is provided in your exam.

7    B    If nothing is spent on advertising, X = 0

∴  Y = 5 + (2 × 0)
   Y = 5 + 0
   Y = 5

Therefore sales revenue is $5 × 10,000 = $50,000 on average when nothing is spent on advertising. II is correct. IV is incorrect.

If $1,000 extra is spent on advertising, then X = X + 1

∴  Y = 5 + 2 (X + 1)
   Y = 5 + 2X + 2
   Y = 7 + 2X

Increase in sales revenue when an extra $1,000 is spent on advertising is $20,000 ((7 − 5) × $10,000). III is correct and I is incorrect.

8    D    When X = 20, we don't know anything about the relationship between X and Y since the sample data only goes up to X = 10. I is therefore true.

Since a correlation coefficient of 0.8 would be regarded as strong (it is a high value) the estimate would be reliable. II is therefore not true.

With such a small sample and the extrapolation required, the estimate is unlikely to be reliable. III is therefore not true.

The sample of only six pairs of values is very small and is therefore likely to reduce the reliability of the estimate. IV is therefore true.

The correct answer is therefore D.

9    B    The coefficient of rank correlation can be interpreted in exactly the same way as the ordinary correlation coefficient with values also ranging from −1 to +1.

10    D    $Y = 30 + 5X$

When nothing is spent on advertising, $X = 0$.

$\therefore Y = 30$, ie sales revenue will be $30 on average (IV is correct).

If advertising expenditure increases by 1, ie if we replace X by $(X + 1)$, we have

$Y = 30 + 5(X + 1)$
$Y = 30 + 5X + 5$
$Y = 35 + 5X$

ie sales revenue increases by $5 on average when expenditure of advertising increases by $1 (II is correct).

# 24 Inter-relationships between variables 3

1    C    **If sales are zero (Y = 0)**

$0 \ \ = \ 54 - 3x$
$3x \ = \ 54$
$x \ \ = \ 18$

If sales (Y) are zero, the temperature is therefore $18°C$.

Therefore I is correct and II and III are incorrect. You should have been able to eliminate options B and D straightaway since sales cannot really be negative.

**If temperature is 0°C (x = 0)**

$\therefore y \ = \ 54 - 3x$
$y \ = \ 54 - (3 \times 0)$
$y \ = \ 54 - 0$
$y \ = \ 54$

If the temperature is $0°C$, sales are $54,000. IV is correct and the correct answer is C (Statements I and IV being true).

2    $\boxed{0.99}$

$$\text{Correlation coefficient, } r \ = \ \frac{n\sum XY - \sum X \sum Y}{\sqrt{(n\sum X^2 - (\sum X)^2)(n\sum Y^2 - (\sum Y)^2)}}$$

$$= \frac{(5 \times 8{,}104) - (100 \times 400)}{\sqrt{(5 \times 2{,}040 - 100^2) \times (5 \times 32{,}278 - 400^2)}}$$

$$= \frac{520}{\sqrt{200 \times 1{,}390}}$$

$$= \frac{520}{527.3}$$

$$= +0.99$$

The formula for the product moment correlation coefficient is provided in your examination. Answering a question such as this is just a matter of plugging the correct numbers into the (given) formula.

ANSWERS

3    B    The least squares method of linear regression analysis involves using the following formulae for a and b in Y = a + bX.

$$b = \frac{n\sum XY - \sum X \sum Y}{n\sum X^2 - (\sum X)^2}$$

$$= \frac{(5 \times 8{,}104) - (100 \times 400)}{(5 \times 2{,}040) - 100^2}$$

$$= \frac{40{,}520 - 40{,}000}{10{,}200 - 10{,}000}$$

$$= \frac{520}{200}$$

$$= 2.6$$

At this stage, you can eliminate options A and C.

$$a = \overline{Y} - b\overline{X}$$

$$= \frac{400}{5} - 2.6 \times \left(\frac{100}{5}\right)$$

$$= 28$$

The formulae above are provided in your examination.

4    False  ✓

The coefficient of determination ($R^2$) explains the percentage variation in the **dependent** variable which is explained by the **independent** variable.

5    11.00

Y = a + bX

If intercept (a) is $248, then Y = 248 + bX

If the value of Y is $523 and X is 25, then using the equation Y = 248 + bX we can determine the unknown value of b (ie the slope) as follows.

523          = 248 + (b × 25)
523 − 248 = 25b
      275 = 25b

$$b = \frac{275}{25} = +11.00$$

6    False  ✓

The rank correlation coefficient can be interpreted in exactly the same way as the ordinary correlation coefficient, but data is given in terms of order or rank. A rank correlation coefficient of 0.94 indicates that there is strong positive correlation between taste and looks of new desserts.

7    A    +0.98

> From the data given, it is clear that the correlation is **positive** and strong. The correlation coefficient describing a strong negative relationship is +0.98.

8    ☑    Weekly fixed costs are approximately $1,500.

       ☑    Variable costs are approximately $15 per unit on average.

       ☑    Next week's production costs are likely to be about $9,000.

A linear equation of the form y = a + bx has fixed costs of a and variable costs per unit of b.

∴   Fixed costs = $1,500

    Variable costs = $15 per unit

If output = 500, total costs   = $1,500 + ($15 × 500)
                                    = $1,500 + $7,500
                                    = $9,000

9    ☑    None of them

If r = 0.9, there is a high degree of correlation between weekly costs of production and production level. Statement (i) is not correct.

If r = 0.9, $r^2$ (coefficient of determination) = 81% ($0.9^2$) and 81% of the variation in weekly costs can be explained by the amount produced. Statement (ii) is not correct.

If r = 0.9 and a linear pattern is evident, forecasts are likely to be reliable, not unreliable. Statement (iii) is not correct.

10    ☑    Slope of a regression line

The correlation coefficient values lie between –1 and +1.

The slope of a regression line is its gradient and it is possible to have a gradient of –2.

The variance is the standard deviation squared and is always a positive value.

# 25 Inter-relationships between variables 4

1    ☑    The slope of the equation if plotted on a graph is 4

       ☑    The line cuts the y-axis at –15 if plotted on a graph

When an equation has the form y = a + bx, b gives the slope which is 4 in the equation y = 4x – 15.

When an equation has the form y = a + bx, a gives the intersection on the y-axis which is –15 in the equation y = 4x – 15.

**ANSWERS**

2

$$\boxed{0.17}$$

$$r = \frac{n\sum xy - \sum x\sum y}{\sqrt{[n\sum x^2 - (\sum x)^2][n\sum y^2 - (\sum y)^2]}}$$

$$= \frac{(6 \times 14) - (2 \times 15)}{\sqrt{[6 \times 30 - 2^2][6 \times 130 - 15^2]}}$$

$$= \frac{84 - 30}{\sqrt{176 \times 555}}$$

$$= \frac{54}{312.54} = 0.172777884$$

$$= 0.17 \text{ (to 2 decimal places)}$$

3    $y = \boxed{2 + 2.2x}$

| $x$ | $y$ | $x^2$ | $xy$ |
|---|---|---|---|
| 1 | 4 | 1 | 4 |
| 2 | 6 | 4 | 12 |
| 3 | 10 | 9 | 30 |
| 4 | 10 | 16 | 40 |
| 10 | 30 | 30 | 86 |

$n = 4$

$$b = \frac{n\sum xy - \sum x\sum y}{n\sum x^2 - (\sum x)^2}$$

$$= \frac{(4 \times 86) - (10 \times 30)}{4 \times 30 - 10^2} = \frac{44}{20} = 2.2$$

$$a = \bar{y} - b\bar{x} = \frac{30}{4} - \left(2.2 \times \frac{10}{4}\right) = 2$$

Therefore $y = 2 + 2.2x$.

4    $$\boxed{0.30}$$

| Astrologer | Rank Technical | Artistic | $d$ | $d^2$ |
|---|---|---|---|---|
| Virgo | 2 | 4 | 2 | 4 |
| Libra | 3 | 3 | 0 | 0 |
| Scorpio | 4 | 5 | 1 | 1 |
| Sagittarius | 5 | 2 | 3 | 9 |
| Aquarius | 1 | 1 | 0 | 0 |
| | | | | 14 |

$$R = 1 - \frac{6\sum d^2}{n(n^2 - 1)}$$

$$= 1 - \frac{(6 \times 14)}{5 \times (25 - 1)}$$

$$= 1 - 0.7$$

$$= 0.30 \text{ (to 2 decimal places)}$$

5    False    ☐ ✓

Correlation does not prove a causal link and this statement is therefore false.

The coefficient of determination is the square of the correlation coefficient.

6    $x =$ ☐ $7.72 + 0.71y$

Since the question asks for the regression line of x on y; x and y must therefore be interchanged in the formula.

| $x$ | $y$ | $y^2$ | $xy$ |
|---|---|---|---|
| 9 | 2 | 4 | 18 |
| 10 | 3 | 9 | 30 |
| 9 | 1 | 1 | 9 |
| 8 | 1 | 1 | 8 |
| 9 | 2 | 4 | 18 |
| 45 | 9 | 19 | 83 |

$n = 5$

$$b = \frac{n\sum xy - \sum x \sum y}{n\sum x^2 - (\sum x)^2}$$

$$= \frac{(5 \times 83) - (45 \times 9)}{(5 \times 19) - 9^2} = \frac{10}{14} = 0.71$$

$$a = \bar{x} - b\bar{y} = \frac{45}{5} - \left(0.71 \times \frac{9}{5}\right) = 7.722 = 7.72 \text{ (to 2 decimal places)}$$

Therefore, the equation is x = 7.72 + 0.71y

7    ☐ ✓    Fixed costs are $200. Variable costs per unit are $30.

If C = 200 + 30P, then fixed costs are the constant, $200 and variable costs are $30 per unit.

8    ☐ 0.4624

The coefficient of determination, $r^2$, measures the proportion of the total variation in the value of one variable that can be explained by variations in the value of the other variable.

$$r^2 = 0.68^2$$

$$= 0.4624$$

Therefore, only just under half of the variation in one variable can be explained by variation in the other.

9    20.09 %

Let growth factor = x

Let original market size = 1

$\therefore$  $x^6$  = 1 × 3

   $x^6$  = 3

   x  = $\sqrt[6]{3}$

     = 1.2009

     = 20.09%

10    330

Perfect negative correlation = –1

$$R(rank) = 1 - \frac{6\sum d^2}{n(n^2 - 1)}$$

$$-1 = 1 - \frac{6\sum d^2}{10(10^2 - 1)}$$

$$-1 = 1 - \frac{6\sum d^2}{10 \times 99}$$

$$-1 = 1 - \frac{6\sum d^2}{990}$$

$$\frac{6\sum d^2}{990} = 1 + 1$$

$$6\sum d^2 = 2 \times 990$$

$$\sum d^2 = \frac{2 \times 990}{6}$$

$$\sum d^2 = 330$$

# 26 Inter-relationships between variables 5

1    False  ✓

When using the regression of Y upon X, X is the independent variable and Y is the dependent variable (the value of Y will depend upon the value of X).

2    Lowest value = 0

Highest value = 1

The correlation coefficient, r, must always fall within the range –1 to +1, therefore the coefficient of determination must always fall in the range 0 to 1 ($-1^2$ = +1).

3    B    The rank correlation coefficient can be interpreted in exactly the same way as the ordinary correlation coefficient, but data is given in terms of order or rank. A rank correlation coefficient of 0.95 indicates that there is strong positive correlation between taste and looks of new drinks.

4    The correlation coefficient of temperature and sales is $\boxed{0.98}$ (to 2 decimal places).

*Workings*

$$\textbf{Correlation coefficient} = \frac{n\sum xy - \sum x \sum y}{\sqrt{[n\sum x^2 - (\sum x)^2][n\sum y^2 - (\sum y)^2]}}$$

$$= \frac{10 \times 4{,}208 - 210 \times 187}{\sqrt{[10 \times 4{,}634 - 210^2][10 \times 3{,}865 - 187^2]}}$$

$$= \frac{2{,}810}{\sqrt{2{,}240 \times 3{,}681}}$$

$$= \frac{2{,}810}{2{,}871.49} = 0.98$$

5

$b = \boxed{10.05}$ (to 2 decimal places)

$a = \boxed{44.50}$ (to 2 decimal places)

*Workings*

| $x$ | $y$ | $xy$ | $x^2$ |
|---|---|---|---|
| 2 | 60 | 120 | 4 |
| 8 | 132 | 1,056 | 64 |
| 6 | 100 | 600 | 36 |
| 8 | 120 | 960 | 64 |
| 10 | 150 | 1,500 | 100 |
| 4 | 84 | 336 | 16 |
| 4 | 90 | 360 | 16 |
| 2 | 68 | 136 | 4 |
| 6 | 104 | 624 | 36 |
| 10 | 140 | 1,400 | 100 |
| 60 | 1,048 | 7,092 | 440 |

$$b = \frac{n\sum xy - \sum x \sum y}{n\sum x^2 - (\sum x)^2}$$

$$b = \frac{(10 \times 7{,}092) - (60 \times 1{,}048)}{(10 \times 440) - 60^2}$$

$$= \frac{8{,}040}{800}$$

$$= 10.05$$

$$a = \bar{y} - b\bar{x}$$

$$a = \frac{1{,}048}{10} - (10.05 \times \frac{60}{10})$$

$$= 44.5$$

The equation to use for predicting the likely maintenance cost per vehicle per annum is

| y = 44.5 + 10.05x |
|---|

where   y = | maintenance costs (£10) |

x = | age |

6    The Spearman's rank correlation coefficient is | 0.8515 | (to 4 decimal places).

*Workings*

It is necessary to complete the following table and to calculate the difference between the ranking of accidents and expenditure before using the formula to calculate the rank correlation coefficient.

| Site | Number of minor accidents | Rank accidents | Expenditure $'000 | Rank expenditure | /d/ | /d/² |
|---|---|---|---|---|---|---|
| A | 17 | 8 | 6 | 9 | 1 | 1 |
| B | 9 | 5 | 15 | 4 | 1 | 1 |
| C | 10 | 6 | 10 | 5 | 1 | 1 |
| D | 4 | 2 | 22 | 2 | 0 | 0 |
| E | 12 | 7 | 8 | 7.5 | 0.5 | 0.25 |
| F | 21 | 9 | 9 | 6 | 3 | 9 |
| G | 25 | 10 | 5 | 10 | 0 | 0 |
| H | 8 | 4 | 8 | 7.5 | 3.5 | 12.25 |
| I | 6 | 3 | 16 | 3 | 0 | 0 |
| J | 3 | 1 | 30 | 1 | 0 | 0 |
| | | | | | | 24.50 |

$$R_s = 1 - \frac{6\sum d^2}{n(n^2 - 1)}$$

$$R_s = 1 - \frac{6 \times 24.5}{10 \times (100 - 1)}$$

$$= 0.8515$$

7    | 0.64 |

The correlation coefficient of determination is calculated by squaring the correlation coefficient.

8    D    b is the slope of the line which measures the increase in the y variable for unit increase in x

9    C    a is the intercept on the y axis which is the value of the dependant variable when the value of the independent variable is zero.

10    C    A correlation coefficient of 0.9 indicates that the relationship between x and y is too strong to have been caused by chance.

BPP
PROFESSIONAL EDUCATION

# 27 Forecasting 1

1   D   Year = 2006

∴ Trend  = $(0.0004 \times 2006^2) + (0.2 \times 2006) + 80.2$
          = 2,091.0144

∴ Forecast = $1.87 \times 2,091.0144 = 3910.196928$

∴ Forecast in whole units = 3,910

2   B   $y = 7.112 + 3.949x$

If $x = 19$, trend in sales for month 19 = $7.112 + (3.949 \times 19) = 82.143$

Seasonally-adjusted trend value = $82.143 \times 1.12 = 92$

If you failed to select the correct option, rework the calculation carefully. You shouldn't have too much trouble with this question since it is just a matter of plugging in a value for x into the equation given in the question.

3   A   If $x = 16$, $y = 345.12 - (1.35 \times 16) = 323.52$

Forecast = trend + seasonal component = $323.52 - 23.62 = 299.9 = 300$ (to nearest unit)

If you selected option B, you calculated the forecast for the fifteenth period and deducted the seasonal component of the sixteenth period.

If you selected option C, you correctly forecast the trend for the sixteenth period but forgot to deduct the seasonal component.

If you selected option D, you simply calculated the trend for the fifteenth period instead of the sixteenth period.

4   ⬚ 5,109

$$\frac{4,700}{0.92} = 5,109 \text{ (to the nearest whole number)}$$

5   D   Depending on the value of b in the equation $y = a + bx$, either of the graphs A, B or C could be used to depict the forecasting model.

If b = negative, $y = a + bx$ could be depicted by graph A.
If b = positive, $y = a + bx$ could be depicted by graph B.
If b = 0, $y = a + bx$ could be depicted by graph C.

6   ⬚ 123

$y$  $= 9.82 + (4.372 \times 24)$

$y$  $= 114.748$

∴ forecast  $= 114.748 + 8.5$
             $= 123.248$
             $= 123$

7    A    $Y = 20 - 0.25X$

$X = 12$

$\therefore Y = 20 - 0.25(12) = 17\%$

8    A    A variation of, for example, +50% means that forecast sales are 50% above the trend value (ie trend $\times$ 150%) whereas a variation of −50% means that forecast sales are 50% below the trend value (ie trend $\times$ 50%).

$\therefore$ Trend $\times$ seasonal variation = actual

$\therefore$ Trend $\times$ 150% = 240 (for $Q_2$)

$\therefore$ Trend = 240 $\div$ 1.5 = 160

Variation in $Q_3$ = − 50%

$\therefore$ Forecast = 160 $\times$ 50% = 80

If you selected option B, you have simply taken 50% of the trend for $Q_2$ (50% $\times$ 240 = 120).

If you selected option C, you calculated the trend and not the forecast for $Q_3$.

If you selected option D, you divided the trend in $Q_3$ by 50% instead of multiplying it by 50%.

9    | 123 |

Forecast for quarter 21 = (28.37 + (4.2 $\times$ 21)) $\times$ 1.055    = 122.98

= 123 whole units

10    B    I    Forecasts are made on the assumption that everything continues as in the past.

II    If the model being used is inappropriate, for example, if an additive model is used when the trend is changing sharply, forecasts will not be very reliable.

III    Provided a multiplicative model is used, the fact that the trend is increasing need not have any adverse effect on the reliability of forecasts.

IV    Provided the seasonal variation remains the same in the future as in the past, it will not make forecasts unreliable.

I and II are therefore necessary and hence the correct answer is B.

# 28 Forecasting 2

1    B    Seasonally adjusting the values in a time series removes the seasonal element from the data thereby giving an instant estimate of the trend.

2    C    I    With an additive model the daily component represents the average value of actual production minus the trend for that day, so a component of +7 means production is 7,000 units above the trend.

           II    You have confused the additive variation of +4 (actually +4,000 units) with the multiplicative variation +4%. Production on Thursdays is on average 4,000 units above the trend.

           III    With an additive model the daily component represents the average value of actual production minus the trend for that day, so a component of –8 means production is 8,000 units below the trend.

           IV    You have confused the additive variation of –6 (actually –6,000 units) with the multiplicative variation of –6%. Production on Mondays is on average 6,000 units below the trend.

Statements I and III are true and the correct answer is therefore C.

3    D    If   t = 1 in the first quarter of 20X5
            t = 8 in the fourth quarter of 20X6

Trend (Y)    = 65 + (7 × 8)
             = 121

Forecast    = trend + seasonal component
            = 121 + (–30)
            = 121 – 30
            = 91

If you selected option A, you used t = 4 instead of t = 8 in the fourth quarter of 20X6.

If you selected option B, you calculated the trend as (65 + 7) × 8 = 576 instead of 65 + (7 × 8) = 121.

If you selected option C, you reduced the trend by 30% instead of subtracting 30 from it.

4    C    In the first month of 20X9, t = 13

∴ Y    = $1,500 – $(3 × 13)
        = $1,461

Forecast    = trend × seasonal component
            = $1,461 × 0.92
            = $1,344

If you selected option A, you substituted t = 1 into the trend equation instead of t = 13.

If you selected option B, you calculated the trend as ($1,500 – $3) × 13 = $19,461 and therefore forecast sales as $19,461 × 0.92 = $17,904.

If you selected option D, you added the seasonal component of 0.92 (as you would for an additive model) instead of multiplying by 0.92.

# ANSWERS

5    | 0.8 |

As this is a multiplicative model, the seasonal variations should sum (in this case) to 4 (an average of 1) as there are four quarters.

Let x = seasonal variation in quarter 4.

$$1.3 + 1.4 + 0.5 + x = 4$$
$$\therefore \quad 3.2 + x = 4$$
$$x = 4 - 3.2$$
$$x = 0.8$$

6    For a multiplicative model, the seasonal component is as follows.

$$S = Y/T$$

$$\therefore T = Y/S$$

|  | Quarter | |
|---|---|---|
|  | 1 | 2 |
| Seasonal component (S) | 1.3 | 1.4 |
| Actual series (Y) | $520,000 | $630,000 |
| Trend (T) | $ | 400,000 | $ | 450,000 |

7    The trend line for sales has therefore

| ✓ |  increased between quarter 1 and quarter 2

8    D

|  | Quarter | | | | |
|---|---|---|---|---|---|
|  | 1 | 2 | 3 | 4 | Total |
| *Unadjusted average* | 1.07 | 0.95 | 1.15 | 0.8 | 3.97* |
| Adjustment | 0.0075 | 0.0075 | 0.0075 | 0.0075 | 0.03 |
| Adjusted average | 1.0775 | 0.9575 | 1.225 | 0.8075 | 4.00 |

* The averages should total 4

$$4 - 3.97 = 0.03$$

We therefore need to add 0.03/4 = 0.0075 to each average.

From the table above, it can be seen that the fourth quarter adjusted average is 0.8075 as per option D.

If you selected option A, you added the entire deficit of 0.03 to the first quarter average instead of spreading it across all four averages.

If you selected option B, you subtracted the entire deficit of 0.03 from the second quarter average rather than sharing it across all four averages.

If you selected option C, you have subtracted the deficit of 0.0075 from each quarter's average, instead of adding it.

9    $\boxed{-20.5}$

Trend for week 7    $= 92 + (0.9 \times 7)$
                    $= 92 + 6.3$
                    $= 98.3$

Seasonal variation  $=$ actual series $-$ trend
                    $= 77.8 - 98.3$
                    $= -20.5$

10   D   I    A correlation coefficient close to +1 or −1 indicates a strong linear relationship between X and Y. The regression equation is therefore more reliable for forecasting.

         II   Working to a high number of decimal places gives spurious accuracy unless both the data itself is accurate to the same degree and the methods used lend themselves to such precision.

         III  Forecasting for values of X outside the range of the original data leads to unreliable estimates, because there is no evidence that the same regression relationships hold for such values.

         IV   The regression equation is worthless unless a sufficiently large sample was used to calculate it. In practice, samples of about ten or more are acceptable.

         I and IV increase the reliability of forecasting.

# 29 Forecasting 3

1

|  | Season | | | |
|---|---|---|---|---|
|  | Spring | Summer | Autumn | Winter |
| Average | $\boxed{-5.5}$ | $\boxed{-4.5}$ | $\boxed{+4.5}$ | $\boxed{+6.5}$ |
| Adjustment | $\boxed{-0.25}$ | $\boxed{-0.25}$ | $\boxed{-0.25}$ | $\boxed{-0.25}$ |
| Average seasonal adjustment | $\boxed{-5.75}$ | $\boxed{-4.75}$ | $\boxed{4.25}$ | $\boxed{6.25}$ |

*Workings*

|  | Season | | | | |
|---|---|---|---|---|---|
|  | Spring | Summer | Autumn | Winter | Total |
| **Year** | | | | | |
| 1 |  |  | +5 | +6 | |
| 2 | −6 | −4 | +4 | +7 | |
| 3 | −5 | −5 |  |  | |
| Total | −11 | −9 | +9 | +13 | |
| Average (÷2) | −5.5 | −4.5 | +4.5 | +6.5 | +1.0* |
|  | −0.25 | −0.25 | −0.25 | −0.25 | −1.0 |
|  |  |  |  |  | 0 |

*Averages must sum to zero, therefore adjustments $= -1 \div 4 = -0.25$

# ANSWERS

2   ☑ Their magnitude is constant from one cycle to the next
    ☑ They always reflect the trade cycle
    ☑ They always repeat every five to ten years

Cyclical variations are of a longer period than seasonal variations, but do not need to be of a particular length. Similarly, cyclical variations do not have constant magnitudes. They are not necessarily connected with the trade cycle, even if the time series is economic in nature. Many time series are unconnected with economics.

3   Trend for April (to 2 decimal places) = ⎡ 24.67 ⎤

    Seasonal variation (to 2 decimal places) for April = ⎡ 1.33 ⎤

| Month | Data | Three-month total | Three month average (trend) | Seasonal variation |
|-------|------|-------------------|-----------------------------|--------------------|
| June | 16 | | | |
| July | 26 | 74 | 24.67 | 1.33 |
| August | 32 | | | |

Remember that the actual series = trend + seasonal variation

∴ 26 = 24.67 + seasonal variation

So seasonal variation = 26 – 24.67
                      = 1.33

4

| Autumn | Winter |
|--------|--------|
| $ | $ |
| 46,483 | 70,453 |

Using the multiplicative model, actual sales = trend × seasonal variation

Seasonally-adjusted data are the same as the trend.

Autumn actual sales = $47,921 × 0.97 = $46,483

Winter actual sales = $65,234 × 1.08 = $70,453

5   ☑ Four-quarter totals

The main features of a time series are:

- A trend
- Seasonal variations
- Cyclical variations
- Random variations

6   ☑ A peak in the first three years of every decade, with a corresponding trough in the last five years of every decade.

Cyclical variations occur over a cycle longer than seasonal variations.

7 ☐✓ They have a period shorter than that of any cyclical variations there may be

Seasonal variations occur over a cycle shorter than that of any cyclical variations. For example, seasonal variations may occur over a year, and cyclical variations over five years. However, seasonal variations could occur over (for example) a week or a month, rather than a year. They need not repeat exactly, but could vary in size from one year, month etc to the next. The data may be a combination not only of trend and seasonal variations, but also of residuals.

8 ☐ 340

The seven-day total for a day will be made up of the data for the three days before that day, that day itself and the three days after that day.

| Week | Day | Data | Seven-day total |
|---|---|---|---|
| 1 | Tuesday | 82 | |
| | Wednesday | 61 | |
| | Thursday | 47 | |
| | Friday | 49 | 340 |
| | Saturday | 42 | |
| | Sunday | 38 | |
| 2 | Monday | 21 | |

The required total is 340. As this total includes one figure from each day of the week, it should not reflect the seasonal variations which affect individual days' figures.

9 ☐ 104

Sales vary according to the day of the week. Fore example, Tuesday is a day of very low sales and Wednesday is a day of very high sales. Therefore the most suitable moving average is one which covers one full weekly cycle, ie a five day moving average. A five day moving total centred on Thursday of week 2 must be calculated:

| | | Sales units | |
|---|---|---|---|
| Week 2 | Monday | 107 | |
| | Tuesday | 80 | |
| | Wednesday | 130 | ◄— centre point |
| | Thursday | 95 | |
| Week 3 | Friday | 107 | |
| Five day moving total | | 519 | |

Moving average = 519 ÷ 5 = 103.8 units = 104 units.

This moving average of 104 units constitutes a trend figure. The fact that it is lower than the actual figure for Wednesday of week 3 (130 units) reflects the fact that Wednesday is a day of high sales.

ANSWERS

10    B    When the trend is increasing or decreasing, additive seasonal components change in their importance relative to the trend whereas multiplicative components remain in the same proportion to the trend. Option B is therefore a circumstance in which the multiplicative model would be preferred to the additive model.

It would generally be agreed that non-numerate people find the multiplicative model more difficult to understand than the additive model, perhaps due to problems with percentages. Option A does not apply in this instance.

When the trend is steady an additive model is acceptable but when it is increasing or decreasing it is important to use the multiplicative model so that the seasonal components remain the same proportion of the trend. Option C does not apply in this instance.

Provided the additive model is appropriate, as it is when the trend is steady, it will give forecasts as accurate as those given by the multiplicative model. Option D does not apply in this instance.

# 30 Forecasting 4

1    ☑    Annual sales are static.

☑    The fourth quarter, $Q_4$, has the highest quarterly sales in each of the three years.

☑    The mean sales for the second quarter ($Q_2$) equals the mean quarterly sales for the whole period, 1997-99.

Annual sales are 200 units each year, ie static.

The fourth quarter, $Q_4$, has the highest quarterly sales in each of the three years.

The mean sales for $Q_2$ = 50 and the mean quarterly sales for 1997-99 = 600 ÷ 12 = 50.

All three statements are correct.

2    B    3-point moving totals are 18, 22, 26, 30 and 34 which change by the same amount (4) each day. The 3-point moving average would also change by a constant amount which would result in a straight line graph if the data were plotted.

3    D    Year = 2000

∴ Trend     $= (0.0002 \times 2000^2) + (0.4 \times 2000) + 30.4$
            $= 800 + 800 + 30.4$
            $= 1,630.4$

∴ Forecast  $= 1.6 \times 1,630.4$
            $= 2,608.64$

∴ Forecast in whole units = 2,609

4    B    If Y = 0.5t – 12

The breakeven point is reached where profit = 0, ie where Y = 0

$0 = 0.5t – 12$

$12 = 0.5t$

$t = \dfrac{12}{0.5}$

$t = 24$

If t = 1 is the first month of 20X0, t = 24 is the last month (12th month) of 20X1.

If you selected option A, you rearranged the formula (12 = 0.5t) to give t = 6 which is incorrect.

If you selected option C, you rearranged the formula (12 = 0.5t) to give t = 12.5 (adding the 0.5 instead of dividing by it) which is incorrect.

If you selected option D you seem to have confused the variables Y and t (and had t = 0 instead of Y = 0 in your equation thus leading to an answer of Y = 12 which you have then interpreted as t = 12, ie the 12th month of 20X0).

5    B    I      A cyclical component of 0.95 means that actual values are 95% of the trend.

II     A cyclical component of 0.6 means that values are only 60% of the trend, ie they are 40% below the trend.

III    A cyclical component of 0.82 means that values are 82% of the trend, ie they are 18% below the trend, not 18% above it.

IV    The seasonal components build up steadily from year 1 to year 3 but whether the actual values do depends on the trend.

Options I and II are correct, and therefore the answer is B.

6    C

|  | Quarter | | | |
|---|---|---|---|---|
|  | 1 | 2 | 3 | 4 |
| Actual value | $500 | $300 | $330 | $610 |
| Seasonal component | +20% | –30% | –25% | +35% |
| Seasonally-adjusted value | $417 | $429 | $440 | $452 |

II is the only correct calculation. The correct answer is therefore C.

7

| Month | No of ice creams sold | Moving total of 3 months ice creams sold | Moving average of 3 months ice creams sold |
|---|---|---|---|
| July | 2,000 | | |
| August | 2,500 | 6,300 | 2,100 |
| September | 1,800 | 5,700 | 1,900 |
| October | 1,400 | 4,100 | 1,367 |
| November | 900 | 3,300 | 1,100 |
| December | 1,000 | | |

8    A    $t = 1$ in the first quarter of 20X8
$t = 6$ in the second quarter of 20X9

$\therefore$   $y = 5t - 1.5$
$y = (5 \times 6) - 1.5$
$y = 30 - 1.5$
$y = 28.5$

If $y = \$28,500$ and the seasonal component is $-7\%$.

Forecast   $= \$28,500 \times 0.93$
           $= \$26,505$

If you selected option B, you used $t = 2$ instead of $t = 6$ (the question is dealing with quarters, not years).

If you selected option C, you have treated the trend equation $Y = 5t - 1.5$ as $Y = (5 - 1.5)t$.

If you selected option D, you have treated the series as if it were an additive model by subtracting 7 from the trend instead of reducing it by 7%.

9     •    Odd number of time periods  $=$   1

     •    Even number of time periods  $=$   2

10     308

If $C = 10$

$P = 273.16 - (1.74 \times 10) = 255.76$

Forecast   $=$ trend + seasonal component
           $= 255.76 + 52.19$
           $= 307.95$
           $= 308$ (to the nearest unit)

# 31 Forecasting 5

1    B    In 20X9, t = 9

$y = 20t - 10$
$y = (20 \times 9) - 10$
$y = 180 - 10 = 170$

∴ Forecast profits for 20X9 = 170 − 30      = 140
                                                            = \$140,000

If you selected option A, you used t = 10 in the trend line equation instead of t = 9.

If you selected option C, you have treated the model as if it were multiplicative instead of additive and reduced the trend by 30% instead of 30.

If you selected option D, you have muddled up the brackets in the trend equation and calculated Y = (20 − 10)t instead of Y = 20t − 10.

2    C    I    Provided the multiplicative model is used, it does not matter if the trend is increasing or decreasing.

II    Forecasts are made on the assumption that the previous trend will continue.

III    In general, extrapolation does not produce reliable estimates but in forecasting the future using time series analysis we have no option but to extrapolate.

IV    Forecasts are made on the assumption that previous seasonal variations will continue.

II and IV are therefore necessary. The correct answer is C.

3    D    Forecast trend, $y = 30.15 + 3.6x$

In month 21,    $y = 30.15 + (3.6 \times 21)$
                        $y = 30.15 + 75.6$
                        $y = 105.75$

Forecast for month 21    = trend × seasonal factor
                                    = 105.75 × 1.02
                                    = 107.865
                                    = 108 (to the nearest whole unit)

If you selected option A, you divided the trend by the seasonal factor instead of multiplying by the seasonal factor.

If you selected option B, you correctly forecast the trend but failed to take account of the seasonal factor.

If you selected option C, you rounded 107.865 down to 107 instead of up to 108.

4    D    Actual value = trend × seasonal factor

Seasonally-adjusted figure = estimate of trend

$$\text{Estimate of trend} = \frac{\text{Actual value}}{\text{Seasonal factor}}$$
$$= \frac{4,000}{0.95}$$
$$= 4,211$$

If you selected option A you used the underlying trend figure of 3,750 instead of the actual value of 4,000. You also multiplied it by the seasonal factor instead of dividing it.

If you selected option B, you used the actual value of 4,000 and multiplied it by the seasonal factor instead of dividing it by the seasonal factor.

If you selected option C, you divided the underlying trend value (instead of the actual value) by the seasonal factor (correct method).

5    B    The additive model

$$Y = T + S + R$$

where  Y = actual value
       T = trend
       S = seasonal
       R = random

∴  R  = Y − T − S
   R  = 170 − 182 − (−12.8)
      = 0.8

If you didn't get the correct answer, work through the solution again. Note that the formula for the additive time series model is provided in your exam.

6    D    As this is a multiplicative model, the seasonal variations should sum (in this case) to 4 (an average of 1) as there are four quarters.

Let X = seasonal variation in quarter 4

1.2 + 1.3 + 0.4 + X = 4

2.9 + X = 4
   X = 4 − 2.9
   X = 1.1

7    A    For a multiplicative model, the seasonal component S = Y/T
             ∴ T = Y/S

|  | Quarter | |
| --- | --- | --- |
|  | 1 | 2 |
| Seasonal component (S) | 1.2 | 1.3 |
| Actual series (Y) | $125,000 | $130,000 |
| Trend (T) (= Y/S) | $104,167 | $100,000 |

The trend line for sales has therefore decreased between quarter 1 and quarter 2.

8   B   The additive model

Y = T + S

where   Y = actual series
        T = trend
        S = seasonal

The seasonally-adjusted value is an estimate of the trend.

∴  Y = T + S
   T = Y – S
   T = 567,800 – (+90,100)
   T = 477,700

9   C   $Y = 300 - 2\sqrt{t}$

In the third quarter t = 3

$Y = 300 - 2\sqrt{3}$
 = 296.54

Forecast costs   = Trend + seasonal
                 = 296.54 + 50
                 = 346.54
                 = $347,000 (to the nearest $'000)

If you selected option A, you calculated $\sqrt{2 \times 3}$ instead of $2\sqrt{3}$.

If you selected option B, you have confused the multiplicative and additive models, and have increased the trend by 50% instead of just adding 50.

If you selected option D, you have subtracted the seasonal variation instead of adding it.

10  B

| Quarter | Y/T value | Adjustment | Adjusted average |
|---|---|---|---|
| 1 | 1.04 | (0.0075) | 1.0325 |
| 2 | 1.15 | (0.0075) | 1.1425 |
| 3 | 0.94 | (0.0075) | 0.9325 |
| 4 | 0.90 | (0.0075) | 0.8925 |
| * must total 4 | 4.03 | (0.03) | 4.0000* |

If you selected option A, you deducted 0.075 instead of 0.0075.

If you selected option C, you added 0.0075 instead of deducting it.

# 32 Forecasting 6

1   B

| Year | Y – T | Adjustment | Adjusted average |
|------|-------|------------|------------------|
| 1 | 18 | 1.0 | 19 |
| 2 | 30 | 1.0 | 31 |
| 3 | −16 | 1.0 | −15 |
| 4 | −36 | 1.0 | −35 |
|   | −4 | 4.0 | 0 |

If you selected option A, you added 4 to −36 instead of adding 1 (4/4 = 1).

If you selected option C, you deducted 1 instead of adding 1 to the −36.

If you selected option D, you deducted 4 from −36 instead of adding 1 (4/4 = 1).

2   A   In 20X9, x = 9

$$\therefore \text{trend} = 850 + \frac{27}{9}$$
$$= 850 + 3$$
$$= 853$$

A 2% reduction in the trend is the same as multiplying the trend by 0.98 (100% − 2% = 98% or 0.98).

Forecast units = 853 × 0.98

= 836 units (to the nearest whole number)

If you selected option B, you calculated trend = $\frac{850 + 27}{9}$ = 97 and failed to take account of the

cyclical factors. Note that trend = $850 + \frac{27}{9}$.

If you chose option C, you have increased the trend by 2% instead of decreasing it by this amount.

If you selected option D, you forecast the number of units correctly but forgot to take account of cyclical factors.

3   C   In month 13, x = 13

y = 4,320 + (5.2 × 13)
y = 4,320 + 67.6
y = 4,387.6

Sales forecast = 4,387.6 × 1.15

= 5,045.74

= 5,046 (to the nearest whole number)

If you selected option A, you have forgotten to add the 15% increase (658) to the trend in order to calculate the forecast.

If you selected option B, you have reduced the trend by 15% instead of increasing it by this amount.

If you selected option D, you correctly calculated the trend but forgot to increase it by 15%.

4    D    Trend, $y = 250 - 1.57x$

In time period 15, $t = 15$

Therefore trend,   $y = 250 - (1.57 \times 15)$
$$y = 250 - 23.55$$
$$y = 226.45$$

Forecast sales    = trend + seasonal
$$= 226.45 + (-28)$$
$$= 198.45$$
$$= \$198{,}000 \text{ (to the nearest } \$'000)$$

If you selected option A, you have calculated the sales forecast using the multiplicative model (ie reduced the trend by 28%) instead of the additive model (deducted 28).

If you selected option B, you seem to have subtracted the 1.57 from the 250 and then multiplied by 15 $((250 - 1.57) \times 15)$. Watch your order of operations!

If you selected option C, you forgot to subtract the seasonal component.

5    C    Options A, B and D are conditions which need to be met if time series forecasts are to be reliable.

If we wish to make a forecast outside the range of known data (for example, forecasting future results from historical data) we start by extrapolating the trend line (or extending the trend line) outside this range. By extrapolating the trend line, judgement is used and it is possible that errors may be introduced. However, extrapolation is an important tool in forecasting future results from historical data and should not, therefore, be avoided.

6    B    As this is a multiplicative model, the seasonal variations should sum (in this case) to 4 (an average of 1) as there are four quarters.

Let x = seasonal variation for quarter 4.

$0.65 + 1.32 + 1.41 = 3.38$

$\therefore$   $3.38 + x$   = 4
$$x\ =\ 4 - 3.38$$
$$x\ =\ 0.62$$

If you selected option A, you forgot to subtract the sum of the seasonal variations for quarters 1-3 from 4.

If you selected option D, you made an error in your calculation. Try again!

7    C    For the multiplicative model, the seasonal component, $S = Y/T$

$\therefore T = Y/S$

|  | Quarter | |
| --- | --- | --- |
|  | 1 | 2 |
| Seasonal component (S) | 0.65 | 1.32 |
| Actual series (Y) | $320,000 | $500,000 |
| Trend (T) = Y/S | $492,308 | $378,788 |

The trend line for sales has therefore decreased between quarter 1 and quarter 2.

If you selected option A, you guessed (incorrectly)!

If you selected option B, you did not take the seasonal component into account and compared $320,000 with $500,000 instead of $492,308 with $378,788.

If you selected option D, you didn't even try to determine the trend line for sales – it can be determined from the information given.

8    D

|                              | Quarter |         |         |         |
|                              | 1       | 2       | 3       | 4       |
|------------------------------|---------|---------|---------|---------|
| Actual value (Y)             | $1,300  | $1,600  | $1,050  | $1,100  |
| Seasonal component (S)       | +$200   | +$400   | –$300   | –$300   |
| Seasonally-adjusted value (T)| $1,100  | $1,200  | $1,350  | $1,400  |

The seasonally-adjusted value is also known as the trend.

If $Y = T + S$

$\therefore T = Y - S$

I and IV are therefore correct.

Remember, $1,050 – (–$300) = $1,050 + $300 – a minus and a minus makes a plus!

9    D    Seasonally-adjusted data $= \dfrac{\text{Actual results}}{\text{Seasonal factor}}$

$$= \dfrac{750}{0.78}$$

$$= 962$$

If you selected option A you multiplied the underlying trend by the seasonal factor instead of dividing the actual results by the seasonal factor.

If you selected option B, you multiplied by the seasonal factor instead of dividing by it.

If you selected option C, you divided the underlying trend (instead of the actual results) by the seasonal factor.

10   B    In a multiplicative model, values are seasonally adjusted by **dividing** by the corresponding seasonal factor.

| Month                     | January | February | March | April |
|---------------------------|---------|----------|-------|-------|
| Actual                    | 550     | 650      | 750   | 1,190 |
| Seasonal component        | 0.54    | 0.60     | 0.73  | 1.09  |
| Seasonally-adjusted sales | 1,019   | 1,083    | 1,027 | 1,092 |

# 33 Financial mathematics 1

1    B    Current rate is 6% pa payable monthly

$\therefore$ Effective rate is 6/12% = ½% compound every month

$\therefore$ In the six months from January to June, interest earned =

$(\$1,000 \times [1.005]^6) - \$1,000 = \$30.38$

Option A is incorrect since it is simply 6% × $1,000 = $60 in one year, then divided by 2 to give $30 in six months.

Option C represents the annual interest payable (6% × $1,000 = $60 pa).

Option D is also wrong since this has been calculated (incorrectly) as follows.

| | | |
|---|---|---|
| 0.05 × $1,000 | = | $50 per month |
| Over six months | = | $50 × 6 |
| | = | $300 in six months |

2 | 270 |

$2,070 = 115% of the original investment

$$\therefore \text{Original investment} = \frac{100}{115} \times \$2,070$$
$$= \$1,800$$

$$\therefore \text{Interest} = \$2,070 - \$1,800$$
$$= \$270$$

Make sure that you always tackle this type of question by establishing what the original investment was first.

3    C    If costs fall by 2½% per annum on a compound basis then at the end of the year they will be worth 0.975 of the value at the start of the year.

Therefore after five years, costs will have fallen to $160,000 × (0.975)^5 = $140,975

Option A is calculated as $160,000 × (0.975)^6 = $137,450, ie the value at the end of six years instead of five which is incorrect.

Option B is wrong because it has been calculated using 0.875 instead of 0.975 in error (2.5 × 5 = 12.5, 100 − 12.5 = 87.5 or 0.875).

Option D is simply 97.5% of $160,000 = $156,000 which is also wrong.

4    C    If a cost declines by 5% per annum on a compound basis, then at the end of the first year it will be worth 0.95 the original value.

| | |
|---|---|
| Now | = $10,000 |
| End of year 1 | = $10,000 × 0.95 |
| End of year 2 | = $10,000 × 0.95^2 |
| End of year 3 | = $10,000 × 0.95^3 |
| End of year 4 | = $10,000 × 0.95^4 |

At the end of year 4, $10,000 will be worth $10,000 × (0.95)^4 = $8,145

Option A was calculated as $10,000 × 0.95^5 = $7,738 which is incorrect as this gives the value of $10,000 after five years, not four.

Option B assumes that the cost will have declined by 5% × 4 years = 20% after four years, ie 20% × $10,000 = $2,000 giving a cost after four years of $10,000 − $2,000 = $8,000. This option is also incorrect.

Option D was incorrectly calculated as $10,000 × 0.95^3 = $8,574 (this is the value of $10,000 after three years, not four).

ANSWERS

5    C    We need to calculate the effective rate of interest.

8% per annum (nominal) is 2% per quarter. The effective annual rate of interest is $[1.02^4 - 1] = 0.08243 = 8.243\%$.

Now we can use
$$S = X(1 + r)^n$$
$$S = 12{,}000\,(1.08243)^3$$
$$S = \$15{,}218.81$$

∴ The principal will have grown to approximately \$15,219.

Option A is incorrect because this represents $\$12{,}000 \times (1.08)^3 = \$15{,}117$. You forgot to calculate the effective annual rate of interest of 8.243%.

Option B represents the present value of \$12,000 at the end of three years, ie $\$12{,}000 \times 0.794$ (from present value tables) at an interest rate of 8%.

Option D represents the cumulative present value of \$12,000 for each of the next three years at an interest rate of 8%.

6    B    Effective annual rate = $[(1 + r)^{12/n} - 1]$ when n = number of months.

We want a monthly rate and so n = 1.

$$0.3 = [(1 + r)^{12} - 1]$$
$$0.3 + 1 = (1 + r)^{12}$$
$$(1.3)^{1/12} = 1 + r$$
$$1.0221 = 1 + r$$
$$0.221 = r$$
$$2.21\% = r$$

The formula for calculating the effective annual rate is not provided in your examination, so **make sure that you can reproduce it** – that is the only way that you'll get the correct answer to this question.

7    $\boxed{32.000}$

$$Sr = R^N(Ar + P) - P$$
$$S \times 0.07 = (1.07)^{20}[(3{,}000 \times 0.07) + 500] - 500$$
$$0.07S = (1.07)^{20}(710) - 500$$
$$S = \frac{(1.07)^{20}(710) - 500}{0.07}$$
$$S = 32{,}106.8$$

∴ S = \$32,000 to the nearest \$'000

Make sure that you can manipulate formulae confidently. In this OT you were given all of the information that you needed to answer the question correctly – you just needed to use it properly!

186

8    C    $S = \dfrac{A(R^2 - 1)}{R - 1}$

$$S \times (R - 1) = A(R^2 - 1)$$

$$\dfrac{S}{A} = \dfrac{R^2 - 1}{R - 1}$$

$$\dfrac{S}{A} = \dfrac{(R - 1)(R + 1)^*}{(R - 1)}$$

$$\dfrac{S}{A} = R + 1$$

$$\therefore \quad R = \dfrac{S}{A} - 1$$

$^*(R - 1)(R + 1) = R^2 + R - R - 1 = R^2 - 1$

This is another OT question that requires you to be able to manipulate formulae accurately and confidently. Make sure that you understand this solution before you move onto the next question.

9    D    Effective quarterly rate    = 1% (4% ÷ 4)

Effective annual rate     = $[(1.01)^4 - 1]$
                               = 0.0406 = 4.06% pa

Remember that the formula for calculating the effective annual rate is not provided in your examination.

You should have been able to eliminate options A and B immediately. 1% is simply 4% ÷ 4 = 1%. 4% is the nominal rate and is therefore not the effective annual rate of interest.

10    C    Using the formula    $S = X(1 + r)^n$

where    X = $2,500
            r = 0.08
            n = 3

S        = $2,500 \times (1 + 0.08)^3$
        = $3,149 (to the nearest $)

Option A is incorrect as it represents a total growth of 8% for 3 years, ie $2,500 × 1.08 = $2,700.

Option B represents an increase of 24% after 3 years (3 × 8% = 24%), ie $2,500 × 1.24 = $3,100. This option is incorrect.

Option D represents $2,500 invested four years ago instead of three, ie $2,500 × $(1.08)^4$ = $3,401. This is incorrect since the question states that the investment was made exactly three years ago.

# 34 Financial mathematics 2

1    A    The actual rate is 1% per calendar month and so the value of the deposit after 6 months is $500 × $(1.01)^6$ = $530.76.

If you selected option B, you incorrectly calculated 12% of $500.

If you selected option C, you calculated 6% of $500 but have not allowed for monthly compounding.

If you selected option D, you have assumed that the 12% is not nominal and that the rate per calendar month is actually 0.95%.

2    D    If the value of the asset falls by 20% per year, it is worth 80% of its value at the beginning of the year at the end of each year.

100% − 20% = 80% = 0.8

∴ $100,000 × $(0.8)^5$ = $32,768

If you selected option A, you incorrectly calculated the present value of $100,000 discounted at 20% over 5 years.

Option B represents 20% of $100,000 which is incorrect.

If you selected option C you incorrectly depreciated $100,000 at 80% per annum instead of 20%.

3    C    If the cost declines by 7% per annum on a compound basis, then at the end of year 5 it will be worth $20,000 × $0.93^5$ = $13,914.

Option A is incorrect as this is the value of $20,000 after 6 years.

Option B assumes that the cost will have declined by 7% × 5 years = 35% after 5 years ie, 35% × $20,000 = $7,000. $20,000 - $7,000 = $13,000.

Option D is incorrect as this is the value of $20,000 after 4 years.

4    B    If house prices rise at 2% per calendar month, this is equivalent to

$(1.02)^{12}$ = 1.268 or 26.8% per annum

If you selected option A, you forgot to take the effect of compounding into account, ie 12 × 2% = 24%.

If you chose answer C, you correctly calculated that $(1.02)^{12}$ = 1.268 but then incorrectly translated this into 12.68% instead of 26.8%.

If you selected option D, you forgot to raise 1.02 to the power 12, and instead you multiplied it by 12.

5    | 8.195 |

Depreciation of 15% = an annual ratio of 0.85
Depreciation of 10% = an annual ratio of 0.90
Depreciation of 2% = an annual ratio of 0.98

∴ Value of car after 8 years    = $17,000 × $0.85^1$ × $0.90^5$ × $0.98^2$
                            = $8,195

6    A    The monthly rate of increase $= [(1.21)^{1/12} - 1]$
$$= 0.01601$$
$$= 1.601\%$$

Therefore, over eight months

$80,000 \times (1.01601)^8 = \$90,840$

If you selected option B, you have incorrectly calculated the increase in house price as

$80,000 \times 8/12 \times 21\% = \$11,200$
$80,000 + \$11,200 = \$91,200$

You have not taken the compounding effect into account.

If you selected option C, you have incorrectly calculated the increase in house price as follows.

$1.21 \times 8/12 = 0.80667$
$80,000 \times 1.080667 = \$86,453$

If you selected option D, you have correctly calculated that $(1.21)^{8/12} = 1.135508$ but then you have incorrectly interpreted this as an increase of 11.35508% rather than 13.5508%.

7    | 10.700 |

Future value $= \$6,500 \times (1.08)^4 \times (1.1)^2$
$$= \$10,700$$

If you didn't get this answer, rework the question, making sure that you apply the correct interest rates to the correct time periods.

8    D    A decline in value of 25% gives an annual value ratio of 0.75 and so the monthly ratio is given by $(0.75)^{1/12} = 0.9763$. This is equivalent to a monthly rate of decline of 2.37% (100 – 97.63).

If you selected option A, you divided 25% by 12 giving 2.08% and have therefore ignored the effect of compounding.

If you selected option B, you have correctly calculated $(0.75)^{1/12} = 0.976$ but have incorrectly translated this into 9.76% decline per month. 0.976 or 97.6% represents a monthly rate of decline of $(100 - 97.6)\% = 2.4\%$.

If you selected option C, you have divided the annual ratio by 12, giving 0.75/12 = 0.0625, and translated this into 6.25%. The correct calculation is $1 - (0.75)^{1/12}$.

9    B    The price of the bond has increased to $\dfrac{75}{50}$ = 150% over 5 years

∴ The annual increase $= (1.5)^{1/5} - 1$
$$= 1.084 - 1$$
$$= 0.084 \text{ or } 8.4\% \text{ pa}$$

If you selected option A, you forgot to take account of compounding and simply divided 50% by 5 = 10% per annum.

If you selected option C, you have incorrectly assumed that a price rise of $25 over 5 years is the same as a percentage increase of 25% over 5 years or 25%/5 = 5% per annum.

If you selected option D, you have calculated the annual ratio correctly, ie 1.084 but you have incorrectly translated this into 10.84% instead of 8.4% per annum.

10   C   The annual rate of increase = 21%.

Six-month rate of increase = $(1.21)^{1/2}$

Let value at beginning of six months = x

$$\therefore \quad x \times 1.1 \quad = \quad \$90,000$$

$$x \quad = \quad \frac{£90,000}{1.1}$$

$$= \quad \$81,818$$

If you selected option A, you incorrectly calculated the six-month rate to be half of the annual rate, ie 21% ÷ 2 = 10.5% and then decreased $90,000 by 10.5%.

If you selected option B, you have forgotten that the original value is not $90,000 × 90% but $90,000 ÷ 1.1 = $81,818.

If you selected option D, you did not take account of compounding when calculating the six-month rate (it is not 21% ÷ 2 = 10.5%).

# 35 Financial mathematics 3

1   D   $1,200 × (1 + cumulative present value factor at 14%) = $5,319.60, where 1 in the brackets takes account of the payment now, at time 0.

∴ 1 + cumulative PV factor at 14% = $5,319.60 ÷ $1,200 = 4.433

∴ Cumulative PV factor at 14% = 4.433 − 1 = 3.433

From looking in cumulative PV tables in the 14% column we see that this PV factor corresponds to that for 5 years from now.

∴ The final payment is 5 years from now but the lease runs out 12 months after the final payment. The length of the lease is therefore 6 years.

Remember that cumulative present value tables show the present value of $1 per annum, receivable or payable at the **end** of each year. Adding 1 to the cumulative present value factor takes account of payments made now, at time 0 as stated above.

2   C   Present value of annuity of $1 for 5 years at 5% is $4.329 (from cumulative PV tables).

If PV = $60,000, annual amount must be $\frac{\$60,000}{4.329}$ = $13,860.

Option A was calculated as follows.

$\frac{\$60,000}{5 \text{ years}}$ = $12,000 pa (incorrect)

Option B was calculated as follows.

$$\frac{\$60,000}{(4.329 + 1)} = \frac{\$60,000}{5.329} = \$11,259 \text{ (incorrect)}$$

This option assumes that the annuity begins **now** and not in one year's time.

Option D was calculated (incorrectly) as follows.

$$\$60,000 \times (1.05)^5 = \$76,577$$

This option is calculating how $60,000 grows at a rate of 5% per annum (which was not the requirement of the question).

3    C

Present value of the lease for years 1 – 5 = $500 × 4.1 (from cumulative present value tables)

$$\therefore \text{ PV of lease for years } 0 - 5 = \$500 \times (1 + 4.1)$$
$$= \$500 \times 5.1$$
$$= \$2,550$$

Option A is incorrect because it uses present value tables over years 1-6, ie PV = $500 × 6 = $3,000. $3,000 × 0.666 = $1,998 (0.666 is from PV tables, 6 years at 7%).

Option B is calculated using cumulative PV tables for 6 years at 7% (instead of 1 plus the value for 5 years), ie $500 × 4.767 = $2,383. This calculation is incorrect.

Option D is also incorrect since it uses the cumulative present value tables at 7% for 1 plus 6 years, ie 1 + 4.767 = 5.767. $500 × 5.767 = $2,883.5 is not the correct answer.

4    A    Present value of the lease for years 1-9    = $8,000 × 5.328

Present value of the lease for years 0-9    = $8,000 × (1 + 5.328)
$$= \$8,000 \times 6.328$$
$$= \$50,624$$

Option B is the present value of the lease for years 1-9 only, ie $8,000 × 5.328 = $42,624. If the first payments are made now then you must remember to add a 1 to the 5.328.

Option C is the present value of the lease for years 1-10 (the first payment being made in one year's time), ie $8,000 × 5.650 = $45,200.

Option D is incorrect because it represents the present value of the lease for years 1-10 plus an additional payment now, ie $8,000 × (1 + 5.650) = $53,200.

5    C

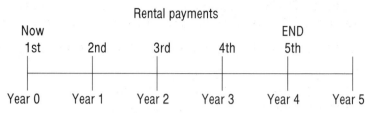

Rental payments

Now
1st    2nd    3rd    4th    END 5th

Year 0    Year 1    Year 2    Year 3    Year 4    Year 5

Let x = annual rental

Present value of the rentals for years 1-4 = x × 3.170

Present value of the rentals for years 0-4 = x × (1 + 3.170) = 4.170x

We know that the present value of the rentals is $32,800.

$\therefore$   $32,800   =   4.170x

$$x = \frac{\$32,800}{4.170}$$

=   $7,866 (to the nearest $)

Option A is incorrect since this is simply equal to 10% × $32,800 = $3,280.

Option B is also incorrect since this represents $32,800 ÷ 5 years = $6,560 per annum.

Option D is the annual rental in years 1-5 at 10% starting in one year's time, ie $32,800 ÷ 3.791 = $8,652.

6    D

|  |  | $ |
|---|---|---|
| PV of $1,200 in one year | = $1,200 × 0.926 = | 1,111.20 |
| PV of $1,400 in two years | = $1,400 × 0.857 = | 1,199.80 |
| PV of $1,600 in three years | = $1,600 × 0.794 = | 1,270.40 |
| PV of $1,800 in four years | = $1,800 × 0.735 = | 1,323.00 |

7    C    There are ten flows but one is at time 0. We therefore need to look up the present value of $1 per annum received at the end of **nine** years at an interest rate of 8% in cumulative present value tables = 6.247.

Present value of cash flows    = $1,000 × (1 + 6.247)*
= $1,000 × 7.247
= $7,247

* We need to add 1 to the annuity factor for years 1-9 since the first rent is to be paid **now**.

Option A is incorrect since it represents the present value of the cashflows in years 1-9 only (and excludes the first payment that is made now). $1,000 × 6.247 = $6,247.

Option B is incorrect because it represents the ten rental payments starting in one year's time for ten years, ie $1,000 × 6.710 = $6,710.

Option D represents the present value of 11 payments, the first payment now followed by 10 further payments = $1,000 × (1 + 6.710) = $1,000 × 7.710 = $7,710. Remember that if there are ten payments and the first one is made now, there will only be nine further payments (not ten).

8    C    The IRR is calculated by equating the present value of costs with present value of benefits.

PV(costs)              = 10,000
PV($7,000 in year 1)   = 7,000/(1 + r) = 7,000/x
PV($5,000 in year 2)   = 5,000/(1 + r)$^2$ = 5,000/x$^2$

Equating the present value of costs with the present value of benefits gives:

$$10,000 = \frac{7,000}{x} + \frac{5,000}{x^2}$$

Multiply each term by x$^2$    $10,000x^2 = 7,000x + 5,000$
So                             $10x^2 - 7x - 5 = 0$

which is the same as $-10x^2 + 7x + 5$

Option C is therefore correct since I, II and III are all equations that would enable you to calculate the IRR.

Once you had established that I and II were valid equations, you should have been able to add III to your list and reject IV straightway.

9    B    The formula to calculate the IRR is $a\% + \left[\frac{A}{A-B} \times (b-a)\right]\%$

where    a = one interest rate
         b = other interest rate
         A = NPV at rate a
         B = NPV at rate b

IRR    $= 9\% + \left[\frac{22}{22+4} \times 1\right]\%$
       $= 9 + 0.85 = 9.85\%$

If you selected option A you took A to be 'the other interest rate', and you subtracted the 0.85 instead of adding it.

You should have spotted that Options C and D were invalid because if the NPV is positive at one rate and negative at another rate, the IRR will be somewhere between the two rates, ie between 9% and 10%.

10   D    Project 4 has the highest NPV. When comparing projects it is the NPVs of each project which should be calculated and compared. The correct answer is therefore D.

Mutually exclusive projects should not be selected by comparing IRRs. The project with the highest NPV should be chosen. Option A is therefore incorrect.

Project 2 does not have the highest NPV - the criteria which should be used to select a project. Option B is therefore incorrect.

Project 3 does not have the highest NPV – the criteria which should be used to select a project. Option C is therefore incorrect.

# 36 Financial mathematics 4

1    B    The discount factor for 10 years at 7% is 0.508.

∴ Original amount invested    = $2,000 × 0.508
                                   = $1,016

If you selected option A, you mixed up the rate and the period in the present value tables and therefore found the discount factor for 7 years at 10%.

If you selected option C, you divided $2,000 by the discount factor instead of multiplying it.

If you selected option D, you used the cumulative present value tables instead of the simple present value tables. Always check your answers for common sense – an investment **growing** at 7% per annum is unlikely to fall in value!

2    C    The following problems arise when using net present values to appraise an investment.

- Estimating future cash flows
- Selecting an appropriate discount rate
- Non-accountants often find it difficult to understand the concept of net present value

Inflation will often be ignored when two alternative investments are being considered since both will be affected by it. III is therefore not (generally) a problem with the use of net present values in appraising projects.

3    D    From present value tables, the relevant discount factor for four years at 4% is 0.855.

∴ Present value of $500,000    = $500,000 × 0.855
                                         = $427,500

From cumulative present value tables, the relevant annuity factor is 2.775 for years 1-3 at 4%. Since investments are taking place at the beginning of the years, we take account of time 0 by adding 1 to the annuity factor (1 + 2.775 = 3.775).

$$\text{Annuity} = \frac{\text{Present value}}{\text{Annuity factor}}$$

$$= \frac{\$427,500}{3.775}$$

$$= \$113,245$$

$$= \$113,000 \text{ (to the nearest } \$'000)$$

If you selected option A, you forgot to allow for the 6% growth per year and have simply divided $500,000 by 4.

If you selected option B, you forgot to take account of the fact that the payments take place at the beginning of each year and not at the end.

If you selected option C, you forgot to take the first payment (at time 0) into account and only accounted for payments at the beginning of years 1-3.

4    B    Let A = annual repayments

These repayments, A, are an annuity for 15 years at 9%.

$$\text{Annuity (A)} = \frac{\text{Present value of mortgage}}{\text{Annuity factor}}$$

Present value of mortgage    = $30,000

Annuity factor    = 8.061 (9%, 15 years from CDF tables)

$$\therefore \text{Annuity} = \frac{\$30,000}{8.061}$$

= $3,720 (to the nearest $10)

If you selected option A, you seem to have confused mortgages with sinking funds and have calculated the present value of the mortgage as if it occurred at time 15 instead of time 0.

If you selected option C, you have forgotten to take account of interest rates (ie 9% for 15 years). You have simply divided $30,000 by 15.

If you selected option D, you have not taken account of the fact that the repayments happen at the year end and that the first repayment is in one year's time, not now.

5    A    If Annuity = $\dfrac{\text{PV of annuity}}{\text{Annuity factor}}$

where annuity factor = 7.943 (12 years, 7%)

PV of annuity    = Annuity × annuity factor
= $1,000 × 7.943
= $7,943

∴ Present value of investments = $7,943

At 7%, and 12 years, the discount factor is 0.444.

$$\text{Final value of investments} = \frac{\text{Present value of investments}}{\text{Discount factor}}$$

$$= \frac{\$7,943}{0.444}$$

= $17,890 (to the nearest $10)

If you selected option B, you forgot to take account of the 7% growth per annum and have simply multiplied $1,000 × 12 = $12,000.

If you selected option C, you have calculated the value of the fund at the end of year 13, instead of year 12.

Option D represents the value of the fund one year after final payments. You should have been able to eliminate this option straightaway since the question asked you to give your answer to the nearest $10.

6    D    I     As the discount rate increases, the NPV decreases. If the discount rate is viewed as the cost of capital, the NPV will fall as financing the project becomes more expensive.

             II     The NPV falls as the discount rate increases and so a lower discount rate will result in a higher NPV.

             III    The algebraic and graphical methods both approximate the behaviour of the IRR as discount rates increase and decrease as linear, whereas the behaviour is curvilinear. Neither can therefore give exact answers.

             IV    By calculating the net present value at two different discount rates, the IRR can generally be obtained by linear interpolation.

             I and IV are correct statements and the answer is therefore D.

7    C    Annual repayment = $5,000 = Annuity

$$\text{If Annuity} = \frac{\text{PV of annuity}}{\text{Annuity factor}}$$

and present value of annuity = $40,000

$$\$5,000 \quad = \quad \frac{\$40,000}{\text{Annuity factor}}$$

$$\text{Annuity factor} \quad = \quad \frac{\$40,000}{5}$$

$$= \quad 8$$

From cumulative present value tables, an annuity factor of 8 corresponds to an interest rate of 7% for a period of between 12 and 13 years (n = 12 and n = 13). Since the mortgage will not quite be repaid after 12 years, the answer is C, 13 years.

If you selected option A, you have ignored the effect of interest and have wrongly concluded that $40,000 ÷ $5,000 = 8 years to pay the mortgage off.

If you selected option B, you have incorrectly assumed that repayments were made at the beginning of each year, rather than the end.

If you selected option D, you seem to have incorrectly calculated that eight payments are required, with the first payment being made immediately.

8    D    The IRR is the discount rate at which the NPV = 0 and hence it is the percentage return paid by the investment.

             There is no special name for the discount rate which should be used in different circumstances.

             If the rate charged on loans was to equal the internal rate of return, the investment would not make a profit.

             There is no special name for the probability of making a profit on an investment.

9    D    Repayments of $3,290 = annuity for fifteen years at 7%
Present value of annuity = $30,000

Mortgage is to be closed immediately after the eighth annual repayment.

PV of annuity = PV of $3,290 at 7% for 8 years + amount outstanding at time 8 at 7%

$30,000   =   ($3,290 × 5.971) + (amount outstanding × 0.582)
$30,000   =   $19,645 + (amount outstanding × 0.582)
$10,355   =   Amount outstanding × 0.582

$$\therefore \text{Amount outstanding} = \frac{\$10,355}{0.582}$$

$$= \$17,792$$

If you selected option A, you have found the amount outstanding at time 9 instead of time 8.

If you selected option B, you have found the amount outstanding immediately before the eighth payment instead of immediately after it.

If you selected option C, you have forgotten to take into account any interest due $30,000 – (8 × $3,290) = $3,680

10   D    I      Net present value is not directly concerned with price inflation, nor does it just measure costs unless specifically described as the net present value of costs.

         II     In general, the project with the highest NPV is preferable but in deciding between two projects there are also other factors to consider.

         III    Net present value is not directly concerned with price inflation although it does, in the very broadest sense, measure profit.

         IV     A net present value is the amount which, if invested now, would generate the net income of a project. So A's NPV of $3,000 can be seen as the current amount which is equivalent to A's net income.

         Statements II and IV are therefore correct and the answer is therefore D.

# 37 Financial mathematics 5

1    A    Future value of annuity = $A \times \dfrac{(R^n - 1)}{(R - 1)}$

where   A   =   $100
        n   =   6
        R   =   1 + 0.04 = 1.04

Future value of annuity    $= \$100 \times \dfrac{(1.04^6 - 1)}{(1.04 - 1)}$

$= \$100 \times 6.63$
$= \$663$

If you selected option B, you used the correct formula but used n = 5 instead of n = 6.

If you selected option C, you seem to have confused the interest rate and the number of time periods in the formula.

If you selected option D, you have calculated the future value of the annuity, $663 and then discounted it using the present value tables, ie $633 × 0.822 = $545. This is obviously incorrect as the question asked for the **future** value of the annuity.

2    D    Annuity = $700

Annuity factor    =   1 + 6.247 (cumulative factor for 9 years, first payment is **now**)
                              =   7.247

$$\text{Annuity} = \frac{\text{PV of annuity}}{\text{Annuity factor}}$$

$$\$700 = \frac{\text{PV of annuity}}{7.247}$$

$700 × 7.247   =   PV of annuity

PV of annuity   =   $5,073 (to the nearest $)

If you selected option A, you have calculated the present value of an annuity from years 1-10 instead of from time 0-9.

If you selected option B, you have used the present value tables instead of the cumulative present value tables, ie $700 × (1 + 0.5) = $1,050.

If you selected option C, you appear to have mixed up the interest rate and periods and obtained an annuity factor for years 0-8 at 10% = $4,435.

3    A    $$\text{IRR} = a\% + \left[ \frac{A}{A - B} \times (b - a) \right]\%$$

Where   a = one interest rate = 8%
              b = other interest rate = 9%
              A = NPV at rate A = $18,000
              B = NPV at rate B = −$11,000

$$\text{IRR} = 8\% + \left[ \frac{\$18,000}{\$18,000 - (-\$11,000)} \times (9 - 8) \right]\%$$

= 8% + 0.62%
= 8.62%

If you selected option B, you used A = NPV at rate B and B = NPV at rate A and therefore divided the range from 8% to 9% in the ratio 11:18 instead of 18:11.

If you selected option C, you have simply taken the midpoint [(8 + 9) ÷ 2 = 8.50%]. The IRR is the discount rate where NPV = 0.

If you selected option D, you have not accounted for the fact that the NPV at 9% is **negative**.

4    A    From PV tables, at 8% and at time 15, discount factor = 0.315.

$\therefore$ PV of final fund    = \$55,000 × 0.315

= \$17,325

$$\text{Annuity} = \frac{\text{PV of annuity}}{\text{Annuity factor}}$$

Annuity = \$2,000

Annuity factor = 8.244 (14 years)

$\therefore$ PV of annuity  = Annuity × annuity factor

= \$2,000 × 8.244

= \$16,488

PV of final payment   = PV final amount − PV of annuity

= \$17,325 − \$16,488

= \$837

However, we need to know the value of \$837 at time 15 (from tables, discount factor = 0.315).

$\therefore$ Payment required at time 15   $= \dfrac{\$837}{0.315}$

= \$2,660 (to 3 significant figures)

If you selected option B, you have failed to account for the growth of the fund at 8%, ie \$55,000 − (14 × \$2,000) = \$27,000.

If you selected option C, you have forgotten to convert the present value of the final payment (\$837) into the value of the actual payment that will be required at time 15.

If you selected option D, you have assumed that \$2,000 will be paid for 15 years (it should be 14 years) so you have carried out the correct method but used an incorrect annuity factor of 8.559 instead of 8.244.

5    B    The present value of an annuity from time 3-10 = present value of annuity from time 1-10 **minus** the present value of annuity from time 1-2.

$\therefore$ PV annuity   = \$3,000 × (7.360 − 1.833)

= \$3,000 × 5.527

= \$16,581

If you selected option A, you forgot to subtract the present value of years 1-2.

If you chose option C, you used the PV tables instead of the cumulative PV tables and subtracted the PV at time 10 from time 2.

If you selected option D, you have used the correct method but you have subtracted the PV of time 1-3 instead of the PV of time 1-2.

6 B The IRR can be calculated using the following formula.

$$IRR = a\% + \left[\frac{A}{A-B} \times (b-a)\right]\%$$

where a = 5%
    b = 12%
    A = \$230
    B = \$160

$$IRR = 5\% + \left[\frac{\$230}{\$230 - \$160} \times (12-5)\right]\%$$

$$= 5\% + [3.2857 \times 7]$$

$$= 28\%$$

If you chose option A, you must realise that it is possible to use either two positive or two negative NPVs as well as a positive and negative NPV. Using the former method, however, the results will be less accurate.

If you selected option C, you have used an NPV of –\$160 instead of +\$160 in your calculation.

If you selected option D, you have taken the arithmetic mean of 5% and 12% instead of using the IRR formula.

7 A Value after 3 years $= \$5,000 \times (1.06)^3$
          $= \$5,955$ (to the nearest \$)

If you selected option B, you have calculated the simple interest for each year as being \$300 (6% of \$5,000). You must take compounding into account.

If you selected option C, you raised 1.06 to the power $^1/_3$ instead of 3.

If you selected option D, you have divided by $1.06^3$ instead of multiplying by this amount. You have therefore found the present value of \$5,000 discounted at 6% for 3 years, instead of the future value.

8 C The payments made on a credit card are an annuity of \$x per month.

From cumulative present value tables (3%, 12 periods) the annuity factor is 9.954.

$$\text{If Annuity} = \frac{\text{PV of annuity}}{\text{Annuity factor}}$$

$$\text{Annuity} = \frac{\$10,500}{9.954}$$

$$= \$1,055$$

If you selected option A, you have simply divided \$10,500 by 12 without any reference to discounting.

If you selected option B, you have misread the cumulative present value tables (and used the annuity factor for 12% and 3 periods instead of 12 periods and 3%).

If you selected option D, you have calculated the present value of $10,500 in 12 time periods at a discount rate of 3% instead of finding the monthly annuity whose present value over 12 months at 3% gives $10,500.

9    D    I     The decision rule for NPV is to accept all investments with a positive NPV

II    NPV is an absolute measure (usually NPV is given in $) and is therefore superior to IRR which is a relative measure (percentage)

III   As the discount rate increases, the NPV decreases

IV    This is the definition of Net Present Value

I, II, III and IV are all correct and option D is therefore the correct answer.

10   A    Future value = $9,000 × $(1.01)^8$ = $9,746

If you selected option B, you confused the future value of an investment with its present value. You should multiply $9,000 by $(1.01)^8$, not divide it by this amount.

If you selected option C, you appear to have confused the rate and the period when using the future value formula. Future value ≠ $9,000 × $(1.08)^1$.

If you selected option D, you have used an interest rate of 1% per annum instead of 1% per quarter. There are therefore 8 periods and not 2.

# 38 Financial mathematics 6

1    | 7 | %

Present value of an annuity    =    PV
Annuity                        =    a

Using the formula a $= \dfrac{PV}{\text{Annuity factor}}$

$1{,}494.87 = \dfrac{10{,}500}{\text{Annuity factor}}$

∴ Annuity factor = 7.024

An annuity factor of 7.024 corresponds to a period of 10 years at an interest rate of 7% (from cumulative present value tables).

2    | 267.65 |

$200 × $(1.06)^5$ = $267.65

ANSWERS

3     $ [ 5,000 ]

$$PV = \text{annuity} \times \left(1 - \frac{1}{(1+r)^n}\right)$$

$$33{,}550 = \$X \times \left(\frac{1}{0.08}\left(1 - \frac{1}{(1+0.08)^{10}}\right)\right)$$

$$\$X = \frac{33{,}550}{6.71}$$

$$\$X = \$5{,}000$$

4     $ [ 84,000 ]

| Year | Payment | Discount factor | Present value |
|------|---------|-----------------|---------------|
|      | $       | 8%              | $             |
| 0    | 20,000  | 1               | 20,000        |
| 1    | X       | 0.926           | 0.926x        |
| 2    | X       | 0.857           | 0.857x        |
| 3    | X       | 0.794           | 0.794x        |
| 4    | X       | 0.735           | 0.735x        |
|      |         |                 | 3.312x        |

The present value of the four equal payments is $26,496.

Therefore each payment = x = $\dfrac{52{,}992}{3.312}$ = $16,000.

The total amount to be paid during the lease period is therefore

($20,000 + (4 × $16,000)) = $20,000 + $64,000 = $84,000.

5     False   [ ✓ ]

The difference between the total present value of a stream of cashflows at a given rate of discount, and the initial capital outlay is known as the internal rate of return.

The internal rate of return is the rate of return on an investment.

6     [ 9 ] %

$$\text{Annuity} = \frac{\text{Present value of annuity}}{\text{Annuity factor}}$$

$$\text{Annuity factor} = \frac{86{,}400}{19{,}260} = 4.486$$

From tables, this annuity factor corresponds to an interest rate of 9% over six years.

7     [ 5.206 ]

Don't get caught out by the irrelevant information given to you in this question. You simply need to look up 8% over 7 periods in the cumulative present value tables which is 5.206.

8    $\boxed{12,656.25}$

Using the compound interest formula, $V = X(I + r)^n$, we have $X = \$40,000$, $r = -0.25$, $n = 4$

∴ $V = 40,000 (1 - 0.25)^4 = 12,656.25$

∴ Written down value = $12,656.25

9    $\boxed{1,084}$

Using the compound interest formula, $V = X(1 + r)^n$, we have

$V = \$2,728.90$, $r = 0.08$, $n = 12$

∴ $2,728.90 = X(1 + 0.08)^{12}$

∴ $\dfrac{2,728.90}{(1 + 0.08)^{12}} = X = \$1,083.68$

∴ The original principal to the nearest $ = $1,084

10    $\boxed{12,167}$

$10,000 is invested at 4% pa for 5 years.
$10,000 \times (1.04)^5 = \$12,166.53 = \$12,167$ (to the nearest $)

# 39 Financial mathematics 7

1    $\boxed{480,000}$

The present value of a perpetuity is:

$PV = \dfrac{a}{r}$

where    $a$    = annuity = $24,000
          $r$    = cost of capital as a proportion = 5% = 0.05

∴ $PV = \dfrac{24,000}{0.05}$

       = $480,000

2    | 11.65 |

There are no excuses for getting this one wrong! Simply insert the values for r and n into the equation, plug the numbers into your calculator (in the correct order of course!). Calculate them step-by-step (as we have shown below) if you are a little uncomfortable using a calculator for more complicated formulae.

$$PV = \frac{1}{0.04} - \frac{1}{0.04(1 + 0.04)^{16}}$$

$$= 25 - \frac{1}{0.04(1.04)^{16}}$$

$$= 25 - \frac{1}{0.04 \times 1.87298}$$

$$= 25 - \frac{1}{0.0749192}$$

$$= 25 - 13.35$$

$$= 11.65$$

3    $ | 10,626 |

| Year | Cashflow $ | Discount factor 9% | Present value $ |
|------|------------|--------------------|-----------------|
| 0 | (45,000) | 1 | (45,000) |
| 1-6 | 12,400 | 4.486 | 55,626 |
| | | NPV = | 10,626 |

Remember to use the cumulative present value tables (and not the present value tables).

4    | 18 | %

The internal rate of return (IRR) of the investment can be calculated using the following formula.

$$IRR = a\% + \left( \frac{A}{A - B} \times (b - a) \right)\%$$

where    a = first interest rate = 12%
         b = second interest rate = 20%
         A = first NPV = $24,000
         B = second NPV = $(8,000)

$$IRR = 12\% + \left( \frac{24,000}{24,000 + 8,000} \times (20 - 12) \right)\%$$

$$= 12\% + 6\%$$

$$= 18\%$$

5    $ 30.19

Current rate is 3% pa payable monthly.

∴ Effective rate is 3/12% = 1/4% compound every month

∴ In the six months from July to December, interest earned
= ($2,000 × (1.0025)$^6$) − $2,000

= $30.19

6    False  ✓

If the value of the asset falls by 15% per year, at the end of each year it is worth 85% of its value at the beginning of the year.

100% − 15% = 85%
∴ $400,000 × (0.85)$^5$ = $177,482.13

However, the question asks you to state your answer to the nearest $, ie $177,482.

Remember to read the requirements of questions *very* carefully!

7    $ 11,269

There are 12 quarters in a three-year period, so n = 12
Future value = $10,000 × (1.01)$^{12}$ = $11,269

8    $ 300,885

If costs fall by 8% per annum on a compound basis then at the end of the year they will be worth 0.92 of the value at the start of the year.

Therefore at the end of four years, costs will have fallen to $420,000 × (0.92)$^4$ = $300,885.

9    12.55  %

Nominal interest rate    = 12% pa

$$= \frac{12\%}{4} = 3\% \text{ compound payable four times per year}$$

APR    $= [(1 + r)^{12/n} − 1]$
       $= (1 + 0.03)^4 − 1$
       $= 12.55\% \text{ pa}$

If you selected one of the other options you used the APR formula incorrectly − make sure you go back and revise this topic.

10    ✓    $510,513

$400,000 × (1.05)$^5$ = $510,513

# 40 Financial mathematics 8

1    Present value of final fund = $ $\boxed{56,700}$ to the nearest $

Present value of annuity = $ $\boxed{41,220}$ to the nearest $

Payment required at time 15 = $ $\boxed{49,143}$ to the nearest $

From PV tables, at 8% and at time 15, discount factor = 0.315.

∴ PV of final fund = $180,000 × 0.315 = $56,700

Annuity = $\dfrac{\text{PV of annuity}}{\text{Annuity factor}}$

Annuity = $5,000

Annuity factor = 8.244 (14 years)

∴ PV of annuity    = Annuity × annuity factor
    = $5,000 × 8.244 = $41,220

PV of final payment    = PV final amount − PV annuity
    = $56,700 − $41,220 = $15,480

However, we need to know the value of $15,480 at time 15 (from tables, discount factor = 0.315)

∴ Payment required at time 15 = $\dfrac{\$15,480}{0.315}$ = $49,143 (to the nearest $)

2    $ $\boxed{10,100}$

Using the formula    $S = X(1 + r)^n$

where    $X = \$8,000$
    $r = 0.06$
    $n = 4$

S    $= \$8,000 × (1 + 0.06)^4$
    = $10,099.82
    = $10,100 (to the nearest $)

3  $\boxed{43,132.42}$

Using the formula    $S = X(1 + r)^n$

where   S = \$84,848
        n = 10
        r = 7\% = 0.07

$84,848 = X(1 + 0.07)^{10}$

$\therefore X = \dfrac{\$84,848}{(1.07)^{10}}$

X = \$43,132.42 (to 2 decimal places)

4  $\boxed{23.16}$ %

Using the formula    $S = X(1 + r)^n$

where   S = \$54,600
        n = 15
        X = \$2,400

$54,600 = \$2,400 \times (1 + r)^{15}$

$\dfrac{\$54,600}{\$2,400} = (1 + r)^{15}$

$\sqrt[15]{\dfrac{54,600}{2,400}} = 1 + r$

$1.2316 = 1 + r$

$\therefore r = 1.2316 - 1$
           = 0.2316
           = 23.16\%

The annual rate of interest is 23.16% to 2 decimal places.

5

| Year | Cashflow $ | Discount factor | Present value $ |
|---|---|---|---|
| 0 | (5,000) | 1.000 | (5,000) |
| 1 | (2,000) | 0.862 | (1,724) |
| 2 | 7,000 | 0.743 | 5.201 |
| 3 | 6,000 | 0.641 | 3,846 |
|  |  | Net present value = | 2,323 |

6  Present value of perpetuity = $ $\boxed{35,000}$ to the nearest $

Net present value of project = $ $\boxed{9,000}$ to the nearest $

The present value of a perpetuity = $\dfrac{a}{r}$

where  a = $4,200

r = 12% = 0.12

PV of cash inflows = $\dfrac{\$4,200}{0.12}$ = $35,000

| | $ |
|---|---|
| Present value of cash inflows | 35,000 |
| Less: initial investment | 26,000 |
| Net present value of project | 9,000 |

7  $ $\boxed{7,855}$

Using cumulative present value tables:

We require the 15% factor for years 3 – 7.

| | |
|---|---|
| Cumulative discount factor for years 1 – 7 at 15% | 4.160 |
| *Less:* cumulative discount factor for years 1 – 2 at 15% | 1.626 |
| Cumulative discount factor for years 3 – 7 at 15% | 2.534 |

$\text{Annuity} = \dfrac{PV}{\text{Cumulative discount factor}}$

$\$3,100 = \dfrac{PV}{2.534}$

∴ PV  = $3,100 × 2.534

= $7,855.4

= $7,855 (to the nearest $)

8  $\boxed{15.6}$ %

The IRR can be calculated using the following formula.

$IRR = a\% + [\dfrac{A}{A - B} \times (b - a)]\%$

where  a = 10%

b = 17%

A = $8,000

B = –$2,000

$IRR = 10\% + [\dfrac{\$8,000}{\$8,000 - (-\$2,000)} \times (17 - 10)]\%$

= 10% + 5.6%

= 15.6%

9    $\boxed{\checkmark}$    $\dfrac{\$40,000}{(1.09)^3}$

We need to find the present value of $40,000 received in three years' time. Using the discounting formula (where x = present value).

$$X = S \times \dfrac{1}{(1+r)^n}$$

$$X = \dfrac{\$40,000}{(1+0.9)^3}$$

10    $ $\boxed{72,564}$

Repayments of $8,000 = annuity for fifteen years at 7%

PV of annuity = $90,000

Mortgage is to be closed **immediately** after the eighth annual repayment.

PV of annuity = PV of $8,000 at 7% for 8 years + amount outstanding at time 8 at 7%.

$90,000 = ($8,000 × 5.971) + (amount outstanding × 0.582)

$90,000 = $47,768 + (amount outstanding × 0.582)

$42,232 = amount outstanding × 0.582

$$\therefore \text{Amount outstanding} = \dfrac{\$42,232}{0.582}$$
$$= \$72,564$$

# 41 Financial mathematics 9

1        If the NPV of an investment at r% is positive, the NPV will be negative at a rate of s% if s% is less than r%

The NPV falls as the discount rate increases and so a lower discount rate will result in a higher NPV.

    The IRR can be obtained exactly using algebra whereas the graphical method provides only an approximate rate for the IRR

The algebraic and graphical methods both approximate the behaviour of the IRR as discount rates increase and decrease as linear, whereas the behaviour is curvilinear.

2     **3.570503**

There are no excuses for getting this one wrong!

Simply insert the values for r and n into the equation, plug the numbers into your calculator (in the correct order of course!). Calculate them step-by-step (as we have shown below) if you are a little uncomfortable using a calculator for a more complicated formula.

$$PV = \frac{1}{0.25} - \frac{1}{0.25(1 + 0.25)^{10}}$$

$$= 4 - \frac{1}{0.25(1 + 0.25)^{10}}$$

$$= 4 - \frac{1}{2.32830643654}$$

$$= 4 - 0.4294967296$$

$$= 3.570503$$

3    $ **1,371**

PV of $8,000 in one year's time $= \dfrac{\$8,000}{1.1} =$      7,272.727272

PV of $6,000 in four years' time $= \dfrac{\$6,000}{(1.1)^4} =$     4,098.080732

                                                  11,370.808004

Less: $10,000 spent *now*                     10,000.000000

                                                  1,370.808004

$1,370.808004 to the nearest whole number = $1,371

4    $ **181,000**

From present value tables, the relevant discount factor for four years at 4% is 0.855.

∴ Present value of $800,000    = $800,000 × 0.855
                                    = $684,000

From cumulative present value tables, the relevant annuity factor is 2.775 for years 1 – 3 at 4%. Since investments are taking place at the beginning of the years, we take account of time 0 by adding 1 to the annuity factor (1 + 2.775 = 3.775).

$$\text{Annuity} = \frac{PV}{\text{Annuity factor}}$$

$$= \frac{\$684,000}{3.775}$$

$$= \$181,192$$

$$= \$181,000 \text{ (to the nearest } \$'000)$$

5     $\boxed{42{,}000}$

We can use compound interest techniques with a negative rate of interest to calculate the depreciation rate per annum.

Let x = depreciation rate per annum

$$\$100{,}000 \times (1 + (-x))^4 = \$50{,}000$$

$$(1 - x)^4 = \frac{\$50{,}000}{\$100{,}000}$$

$$(1 - x)^4 = 0.5$$

$$1 - x = \sqrt[4]{0.5}$$

$$1 - x = 0.841$$

$$x = 1 - 0.841$$

$$x = 0.159$$

$$= 16\%$$

Therefore, after another year, the machine will have depreciated by a further 16%, ie

$\$50{,}000 \times 16\% = \$8{,}000$

$\therefore$ Value of machine $= \$50{,}000 - \$8{,}000$
$= \$42{,}000$

6     $\boxed{16{,}980}$

Final value of mortgage $= \$100{,}000 \times (1.11)^{10}$
$= \$283{,}942$

The final value of the mortgage must equal the sum of the repayments.

The sum of the repayments is a geometric progression with

X = X (annuity)

R = 1.11

n = 10

$$\$283{,}942 = \frac{X(1.11^{10} - 1)}{1.11 - 1}$$

$$\frac{\$283{,}942 \times 0.11}{(1.11^{10} - 1)} = X$$

$$X = \$16{,}980$$

(The difference of $1 is due to rounding)

7

| Value now $ | Investment period Years | Interest rate % | Final value $ |
|---|---|---|---|
| 55,000 | 4 | 7 | 72,093.78 (1) |
| 55,000 | 5 | 14 | 105,897.80 (2) |
| 55,000 | 4 | 21 | 117,897.38 (3) |

*Workings*

(1)  $\$55,000 \times (1.07)^4 = \$72,093.78$
(2)  $\$55,000 \times (1.14)^5 = \$105,897.80$
(3)  $\$55,000 \times (1.21)^4 = \$117,897.38$

8  False  ✓

A perpetuity is an annuity which lasts **forever**.

9  $  2,817.55

The value of the fund at the end of eight years is a geometric progression with:

A = $A × 1.04
R = 1.04
n = 8

The value of the sinking fund at the end of eight years is $27,000

$$\therefore \$27,000 = \frac{A \times 1.04 (1.04^8 - 1)}{1.04 - 1}$$

$$A = \frac{\$27,000 \times 0.04}{1.04 (1.04^8 - 1)}$$

$$= \frac{\$1,080}{0.383311812}$$

$$= \$2,817.55$$

BPP
PROFESSIONAL EDUCATION

10

| Year | Cashflow $ | Discount factor 12% | Present value $ |
|------|------------|---------------------|-----------------|
| 0 | (56,000) | 1.000 | (56,000) |
| 1 | 18,000 | 0.893 | 16,074 |
| 2 | 18,000 | 0.797 | 14,346 |
| 3 | 18,000 | 0.712 | 12,816 |
| 4 | 18,000 | 0.636 | 11,448 |
| | | NPV = | (1,316) |

Project viable   No   ✓

# 42 Spreadsheets 1

1.   A   A line graph is the best way of illustrating a trend over time.

2.   False

A macro is used for automating frequently repeated tasks

3   D   II only

Relative cell references (B3) change when you copy formulae to other locations. Absolute cell references ($B$3) stay the same when you copy formulae to other locations.

4   A   =$D$1/4*B4

This formula will divide the annual turnover by 4 and multiply the result by the seasonal variation. The $ signs show that the cell reference for D1 is absolute so the reference will stay the same when the formula is copied into the cells below.

5   D   =($D$1/4)+B10

This formula will divide the annual turnover by 4 and add the result to the seasonal variation found in cell B10. The $ signs show that the cell reference for D1 is absolute so the reference will stay the same when the formula is copied into the cells below. Brackets are needed so that Excel does the multiplication before the addition.

6   C   =C10*$B$1

This formula will multiply the quarterly volume in units from cell C10 by the unit selling price in cell B1. The $ signs show that the cell reference for B1 is absolute so the reference will stay the same when the formula is copied into the cells below

7    B    =SUM(E4:E8)

This formula will add up the values of XY in the column above to give a total.

8

| | A | B |
|---|---|---|
| 1 | a | 10000 |
| 2 | b | 400 |
| 3 | x at December 20X4 | 36 |
| 4 | Period | 3 months to 31 March 20X5 |
| 5 | Quarter | 1 |
| 6 | Seasonal variation | +500 |
| 7 | Trend = y | =B1+B2*(B3+B5) |
| 8 | Forecast | =B7+B6 |

You need to substitute the appropriate spreadsheet cell references for the a, b and x in the formula y = a + bx for the quarter in question. The value of a is found in cell B1 whatever the quarter, and so a in the spreadsheet formula is B1. Likewise the value of b does not change with time. But the value of x does change and so you cannot simply use B3 but must amend the value in B3 to reflect the quarter you are dealing with ie add 1 (the value in cell C5) to the value in B3 to get the appropriate value for x. The forecast is the trend value in cell B7 adjusted by the seasonal variation (the value in cell B6).

9

| | Tick box |
|---|---|
| Cashflow forecasting | / |
| Monthly sales analysis by market | / |
| Writing a memo | |
| Calculation of depreciation | / |

Spreadsheets are useful for many types of calculation, but are not generally used for memoranda or report writing, except as an import of eg a table of data.

10    B    The formula bar displays the location of the active cell and the formula in the active cell.

# 43 Spreadsheets 2

1    B    I and III only
=C4*117.5% adds 17.5% to the value in C4

2      D

The formulae on the spreadsheet compute as follows.

| =11-3*2 | 5.00 |
|---|---|
| =32^(1/2) | 5.66 |
| =4^4 | 256.00 |
| =4^2 | 16.00 |

A spreadsheet will always carry out a multiplication or division before an addition or a subtraction, so the formula in option A would only work if parentheses are used: =(11-3)*2. The symbol ^ means 'to the power of', so B is 32 to the power of ½, in other words the square root of 32. C is 4 to the power of 4.

3      =B4*17.5%    or    =B4*17.5/100

4      =B5+C5

5      =B4*B9      or      =B4*$B$9

6      False. The keys Ctrl + ` should be used for this.

7      A      Ctrl + s will save your work, Ctrl + t does nothing and F2 allows you to amend your entries in a cell.

8      =B17/12 or =SUM(B4:B15)/12

9      D

10     C      The product names in B3:D3 are needed for the names of the columns. The cost of sales (B10:D10) and profit (B11:D11) are then needed for the two components of each column. The sales data has not been used; if this had been selected also, it would have been stacked on top of the profit and cost of sales to give a meaningless total. As it is, the cost of sales and profit together give the sales as the total height of each column.

# 44 Spreadsheets 3

1      A      I and II only

The formula =C4+C5+C6/3 will first divide the value in C6 by 3 then add the result to the total of the values in C4 and C5. The formula =(C4+C5+C6)/3 will add C4, C5 and C6 together and divide the result by 3.

2      A      The general format shows the number to as many decimal places as are input or result from the computation of a formula, none in this case. Answer B is incorrect as the number is not shown to 2 decimal places: 341.00. C and D are incorrect as both the currency and accounting fonts show the currency unit in front of the number:$341.

3      C      A custom format has to be adapted to give brackets instead of a negative number.

| 4 | D | The percentage format is the only one of the four options given that would show the result of the formula as a percentage. The custom format has a percentage option, but that was not listed in the question. |
|---|---|---|

5    =B11*C11

| 6 | D | Whilst only one figure needs to be re-entered: the new labour rate in C20, the figures in the other cells will all change to reflect the new rate. |
|---|---|---|

| 7 | C | B11 and B14 would have to be amended to the new value of 2.5. The values in D11 and D14 would then change as a result, as would the total, D16. The rate per hour referred to in cells C11 and C14 are unaffected. |
|---|---|---|

| 8 | C | A smaller font size and a wider cell would allow more text to be included in the cell. Increasing the row height will have no effect on the amount of text that can be included on one line. |
|---|---|---|

9    B

| 10 | A | B and C are incorrect as if there is too much text for the size of the cell, it will spill into adjacent cells if they are empty, or will be hidden by the contents of the adjacent cell. If a nonsensical formula is entered into a cell, a different response will be given. For example, if your formula results in a value being divided by 0, #DIV/0! will appear. |
|---|---|---|

# 45 Spreadsheets 4

1

|  | Tick box |
|---|---|
| B15 | |
| B16 | |
| C7 | / |
| C10 | |

The production figures have to be input to this spreadsheet, but the figures in the other three cells can be calculated as follows.

B15    =C14*0.04

B16    =-B14*0.04

C10    =C7*B25        or =C7*$B$25 if replicated from B10

2

| D14 | =D10 or =D7*B25 |
|---|---|
| C16 | =-B15 or =-C14*0.04 |
| D17 | =SUM(D14:D16) |
| C21 | =C17*B26 or =C17*$B$26 |

3

| E10 | | =SUM(B10:D10) |
|---|---|---|
| E14 | | =E10 |
| E15 | | =D15 |
| E16 | | =B16 |

4    =IF(F7<=C7,"YES","NO")    or    =IF(F7>C7,"NO","YES")

5    =IF(G7="NO",0,(D7*E7))    or    =IF(F7<=C7,(D7*E7),0)

6    D    A and B are incorrect as they calculate the price at 5%, rather than deducting the discount from the price. C is incorrect as the discount is applied to orders below 1000 units by using the > sign incorrectly.

7    C    A and B are incorrect as they ignore the discount that this order qualifies for. D is incorrect as it applies the price as though it were a price per unit when, in fact, the price given is per hundred units.

8    False    The spreadsheet would read this as 0.05 instead of 5, so the existing formulae would calculate discount at 1/100th of its intended value.

9    A    You should save your work as often as possible to minimise the loss of work should the system crash: this happens to everyone once in a while.

10    D    Look on Tools, Protection for details of how to do this.

# Mock assessments

# CIMA

# Paper C3 (Certificate)

# Fundamentals of Business Mathematics

# Mock Assessment 1

| Question Paper | |
|---|---|
| Time allowed | **2 hours** |
| **Answer ALL forty-five questions** | |

**DO NOT OPEN THIS PAPER UNTIL YOU ARE READY TO START UNDER EXAMINATION CONDITIONS**

# Answer ALL 45 questions

1   $700 is to be shared out between Mr Singh, Mr Lal and Mr Smith in the ratio 8:5:1. Mr Singh receives

$ [          ]

2   $(70 + 2)/12 + (33 - 6)/-3$

The term above equals [          ] (to 3 decimal places)

3   The price of a job including sales tax at 17.5% is $843. The price of the job excluding sales tax to the nearest

$ is $ [          ]

4   A histogram has a standard interval width of 10 units. One interval has a width of 15 units. If the frequency

of this interval is 30, the height of the corresponding bar is [          ] (to 1 decimal place)

5   Which of the following statements defines differences between bar charts and histograms?

[          ]   Gaps may be left between the bars of a bar chart but not between those of a histogram

[          ]   A histogram may not be shaded or coloured

[          ]   The bases of the bars of a bar chart may be labelled rather than mathematically scaled

[          ]   It is the area rather than the height of a bar which represents the frequency in a histogram

6   A table has five rows showing educational attainment and three columns showing three wards of a town. Which of the following charts could be used to represent the data in the table?

[          ]   A single pie chart

[          ]   A multiple bar chart

[          ]   A simple bar chart

[          ]   A component bar chart

7   The exam marks for nine students were:

48, 51, 47, 75, 52, 52, 68, 62, 79

(a)   The mode of the exam marks is   [          ]

(b)   The median of the exam marks is   [          ]

8   In a group of 100 CIMA students, 40 are male, 42 are studying for Certificate level and 8 of the male students are not studying for Certificate level. A student chosen at random is female. What is the probability that she is not studying Certificate level?

[          ]

9    In a single throw of a pair of fair (six-sided) dice, what is the probability that the result is two numbers which sum to 7?

A    1/12
B    1/6
C    1/4
D    1/2

10   If five units at $1 each, ten units at $1.25 each and another ten units at $X each have an arithmetic mean of $1.22, the value of X is $ [_____] (to 2 decimal places)

11   The following spreadsheet can be used to investigate the inter-relationship between output and costs.

|     | A | B | C | D |
|-----|-----|-----|-----|-----|
| 1   | *Output* | *Cost* | | |
| 2   | *000s of units* | *$'000* | | |
| 3   | X | Y | $X^2$ | $Y^2$ |
| 4   | 2 | 9 | 18 | 81 |
| 5   | 3 | 11 | 33 | 121 |
| 6   | 1 | 7 | 7 | 49 |
| 7   | 4 | 13 | 52 | 169 |
| 8   | 3 | 11 | 33 | 121 |
| 9   | 5 | 15 | 75 | 225 |
| 10  | 18 | 66 | 218 | 766 |

The cell D10 shows the total of the $Y^2$ values. Which of the following would be a correct entry for this cell?

A    =A10*B10
B    =SUM(D4:D9)
C    =SUM(A10:C10)
D    =B10*B10

12   The average annual wage of eighty people surveyed was found to be $17,500. The standard deviation was found to be $3,000. The coefficient of variation (correct to two decimal places) is [_____]

13   A company is deciding between two projects, Project A and Project B. The expected profits from each project are shown below.

| | Project A | | Project B | |
|---|---|---|---|---|
| | *Profit* | *Probability* | *Profit/(Loss)* | *Probability* |
| | $ | | $ | |
| | 4,000 | 0.45 | 8,000 | 0.64 |
| | 2,000 | 0.55 | (1,000) | 0.36 |

The company should chose Project [_____] which has an expected value of $ [_____]

14 A saleswomen visits areas A, B and C in the ratio 2:1:1. The probabilities that her visits will be successful are 0.35, 0.15 and 0.12 respectively. The expected probability that any given visit is successful is ⬚ (to 4 decimal places)

15 A normal distribution has a mean of 200 and a standard deviation of 40. Approximately 80% of frequencies are less than ⬚ (to the nearest whole number)

16 In a time series of the unit sales of shoes, random variation could be caused by

⬚ a general trend

⬚ seasonal effects due to the weather

⬚ cyclical effects resulting from a change in fashion

⬚ unexplained or freak events

17 The present value of an annuity of $300, discounted for twenty years at 4.2% per year, with cash flows arising at the end of each year is $ ⬚ (to the nearest $)

18 Based on the past 10 quarters, an underlying trend equation has been derived as $Y = 21.5 + 2.6X$. If quarter 11 has a seasonal factor of 1.08, using a multiplicative model, the forecast for the quarter to the nearest whole number is ⬚

19 A machine costs $30,000 now and will yield net revenues of $25,000 at the end of year 1, $15,000 at the end of year 2 and $10,000 at the end of year 3. At an interest rate of 6%, the net present value is $ ⬚ (to the nearest $)

20 A sum of $40,000 is invested at an interest rate of 3% per six-month period. By the end of year 4, the principal investment will have grown to $ ⬚ (to the nearest $)

21 An investment has a Net Present Value of $4,000 at 10% and a Net Present Value of –$2,000 at 15%. The approximate internal rate of return of the investment is ⬚ % (to 2 decimal places)

22    In a time series analysis, the multiplicative model is used to forecast sales and the following seasonal variations apply.

| Quarter | 1 | 2 | 3 | 4 |
|---------|-----|-----|-----|-----|
| Seasonal variation | 0.75 | 1.6 | 0.9 | ? |

The actual sales value for the last two quarters of 20X1 were:

Quarter 3          $520,000
Quarter 4          $540,000

(a)    The seasonal variation for the fourth quarter is [＿＿＿] (to 2 decimal places)

(b)    The trend line for sales:

[＿＿＿]    Remained constant between quarter 3 and quarter 4

[＿＿＿]    Increased between quarter 3 and quarter 4

[＿＿＿]    Decreased between quarter 3 and quarter 4

[＿＿＿]    Cannot be determined from the information given

23    If $\Sigma x = 10$            $\Sigma Y = 78$            $\Sigma X^2 = 30$
      $\Sigma Y^2 = 1,266$        $\Sigma XY = 134$

and n = 5, the correlation coefficient is [＿＿＿] (to 3 decimal places)

24    The straight lines $Y = 2X + 4$ and $Y = 12 - 2X$ intersect where

X = [＿＿＿]

Y = [＿＿＿]

25    The following formula is used in loan calculations:

$$R = \frac{2PC}{B(N + 1)}$$

When the formula is rearranged, with N in terms of the other letters, N is equal to

[＿＿＿]    $\dfrac{2PC}{RB} - 1$

[＿＿＿]    $\dfrac{2PC - 1}{RB}$

[＿＿＿]    $2PC - 1$

[＿＿＿]    none of these

26   The formula $\dfrac{1}{1.1} S^2 \div \left(1 - \dfrac{1}{1.1}\right)$ simplifies to

☐   $\dfrac{S^2}{1.1}$

☐   $S^2$

☐   $\dfrac{10S^2}{1.1}$

☐   $10S^2$

---

27   In the equation $C = 6 + 0.5Q$, C denotes the total cost of sales (in thousands of $) and Q denotes the number of units sold (in thousands).

The total cost of sales for 3,000 units is therefore $ ☐ (to 2 decimal places)

---

28   The rank correlation coefficient between the ages and the scrap values of a certain type of machine equals –1.

This value means that

☐   no correlation exists between the ages and the scrap values of these machines.

☐   perfect negative correlation exists.

☐   weak negative correlation exists.

☐   a calculation error has been made.

---

29   The following statements relate to spreadsheet formulae

I      The formula =C4/E5 multiplies the value in C4 by E5

II     The formula =C4*117.5% reduces the value in C4 by 17.5%

III    The formula =C4*B10-D1 multiplies the value in C4 by that in B10 and then subtracts the value in D1 from the result

Which statements are correct?

A      I and II only
B      III only
C      II and III only
D      I, II and III

---

30   The staff in the Complaints Department of an airline are available to answer the telephone at random times, which amount to 20% of the working day on average.

The probability that a customer's call is answered **for the first time**, on their **fifth** attempt is ☐ (to 3 decimal places)

# The following data relate to questions 31 and 32

A credit card company charges its customers 2.2% interest each month on the outstanding balance on their account.

31 The effective annual interest that the company is charging is [＿＿＿＿] % (to 2 decimal places)

32 The company decides to reduce its monthly interest rate to 1.8% but also charges customers $8 per year for having the card. The outstanding balance that a customer should keep on the card in order to benefit from this change is $ [＿＿＿＿] (to the nearest $)

33

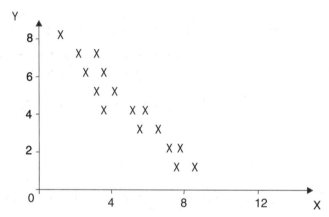

On the basis of the scatter diagram above, which of the following equations would best represent the regression line of Y on X?

A $Y = -X + 8$
B $Y = X + 8$
C $Y = X - 8$
D $Y = -X - 8$

34 For a certain group of students, the coefficient of rank correlation between their performance in Accounting and their performance in Law is −1. The coefficient of rank correlation between their performance in Law and FBSM is also −1. Therefore, the coefficient of rank correlation between their performance in Accounting and their performance in FBSM is

[＿＿＿＿] −2

[＿＿＿＿] zero

[＿＿＿＿] +1

[＿＿＿＿] impossible to determine from the information given.

35  In exactly three years from now, a company will have to replace capital equipment which will then cost $0.5 million. The managers have decided to set up a sinking fund into which twelve equal sums will be put at quarterly intervals, with the first being made three months from now. The rate of compound interest is 2% a quarter.

The quarterly sums required for the sinking fund are $ [＿＿＿＿] (to the nearest $)

## The following data relate to questions 36 and 37

A travel agency has kept records of the number of holidays booked and the number of complaints received over the past ten years. The data are as follows.

| Year | 1 | 2 | 3 | 4 | 5 | 6 | 7 | 8 | 9 | 10 |
|---|---|---|---|---|---|---|---|---|---|---|
| Number of holidays booked | 246 | 192 | 221 | 385 | 416 | 279 | 343 | 582 | 610 | 674 |
| Number of complaints received | 94 | 80 | 106 | 183 | 225 | 162 | 191 | 252 | 291 | 310 |

The agency suspects there is a relationship between the number of bookings and the volume of complaints and wishes to have some method of estimating the number of complaints, given the volume of bookings.

36  Using the method of least squares, the coefficients in the regression line y = a + bx using the above data are

a = [＿＿＿＿] (to 3 decimal places)

b = [＿＿＿＿] (to 3 decimal places)

37  Using the regression line y = a + bx (with the values you have calculated in question 36) the forecast number of complaints when 750 holidays are booked is [＿＿＿＿]

38  A pilot training school is trying to assess whether there is any correlation between the results of the initial aptitude tests given to all trainees and the practical examination given after 3 months' training.

The marks awarded for the test and examination for 6 trainees are given below.

| Trainee number | 1 | 2 | 3 | 4 | 5 | 6 |
|---|---|---|---|---|---|---|
| Aptitude test | 11 | 14 | 14 | 18 | 19 | 26 |
| Practical examination | 15 | 16 | 22 | 14 | 17 | 24 |

(a)  The coefficient of correlation, r, between the marks for the test and the examination is [＿＿＿＿] (to 2 decimal places)

(b)  The coefficient of determination is [＿＿＿＿] (to 2 decimal places)

39    A statistician is carrying out an analysis of a company's production output. The output varies according to the
      season of the year and from the data she has calculated the following seasonal variations, in units of production.

| | Spring | Summer | Autumn | Winter |
|---|---|---|---|---|
| Year 1 | | | + 11.2 | + 23.5 |
| Year 2 | – 9.8 | – 28.1 | + 12.5 | + 23.7 |
| Year 3 | – 7.4 | – 26.3 | + 11.7 | |

The average seasonal variation for each season is (to 1 decimal place)

Spring  [        ]

Summer  [        ]

Autumn  [        ]

Winter  [        ]

40    You are assisting with the work on a maintenance department's budget for the next quarter of 20X4. The
      maintenance department's budget for the current quarter (just ending) is $200,000. Its use of materials and
      their respective prices, are shown below.

| | Quantity used in current quarter | Average price payable per unit | |
|---|---|---|---|
| | | Current quarter | Next quarter |
| | Units | $ | $ |
| Material A | 9 | 10 | 10.20 |
| Material B | 13 | 12 | 12.50 |
| Material C | 8 | 9 | 9.00 |
| Material D | 20 | 25 | 26.00 |

One all-items price index for materials for the next quarter, using the current quarter as base, and the current

quantities as weights is calculated as [        ] (to 1 decimal place)

# The following data should be used for questions 41 and 42

In an internal audit of 200 invoices, the following numbers of errors were discovered:

| Number of errors: | 0 | 1 | 2 | 3 | 4 | 5 | 6 or more |
|---|---|---|---|---|---|---|---|
| Number of invoices: | 60 | 30 | 40 | 40 | 20 | 10 | 0 |

41    The percentage of invoices with errors is

A    30%
B    70%
C    80%
D    None of these

42    The expected value of the number of errors per invoice is

| | 1.8 |
| | 2 |
| | 2.1 |
| | 3 |

## The following data should be used for questions 43 and 44

A retailer sells computer games. Tabulated below are the unit sales of one of its games for the last 13 quarters. The trend in sales is linear and described by the equation SALES = 180 – 10T, where T denotes the time period. (T = 1 indicates the first quarter in 1998, T = 2 the second quarter in 1998, T = 5 the first quarter of 1999 and so on.) For planning purposes, forecasts of sales are required for the remaining three quarters of this year. [The brand was introduced in 1997.]

| Sales | $Q_1$ | $Q_2$ | $Q_3$ | $Q_4$ |
|-------|-------|-------|-------|-------|
| 1998 | 105 | 95 | 150 | 250 |
| 1999 | 80 | 70 | 110 | 180 |
| 2000 | 50 | 50 | 70 | 110 |
| 2001 | 30 | | | |

Average seasonal variations for the years 1998-2001

| $Q_1$ | $Q_2$ | $Q_3$ | $Q_4$ |
|-------|-------|-------|-------|
| –40% | –40% | 0 | +80% |

43    Using the trend equation, predict the trend value for $Q_2$ 2001.  ☐

44    Forecast sales (units) for the next three quarters of 2001 are

(a)    Forecast for $Q_2$ 2001  ☐

(b)    Forecast for $Q_3$ 2001  ☐

(c)    Forecast for $Q_4$ 2001  ☐

45

| | A | B | C | D | E |
|---|---|---|---|---|---|
| 1 | **BUDGETED SALES FIGURES** | | | | |
| 2 | | *Jan* | *Feb* | *Mar* | *Total* |
| 3 | | $'000 | $'000 | $'000 | $'000 |
| 4 | North | 2431 | 3001 | 2189 | 7621 |
| 5 | South | 6532 | 5826 | 6124 | 18482 |
| 6 | West | 895 | 432 | 596 | 1923 |
| 7 | Total | 9858 | 9259 | 8909 | 28026 |
| 8 | | | | | |

If the February sales figure for the South changed from $5,826 to $5,731, what other figures would change as a result? Give cell references.

```
┌─────────────┐
│             │
└─────────────┘

┌─────────────┐
│             │
└─────────────┘

┌─────────────┐
│             │
└─────────────┘
```

# Answers

DO NOT TURN THIS PAGE UNTIL YOU HAVE
COMPLETED MOCK ASSESSMENT 1

1    $ [ 400 ]

$700 must be divided by (8 + 5 + 1) = 14. $\frac{\$700}{14}$ = $50.

Therefore Mr Singh receives 8 × $50 = $400.

2    [ −3 ] (to 3 decimal places)

$(70 + 2)$   =   72

$\frac{72}{12}$   =   6

$(33 − 6)$   =   27

$\frac{27}{-3}$   =   −9

Therefore, the answer is $6 − 9 = −3$

3    $ [ 717 ] (to the nearest $)

Price excluding sales tax × 1.175  = $843

Price excluding sales tax      =   $\frac{\$843}{1.175}$

                   =   $717.45

                   =   $717 (to the nearest $)

4    [ 20 ] (to 1 decimal place)

The area of a bar represents the frequency of an interval, therefore when the width is increased by 1.5 (10 × 1.5 = 15) then the height must be reduced by 1.5 (30/1.5 = 20).

5    [ ✓ ]    Gaps may be left between the bars of a bar chart but not between those of a histogram

     [ ✓ ]    The bases of the bars of a bar chart may be labelled rather than mathematically scaled

     [ ✓ ]    It is the area rather than the height of a bar which represents the frequency in a histogram

6    [ ✓ ]    A multiple bar chart

     [ ✓ ]    A component bar chart

It would require three pie charts to represent this data.

A multiple bar chart would display all aspects of the data apart from totals.

A simple bar chart could display very little of the data.

A component bar chart could display all aspects of the data.

7    (a)    | 52 |

The mode is an average which means the 'most frequently occurring value'. 52 is the only mark which appears more than once. It is therefore the most frequently occurring item. Therefore mode = 52.

(b)    | 52 |

The median is the value of the middle item of a distribution once all of the items have been arranged in order of magnitude.

47, 48, 51, 52, 52, 62, 68, 75, 79

There are an odd number of items, so the middle item of an odd number of items is calculated as the $\frac{(n + 1)}{2}$ th item = $\frac{9 + 1}{2}$ = 5th item = 52.

Median = 52.

8    | 0.5 |

The easiest way to answer this questions is using a table:

|  | Not Certificate | Certificate | Total |
|---|---|---|---|
| Male | 8 | 40 − 8 = 32 | 40 |
| Female | 58 − 8 = 50 | 60 − 50 = 10 | 100 − 40 = 60 |
| Total | 100 − 42 = 58 | 42 | 100 |

The probability that a randomly chosen female student is not studying for Certificate level is 50/100 = 0.5

9    B    **Possible ways of two numbers summing to 7**

| First die | Second die | Probability |
|---|---|---|
| 1 | 6 | $1/6 \times 1/6 = 1/36$ |
| 2 | 5 | $1/6 \times 1/6 = 1/36$ |
| 3 | 4 | $1/6 \times 1/6 = 1/36$ |
| 4 | 3 | $1/6 \times 1/6 = 1/36$ |
| 5 | 2 | $1/6 \times 1/6 = 1/36$ |
| 6 | 1 | $1/6 \times 1/6 = 1/36$ |

Probability of two numbers summing to 7    = 1/36 + 1/36 + 1/36 + 1/36 + 1/36 + 1/36
   = 6/36
   = 1/6

10  $\boxed{1.30}$ (to 2 decimal places)

Arithmetic mean $= \dfrac{\text{Sum of values of items}}{\text{Number of items}}$

$\$1.22 = \dfrac{(5 \times \$1) + (10 \times \$1.25) + (10 \times \$X)}{5 + 10 + 10}$

$\$1.22 = \dfrac{\$5 + \$12.50 + \$10X}{25}$

$\$1.22 \times 25 = \$17.50 + \$10X$

$\$30.5 - \$17.50 = \$10X$

$\$13 = \$10X$

$\dfrac{£13}{10} = \$X$

$X = \$1.30$

11  B  =SUM(D4:D9) is the correct answer as it adds up the numbers in the D column

12  $\boxed{0.17}$ (correct to 2 decimal places)

**Coefficient of variation** $= \dfrac{\text{Standard deviation}}{\text{Mean}}$

$= \dfrac{\$3,000}{\$17,500}$

$= 0.17$

13  The company should chose Project $\boxed{B}$ which has an expected value of $\$\boxed{4,760}$

**Project A**  $= (\$4,000 \times 0.45) + (\$2,000 \times 0.55)$
$= \$2,900$

**Project B**  $= (\$8,000 \times 0.64) + ((\$1,000) \times 0.36)$
$= \$5,120 + (-\$360)$
$= \$5,120 - \$360$
$= \$4,760$

14  $\boxed{0.2425}$ (to 4 decimal places)

Expected value $= \sum px$

where  $x$ = value
$p$ = probability of value occurring

**Expected value**  $= (2/4 \times 0.35) + (1/4 \times 0.15) + (1/4 \times 0.12)$
$= 0.175 + 0.0375 + 0.03$
$= 0.2425$

15    | 234 |  (to the nearest whole number)

We need to find the point Z standard deviations above the mean, such that 80% of frequencies are below it and 20% are above it. This means that 50% − 20% = 30% of the frequencies lie between the point Z and the mean.

From normal distribution tables, 30% of frequencies lie between the mean and 0.84 standard deviations from the mean.

$$If \quad Z = \frac{X - \mu}{\sigma}$$

$$0.84 = \frac{X - 200}{40}$$

$$0.84 \times 40 = X - 200$$

$$33.6 = X - 200$$

$$33.6 + 200 = X$$

$$233.6 = X$$

$$X = 234$$

16    | ✓ |    Unexplained or freak events

17    $ | 4,006 |  (to the nearest $)

$$PV = \frac{1}{r}\left(1 - \frac{1}{(1+r)^n}\right)$$

with    r = 0.042
        n = 20

$$PV = \frac{1}{0.042}\left(1 - \frac{1}{(1+0.042)^{20}}\right) \times \$300$$

$$= \$4,006$$

18    | 54 |

Y = 21.5 + 2.6X

If X = 11, trend for month 11 = 21.5 + (2.6 x 11) = 50.1

Seasonally adjusted forecast = 50.1 x 1.08 = 54.108 = 54 to nearest whole number

19    $ | 15,325 |  (to the nearest $)

| Year | Cashflow $ | Discount factor 6% | PV $ |
|---|---|---|---|
| 0 | (30,000) | 1 | (30,000) |
| 1 | 25,000 | 0.943 | 23,575 |
| 2 | 15,000 | 0.890 | 13,350 |
| 3 | 10,000 | 0.840 | 8,400 |
|  |  | NPV = | 15,325 |

20    $ | 50,671 | (to the nearest $)

Future value    $= \$40,000 \times (1.03)^8$
                $= \$50,671$

21    | 13.33 | % (to 2 decimal places)

$$IRR = a\% + \left[\frac{A}{A - B} \times (b - a)\right]\%$$

where    $a = 10\%$
         $b = 15\%$
         $A = \$4,000$
         $B = -\$2,000$

$IRR$    $= 10\% + \left[\dfrac{4,000}{4,000 - (-2,000)} \times (15 - 10)\right]\%$

         $= 10\% + 3.33\%$

         $= 13.33\%$

22    (a)    The seasonal variation for the fourth quarter is | 0.75 | (to 2 decimal places)

As this is the multiplicative model, the seasonal variations should sum to 4 (giving an average of 1 per quarter).

Let X = seasonal variation in quarter 4

$0.75 + 1.6 + 0.9 + X$    $= 4$
            $3.25 + X$    $= 4$
                    $X$    $= 4 - 3.25$
                    $X$    $= 0.75$

(b)    The trend line for sales:

| ✓ |    Increased between quarter 3 and quarter 4

*Workings*

For a multiplicative model, the seasonal component is as follows.

   $S = Y/T$

$\therefore$    $T = Y/S$

| | Quarter | |
| --- | --- | --- |
| | *3* | *4* |
| Seasonal component (S) | 0.9 | 0.75 |
| Actual series (Y) | $520,000 | $540,000 |
| Trend (T = Y/S) | $577,778 | $720,000 |

The trend for sales has therefore increased between quarters 3 and 4.

23 $\boxed{-0.992}$ (to 3 decimal places)

The formula for the Pearson correlation coefficient is provided in your exam. There are no excuses for getting this question wrong.

$$\text{Correlation coefficient, } r = \frac{n\sum XY - \sum X \sum Y}{\sqrt{[n\sum X^2 - (\sum X)^2][n\sum Y^2 - (\sum Y)^2]}}$$

$$= \frac{(5 \times 134) - (10 \times 78)}{\sqrt{(5 \times 30 - 100) \times (5 \times 1{,}266 - 6{,}084)}}$$

$$= \frac{670 - 780}{\sqrt{(150 - 100) \times (6{,}330 - 6{,}084)}}$$

$$= \frac{-110}{\sqrt{(50 \times 246)}}$$

$$= \frac{-110}{\sqrt{12{,}300}}$$

$$= \frac{-110}{110.90537}$$

$$= -0.992$$

24 $X = \boxed{2}$

$Y = \boxed{8}$

*Workings*

$$Y = 12 - 2X$$
$$\text{or} \quad Y = -2X + 12$$

$$Y = -2X + 12 \quad\quad (1)$$
$$Y = 2X + 4 \quad\quad (2)$$
$$0 = -4X + 8 \quad\quad (1) - (2)$$
$$4X = 8$$
$$X = 2$$

$$\text{If } X = 2, \quad Y = 12 - (2 \times 2)$$
$$= 12 - 4$$
$$= 8$$

25  [ ✓ ]  $\dfrac{2PC}{RB} - 1$

*Workings*

$R = \dfrac{2PC}{B(N+1)}$

$N + 1 = \dfrac{2PC}{RB}$

$N = \dfrac{2PC}{RB} - 1$

26  [ ✓ ]  $10S^2$

*Workings*

$\dfrac{1}{1.1}S^2 \div \left(1 - \dfrac{1}{1.1}\right) = \dfrac{0.909090909S^2}{0.09090909} = 10S^2$

27  $ [ 7,500.00 ] (to 2 decimal places)

*Workings*

$C = 6 + 0.5Q$

If $Q = 3$        (3,000 units)

$C \quad = 6 + (0.5 \times 3)$
$\quad\quad = 6 + 1.5$
$\quad\quad = 7.5$

Total cost  $= 7.5 \times \$1,000$
$\quad\quad\quad\quad = \$7,500.00$

28  [ ✓ ]  perfect negative correlation exists

The coefficient of rank correlation can be interpreted in exactly the same way as the ordinary correlation coefficient. Its value can range from –1 to +1.

29  B     The formula =C4/E5 divides the value in C4 by E5
        The formula =C4*117.5% increases the value in C4 by 17.5%
        Only (III) is therefore correct

30  $\boxed{0.082}$ (to 3 decimal places)

*Workings*

Pr(call answered) = 0.2

Pr(call not answered) = 1 − 0.2 = 0.8

|  | | Attempt | | | |
|---|---|---|---|---|---|
|  | 1 | 2 | 3 | 4 | 5 |
| *Not answered* | ✓ | ✓ | ✓ | ✓ |  |
| *Answered* |  |  |  |  | ✓ |
| *Probability* | 0.8 | 0.8 | 0.8 | 0.8 | 0.2 |

∴ Probability (call answered for first time on fifth attempt) $= 0.8^4 \times 0.2$
$= 0.082$ (to 3 decimal places)

31  $\boxed{29.84}$ % (to 2 decimal places)

*Workings*

**Effective annual rate** $= [(1 + r)^{12/n} − 1]$

Where    r = rate for each time period
          n = number of months in time period

∴ **Effective annual rate**    $= (1 + 0.022)^{12/1} − 1$
$= 0.2984$
$= 29.84\%$

32  $\$\boxed{134}$ (to the nearest $)

*Workings*

The new effective annual rate   $= (1 + 0.018)^{12/1} − 1$
$= 0.2387$
$= 23.87\%$

The annual saving in interest per $ outstanding = $(0.2984 − 0.2387) = $0.0597

The **minimum balance** to be kept on the card to benefit from the change = $8/$0.0597 = $134.

33  A    The scatter diagram displays perfect negative correlation. The gradient of the regression line has a gradient of −1 and cuts the y axis at y=8 (ie when x=0, y=8).

34  $\boxed{\checkmark}$  +1

Say, performance in Accounting is HIGH , Law is LOW

Say, performance in FBSM is HIGH, Law is LOW

∴ Performance in Accounting is HIGH when performance in FBSM is HIGH and they are therefore positively correlated, ie R = +1

BPP
PROFESSIONAL EDUCATION

35  $ $\boxed{37,280}$ (to the nearest $)

*Workings*

*Note.* If you find it useful to do so, you should draw a time line to identify the time periods and interest rates involved in the question you are tackling. The formula for the sum of a geometric progression is provided in your examination.

Use the formula S = $\dfrac{A(R^n - 1)}{(R - 1)}$, where R = 1.02, S is the value of the fund at the end of 12 quarters and A is the quarterly sum invested.

Using this formula, the first payment into the fund must be one time period from now.

After 3 years  (12 quarters), value of sinking fund = $\dfrac{A(1.02^{12} - 1)}{(1.02 - 1)}$ = 13.412 A

After 12 quarters, the sinking fund must equal $500,000

∴ 500,000 = 13.412 A

∴  A = $37,280 = quarterly sum

36  a = $\boxed{10.560}$ (to 3 decimal places)

b = $\boxed{0.453}$ (to 3 decimal places)

*Workings*

The method of least squares involves using the following formulae for a and b in y = a + bx.

Let x = the number of holidays booked

Let y = the number of complaints received

b = $\dfrac{n\sum xy - \sum x \sum y}{n\sum x^2 - (\sum x)^2}$

a = $\bar{y} - b\bar{x}$

where  n = the number of pairs of data
$\bar{x}$ = the average x value of all the pairs of data
$\bar{y}$ = the average y value of all the pairs of data

| $x$ | $y$ | $xy$ | $x^2$ | $y^2$ |
|---|---|---|---|---|
| 246 | 94 | 23,124 | 60,516 | 8,836 |
| 192 | 80 | 15,360 | 36,864 | 6,400 |
| 221 | 106 | 23,426 | 48,841 | 11,236 |
| 385 | 183 | 70,455 | 148,225 | 33,489 |
| 416 | 225 | 93,600 | 173,056 | 50,625 |
| 279 | 162 | 45,198 | 77,841 | 26,244 |
| 343 | 191 | 65,513 | 117,649 | 36,481 |
| 582 | 252 | 146,664 | 338,724 | 63,504 |
| 610 | 291 | 177,510 | 372,100 | 84,681 |
| 674 | 310 | 208,940 | 454,276 | 96,100 |
| 3,948 | 1,894 | 869,790 | 1,828,092 | 417,596 |

Therefore, n = 10 (there are ten pairs of data for x and y values)

$\sum x$ = 3,948

$\sum y$ = 1,894

$\sum xy$ = 869,790

$\sum x^2$ = 1,828,092

$\sum y^2$ = 417,596

$$b = \frac{n\sum xy - \sum x \sum y}{n\sum x^2 - (\sum x)^2} = \frac{(10 \times 869,790) - (3,948 \times 1,894)}{10 \times 1,828,092 - (3,948)^2}$$

$$= \frac{8,697,900 - 7,477,512}{18,280,920 - 15,586,704} = \frac{1,220,388}{2,694,216} = 0.453$$

Therefore $a = \bar{y} - b\bar{x}$ $= (\frac{1,894}{10}) - (0.453 \times \frac{3,948}{10})$

$$= 189.4 - 178.84$$

$$= 10.56$$

Thus y = 10.56 + 0.453x

37    | 351 |

*Workings*

If the number of holidays booked is 750, then x = 750 and the number of complaints (y) may be forecast as follows.

y  = 10.56 + (0.453 × 750)
   = 10.56 + 339.75
   = 350.31, say 351 complaints

38    The coefficient of correlation, r, between the marks for the test and the examination is $\boxed{0.56}$ (to 2 decimal places)

The coefficient of determination is $\boxed{0.31}$ (to 2 decimal places)

*Workings*

Let    X = Aptitude test results
       Y = Practical examination results
       n = 6

| Trainee number | X | Y | XY | $X^2$ | $Y^2$ |
|---|---|---|---|---|---|
| 1 | 11 | 15 | 165 | 121 | 225 |
| 2 | 14 | 16 | 224 | 196 | 256 |
| 3 | 14 | 22 | 308 | 196 | 484 |
| 4 | 18 | 14 | 252 | 324 | 196 |
| 5 | 19 | 17 | 323 | 361 | 289 |
| 6 | 26 | 24 | 624 | 676 | 576 |
| | $\sum X = \underline{102}$ | $\sum Y = \underline{108}$ | $\sum XY = \underline{1,896}$ | $\sum X^2 = \underline{1,874}$ | $\sum Y^2 = \underline{2,026}$ |

Using the formula for the coefficient of correlation (r) provided in the examination:

$$r = \frac{n\sum XY - \sum X \sum Y}{\sqrt{[n\sum X^2 - (\sum X)^2][n\sum Y^2 - (\sum Y)^2]}}$$

$$r = \frac{(6 \times 1,896) - (102 \times 108)}{\sqrt{[(6 \times 1,874) - (102)^2][(6 \times 2,026) - (108)^2]}}$$

$$r = \frac{11,376 - 11,016}{\sqrt{(11,244 - 10,404)(12,156 - 11,664)}}$$

$$= \frac{360}{\sqrt{840 \times 492}}$$

$$= \frac{360}{\sqrt{413,280}} = 0.56$$

∴ The coefficient of correlation, r, between the marks for the test and the examination is 0.56.

The coefficient of determination, $r^2 = 0.56^2 = 0.31$ (to 2 decimal places)

39    The average seasonal variation for each season is (to 1 decimal place)

Spring     | −8.5 |

Summer     | −27.1 |

Autumn     | +11.9 |

Winter     | +23.7 |

*Workings*

|  | *Spring* | *Summer* | *Autumn* | *Winter* | *Total* |
|---|---|---|---|---|---|
| Year 1 |  |  | +11.2 | +23.5 |  |
| Year 2 | −9.8 | −28.1 | +12.5 | +23.7 |  |
| Year 3 | −7.4 | −26.3 | +11.7 |  |  |
| Average variation | −8.6 | −27.2 | +11.8 | +23.6 | −0.4 |
| Adjust total variation to nil | +0.1 | +0.1 | +0.1 | +0.1 | +0.4 |
| Estimated seasonal variation | −8.5 | −27.1 | +11.9 | +23.7 | 0.0 |

40    | 103.5 | (to 1 decimal place)

*Workings*

An aggregate price index is calculated as follows.

**Aggregate price index** $= \dfrac{\sum P_1 W}{\sum P_0 W} \times 100$

|  | *(W)* | $P_0$ | $P_1$ | $P_0 W$ | $P_1 W$ |
|---|---|---|---|---|---|
| Material A | 9 | 10 | 10.20 | 90 | 91.80 |
| Material B | 13 | 12 | 12.50 | 156 | 162.50 |
| Material C | 8 | 9 | 9.00 | 72 | 72.00 |
| Material D | 20 | 25 | 26.00 | 500 | 520.00 |
|  |  |  |  | 818 | 846.30 |

W = quantity used in current quarter
$P_0$ = Average price payable per unit in current quarter
$P_1$ = Average price payable per unit in next quarter

**Aggregate price index**    $= \dfrac{846.30}{818} \times 100$

$= 103.5$ (to 1 decimal place)

41    B    Percentages of invoices with errors

Total number of invoices  = 60+30+40+40+20+10+0
                          = 200

Number of invoices without errors  = 60

∴ Number of invoices with errors  = 200 – 60
                                   = 140

∴ Percentage of invoices with errors  = $\dfrac{140}{200} \times 100\%$

                                       = 70%

42    ☐ ✓    1.8

| Number of errors | 0 | 1 | 2 | 3 | 4 | 5 | 6 or more |
|---|---|---|---|---|---|---|---|
| Number of invoices | 60 | 30 | 40 | 40 | 20 | 10 | 0 |
| Probability | 0.3 | 0.15 | 0.2 | 0.2 | 0.1 | 0.05 | 0 |

Expected value of number of errors per invoice

$= (0 \times 0.3) + (1 \times 0.15) + (2 \times 0.2) + (3 \times 0.2) + (4 \times 0.1) + (5 \times 0.05) + (6 \times 0)$
$= 0 + 0.15 + 0.4 + 0.6 + 0.4 + 0.25 + 0$
$= 1.8$ errors

43    The trend value for $Q_2$ 2001 is ☐ 40 ☐ units.

*Workings*

$Q_2$ 2001 is T = 14

∴ If trend  = 180 – 10T
            = 180 – (10 × 14)
            = 180 – 140
            = 40 units

44    (a)    Forecast for $Q_2$ 2001:    | 24 |    (W1)

      (b)    Forecast for $Q_3$ 2001:    | 30 |    (W2)

      (c)    Forecast for $Q_4$ 2001:    | 36 |    (W3)

*Workings*

   (1)    $Q_2$ 2001 is T = 14, trend = 40 units
        ∴ Forecast sales = 40 × 0.6* = 24 units
        * (100% − 40%) = 60% = 0.6

   (2)    $Q_3$ 2001 is T = 15, trend = 180 − (10 × 15) = 180 − 150 = 30 units

        ∴ Forecast sales = 30 × 1 = 30 units*
        * No seasonal variation in this quarter

   (3)    $Q_4$ 2001 is T = 16, trend = 180 − (10 × 16) = 180 − 160 = 20 units
        ∴ Forecast sales = 20 × 1.8 = 36 units

45    | C7 |

      | E5 |

      | E7 |

# CIMA

# Paper C3 (Certificate)

# Fundamentals of Business Mathematics

# Mock Assessment 2

| Question Paper | |
| --- | --- |
| Time allowed | **2 hours** |
| **Answer ALL forty-five questions** | |

**DO NOT OPEN THIS PAPER UNTIL YOU ARE READY TO START UNDER EXAMINATION CONDITIONS**

# CIMA

# Paper C3 (Certificate)

# Fundamentals of Business Mathematics

# Mock Assessment 2

# Answer ALL 45 questions

1   An index number increases each year by 10% of its value in the previous year. If its value in 1999 was 120, its value in 2002 is closest to

    A     150
    B     156
    C     160
    D     162

2   Product X needs 2 labour hours, product Y needs 5 labour hours, there are 500 hours available.  How would this be expressed as an inequality?

    A     $2X + 5Y \leq 500$
    B     $5X + 2Y \geq 500$
    C     $2X + 5Y \geq 500$
    D     $5X + 2Y \leq 500$

3   $10,000 was invested on 1 January 1999, earning interest of 5% per annum. The value of this investment on 31 December 2003 will be (to the nearest $)

    A     $12,155
    B     $12,763
    C     $35,460
    D     $43,290

4   An annual year-end income of $15,000 is required in perpetuity. Assuming a fixed rate of interest of 9% each year, and ignoring administrative charges, the sum required now to purchase the annuity is closest to

    A     $13,650
    B     $135,000
    C     $150,000
    D     $167,000

5   George does a number of cycle rides in a week. In a week where his average ride was 22 miles, his individual ride distances, in miles, were

35, 24, x, 17, y, 23

When x = 2y, the value of x is                 

6    A Health & Fitness Centre has to buy one of two types of machine, A or B. Machine A would cost $200,000, half of which would be due on delivery, the remainder a year later. Machine B would cost $240,000, with payment due in the same way as for machine A. Both machines last for 6 years and have an expected scrap value of 10% of their original cost price. Taking into account operating costs and maintenance, machine A would produce year-end net operational cash flows of $40,000 and machine B year-end net operational cash flows of $50,000. In both cases the relevant cost of capital is 10% each year throughout the period.

The net present value of machine A is $ ⎡＿＿＿＿⎤ (to the nearest $)

7    In Excel, a macro is used for

A    Occasional complicated tasks in spreadsheets
B    Generating graphs
C    Automating frequently repeated tasks
D    Tidying up the presentation of the spreadsheet

8    An accountant has marked some performance criteria out of 20 and found the mean to be 10 marks and the standard deviation to be 2 marks. The marks now have to be expressed as a percentage.

What would be the new value of the standard deviation?

A    $\sqrt{10}$%

B    $\sqrt{20}$%

C    10%

D    20%

9    A company is considering purchasing a new machine for $25,000. This would increase the annual cash flow of the company by $6,500 in each of the next six years. If the cost of capital is 9% per annum, the net present value of this investment is

A    $4,159
B    $10,780
C    $10,901
D    $14,000

10   An index number is made up of two items, food and non-food.

| Sub-group | Weight | Index |
|---|---|---|
| Non-food | 7 | 130 |
| Food | 3 | ? |
| All items | 10 | 127 |

The index number for the sub-group Food is closest to

A    120
B    122
C    124
D    126

11    The diagram below shows an ogive (cumulative frequency) for a sample of 400 items.

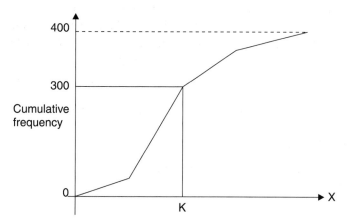

The point K on the X-axis represents the value

| | which 75% of the sample take |

| | below which 75% of the sample values lie |

| | which 25% of the sample take |

| | above which 75% of the sample values lie |

---

12    Sample 1:    2, 5, 5, 12
      Sample 2:    1, 3, 5, 8, 8

Which of the following statistics has the same value in both samples?

A     Arithmetic mean
B     Standard deviation
C     Median
D     Mode

---

13    A company's market value has fallen from $32 billion to $2 billion in four years. The average annual percentage decline in market value is closest to

  20%

                      40%

                      50%

                      100%

---

14    The net present value of an investment at 10% is $12,000, and at 18% is – $4,000. The internal rate of return of this investment is

    A    12%
    B    14%
    C    16%
    D    22%

15    The formula for the internal rate of return is

$$IRR = R_1 + \frac{(R_2 - R_1)*NPV_1}{NPV_1 - NPV_2}$$

If the net present value of an item of farming equipment is –$9,442 when r = 12% and $2,206 when r = 10%, the internal rate of return of the equipment is ⌷ (to 2 decimal places).

16    The following table shows the typical salary of part qualified management accountants in five different regions of England.

| Area | Typical salary $ |
|------|------------------|
| South-east | 21,500 |
| Midlands | 20,800 |
| North-east | 18,200 |
| North-west | 17,500 |
| South-west | 16,700 |

The best diagram to draw to highlight the differences between areas is

    A    A pie diagram.
    B    A multiple bar chart.
    C    A percentage component bar chart.
    D    A simple bar chart.

17    A company is bidding for three contracts which are awarded independently of each other. The board estimates its chances of winning Contract A as 40%, of winning Contract B as 1 in 4 and of winning Contract C as 1 in 5. The profits from A, B and C are estimated to be $600,000, $700,000 and $800,000 respectively.

The expected value to the company of the profits from all three contracts will be closest to:

    A    $240,000
    B    $575,000
    C    $700,000
    D    $800,000

18  For a set of six data pairs for the variable x (profit) and y (sales) the following values have been found.

$\Sigma x = 2$

$\Sigma y = 15$

$\Sigma x^2 = 30$

$\Sigma y^2 = 130$

$\Sigma xy = 14$

Calculate the values for the intercept and gradient of the linear regression line for this data (to 2 decimal places).

a = [          ]

b = [          ]

19  When x = 4 the value (to 2 decimal places) of $(x^{-0.65})^{-6}$ = [          ]

20  The sales of a product are recorded monthly for 24 months. The four-point (centred) moving averages are calculated and plotted on a graph.

How many moving average points are plotted?

[          ] 20

[          ] 21

[          ] 22

[          ] 24

21  A company's weekly costs ($C) were plotted against production level (P) for the last 50 weeks and a regression line calculated to be C = 2,000 + 300P. Which statement about the breakdown of weekly costs is true?

A    Fixed costs are $2,000. Variable costs per unit are $5.

B    Fixed costs are $300. Variable costs per unit are $4.

C    Fixed costs are $300. Variable costs per unit are $2,000.

D    Fixed costs are $2,000. Variable costs per unit are $300.

## Questions 22,23 and 24 refer to the spreadsheet shown below.

|  | A | B | C | D | E | F |
|---|---|---|---|---|---|---|
| 1 |  |  |  | Cash forecast for Peter & Sons | | |
| 2 |  |  |  |  |  |  |
| 3 |  |  |  | Month 1 | Month 2 | Month 3 |
| 4 |  |  |  | $ | $ | $ |
| 5 | Opening cash |  |  | 0 | 7482 | 15710 |
| 6 |  |  |  |  |  |  |
| 7 | Receipts |  |  | 16500 | 17250 | 18300 |
| 8 |  |  |  |  |  |  |
| 9 | Payments |  |  |  |  |  |
| 10 | Staff: |  |  |  |  |  |
| 11 | Project manager |  |  | 1800 | 1800 | 1900 |
| 12 | Supervisor |  |  | 1500 | 1500 | 1500 |
| 13 | Mechanic 1 |  |  | 1200 | 1200 | 1200 |
| 14 | Mechanic 2 |  |  | 1100 | 1100 | 1100 |
| 15 | Mechanic 3 |  |  | 1000 | 1000 | 1000 |
| 16 | Admin staff |  |  | 1050 | 1050 | 1050 |
| 17 | National insurance @ |  | 10% | 765 | 765 | 775 |
| 18 | Total staff costs |  |  | 8415 | 8415 | 8525 |
| 19 |  |  |  |  |  |  |
| 20 | Insurance |  |  | 35 | 35 | 35 |
| 21 | Telephone |  |  | 120 | 120 | 120 |
| 22 | Computer supplies |  |  | 58 | 60 | 62 |
| 23 | Rent |  |  | 250 | 250 | 250 |
| 24 | Stationery |  |  | 10 | 12 | 14 |
| 25 | Accountancy |  |  | 45 | 45 | 45 |
| 26 | Marketing |  |  | 55 | 55 | 55 |
| 27 | Other costs |  |  | 30 | 30 | 30 |
| 28 | Total other costs |  |  | 603 | 607 | 611 |
| 29 |  |  |  |  |  |  |
| 30 | Total payments |  |  | 9018 | 9022 | 9136 |
| 31 |  |  |  |  |  |  |
| 32 | Closing cash |  |  | 7482 | 15710 | 24874 |

22     The cell F5 (column F row 5) shows the opening position for month 3. The value in this cell is a formula.

Which of the following would not be a correct entry for this cell?

A     =E7-E30+D32

B     =E5+E7-E30

C     =E32

D     =15710

23   The formula in D17 (column D row 17) adds a percentage national insurance charge to the sub total of staff costs. Which of the formulae shown below would be the **best** formula for cell D17?

   A    =SUM(D11:D16)*0.1
   B    =SUM(D11:D16)*$C17
   C    =SUM(D11:D16)*10%
   D    =SUM(D11:D16)*C17

24   The cell D30 (column D row 30) shows the total payments. Which of the following is the **correct** formula for this cell?

   A    =D28+D18
   B    =SUM(D11:D28)
   C    =SUM(D7:D28)
   D    D18+D28

25   The correlation coefficient between two variables, x and y, is +0.65. The proportion of variation in x that is explained by variation in y is ⬚ (to 4 decimal places)

26   The number of daily complaints to a railway company has an average (arithmetic mean) of 12 and a standard deviation of 3 complaints.

   The coefficient of variation is

   A    0.25%
   B    4%
   C    25%
   D    400%

27   The following formula is used in the financial analysis of dividends:

$$R = \left(\frac{V}{P}\right) + G$$

   When the formula is rearranged, with P in terms of the other variables, P is equal to

   ⬚  $\left(\dfrac{R}{V}\right) - G$

   ⬚  $\dfrac{(R-G)}{V}$

   ⬚  $\left(\dfrac{V}{R}\right) - G$

   ⬚  $\dfrac{V}{(R-G)}$

28    The length of telephone calls to a Software Support line is approximately normally distributed with a mean of 20 minutes and a standard deviation of 5 minutes.

The percentage of calls lasting under 30 minutes is closest to

|      | 2% |
|------|-----|
|      | 48% |
|      | 83% |
|      | 98% |

29    A fixed-interest $200,000 mortgage, with annual interest compounded at 6% each year, is to be repaid by 15 equal year-end repayments of $R.

The annual repayment $R will be closest to

|      | $14,133 |
|------|---------|
|      | $20,593 |
|      | $31,954 |
|      | $83,400 |

30    A company's security system is made up of three separate electronic alarms, which operate independently. The security system operates provided that at least one of the three alarms is working. The probability of an alarm failing at any time is 1 in 100.

The probability of the security system failing is

|      | 1 in 100 |
|------|----------|
|      | 3 in 100 |
|      | 1 in 10,000 |
|      | 1 in 1,000,000 |

31    You borrow $3,000 and pay 10% each year interest. Ignoring capital, if you pay this interest at the end of each year, what is the present value of the *interest* payable at the end of the third year?

|      | $(3/10) \times \$300 \times 3$ |
|------|--------------------------------|
|      | $(7/10) \times \$300$ |
|      | $(10/11)^3 \times \$300$ |
|      | $(11/10)^3 \times \$400$ |

32 A manufacturer supplies components in boxes of 10, stating that there is a (independent) chance of 10% of any one component being faulty.

In large batch, the percentage of boxes containing *no* faulty components will be closest to

| | |
|---|---|
| | 10% |
| | 35% |
| | 50% |
| | 90% |

33 A new lake is to be stocked with fish, according to the numbers in the table below.

| Type of fish | A | B | C | D |
|---|---|---|---|---|
| Number of fish | 400 | 300 | 200 | 100 |
| Annual % increase | 10 | 20 | 30 | 40 |

After one year, the percentage of fish of Type D in the lake will be closest to

| | |
|---|---|
| | 10% |
| | 12% |
| | 14% |
| | 20% |

34 In a time series analysis, the trend equation for a particular product is given by

$$\text{TREND} = 0.0002 \times \text{YEAR}^2 + 0.4 \times \text{YEAR} + 30.4$$

Due to the cyclical factor, the forecast for the year 2007 is estimated at 1.6 times trend.

In whole units, the forecast for the year 2007 is

A 1,639         B 3,211         C 2,608         D 2,622

35 A company's annual profits have a trend line given by $Y = 30t - 10$, where Y is the trend in $'000 and t is the year with t = 0 in 20X0. Forecast profits for the year 20X8 using an additive model if the cyclical component for that year is −25 are

A $235,000         B $205,000         C $161,000         D $260,000

36     The mail-order sales (units) of Brand X in a certain country are shown below. In this country, the populations of all twenty sub-groups are equal. Each customer buys one unit. Ages are given in years.

**Mail-order sales of Brand X (units) by region and age in 20X6**

| Region/Age | 21–29 | 30–39 | 40–49 | 50–59 | 60 + | Total |
|---|---|---|---|---|---|---|
| North | 100 | 80 | 50 | 40 | 30 | 300 |
| South | 55 | 50 | 45 | 30 | 20 | 200 |
| East | 65 | 60 | 65 | 60 | 50 | 300 |
| West | 20 | 30 | 40 | 50 | 60 | 200 |
| | 240 | 220 | | | | 1,000 |

A customer is to be randomly selected for a holiday prize. The probability that this customer is from the East **and** over 39 years of age is ⌷ to 3 decimal places.

37     The mail-order sales (units) of Brand X in a certain country are shown below. In this country, the populations of all twenty sub-groups are equal. Each customer buys one unit. Ages are given in years.

**Mail-order sales of Brand X (units) by region and age in 20X6**

| Region/Age | 21–29 | 30–39 | 40–49 | 50–59 | 60 + | Total |
|---|---|---|---|---|---|---|
| North | 100 | 80 | 50 | 40 | 30 | 300 |
| South | 55 | 50 | 45 | 30 | 20 | 200 |
| East | 65 | 60 | 65 | 60 | 50 | 300 |
| West | 20 | 30 | 40 | 50 | 60 | 200 |
| | 240 | 220 | | | | 1,000 |

For the North and South the rank correlation coefficient between sales and age is ⌷ (to the nearest whole number).

38     If $y = aX^b$ and a = 8 minutes, X = 12 and b = –0.23. What is the value of Y to two decimal places?

⌷

39     An item is made in two stages. At the first stage it is processed by one of four machines – A, B, C, or D – with equal probability. At the second stage it is processed by one of two machines – E or F – and is twice as likely to go through F as this machine works twice as quickly.

The probability that an item is processed on A or E is:

A     1/12
B     2/7
C     1/2
D     7/12

40   A bakery produces fresh cakes each day. The variable costs of production are $0.20 per cake and the retail
     price is $0.50 per cake. The daily demand for cakes over the last four months is shown in the table below. At
     the end of each day, any unsold cakes are sold to a local pig farmer for $0.05 per cake.

| Daily demand (cakes) | 1-39 | 40-79 | 80-119 | 120-159 | 160-199 |
|---|---|---|---|---|---|
| Number of days: | 10 | 20 | 30 | 30 | 10 |

[For simplicity, the midpoints of the intervals are assumed to be 20, 60, 100 etc]

Complete the daily contribution ($) table shown below.

|  |  | Daily demand for cakes | | | | |
|---|---|---|---|---|---|---|
|  |  | 20 | 60 | 100 | 140 | 180 |
| Daily production | 20 | 6 | 6 | 6 | 6 | 6 |
| of cakes | 60 | A | 18 | 18 | 18 | 18 |
|  | 100 |  | B | 30 | 30 | 30 |
|  | 140 |  | C |  | 42 | 42 |
|  | 180 |  |  |  |  | D |
| Probability of demand |  |  |  | E |  |  |

A  [          ]

B  [          ]

C  [          ]

D  [          ]

E  [          ]

---

# The following information is to be used for questions 41 and 42

In a time series analysis, the multiplicative model is used to forecast sales and the following seasonal variations
apply:

| Quarter | 1 | 2 | 3 | 4 |
|---|---|---|---|---|
| Seasonal variation | 1.3 | 1.6 | 0.5 | ? |

The actual sales values for the first two quarters of 2006 were:

Quarter 1: $125,000
Quarter 2: $135,000

41   The seasonal variation for the fourth quarter is:

A   3.4
B   0.6
C   1.0
D   1.1

42     The trend line for sales:

   A     Decreased between quarter 1 and quarter 2 .
   B     Increased between quarter 1 and quarter 2.
   C     Remained constant between quarter 1 and quarter 2.
   D     Cannot be determined from the information given.

43     In an additive time series analysis, the seasonal variations given by averaging the $(Y - T)$ values are as follows.

| Year | $Y - T$ |
|:----:|:-------:|
| 1 | 16 |
| 2 | 32 |
| 3 | -18 |
| 4 | -34 |

The averages are subsequently adjusted so that their total is 0.  What is the new value of the current average for year 4?

_____

44     Which of these scatter diagrams shows no linear correlation between x and y?

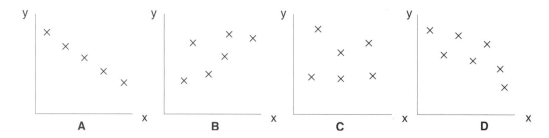

45   A gas supplier has monitored the monthly volume of gas consumed in an area against the mean temperature each month. The following results have been produced.

| Mean temperature | Gas consumption | | | |
| X | Y | $X^2$ | $Y^2$ | XY |
| --- | --- | --- | --- | --- |
| 2.50 | 26.70 | 6.25 | 712.89 | 66.75 |
| 0.80 | 33.10 | 0.64 | 1,095.61 | 26.48 |
| 4.60 | 28.60 | 21.16 | 817.96 | 131.56 |
| 8.90 | 22.40 | 79.21 | 501.76 | 199.36 |
| 14.60 | 17.30 | 213.16 | 299.29 | 252.58 |
| 15.10 | 10.10 | 228.01 | 102.01 | 152.51 |
| 18.30 | 5.10 | 334.89 | 26.01 | 93.33 |
| 21.20 | 4.20 | 449.44 | 17.64 | 89.04 |
| 20.30 | 4.40 | 412.09 | 19.36 | 89.32 |
| 14.20 | 11.60 | 201.64 | 134.56 | 164.72 |
| 10.60 | 23.50 | 112.36 | 552.25 | 249.10 |
| 6.50 | 24.50 | 42.25 | 600.25 | 159.25 |
| 137.60 | 211.50 | 2,101.10 | 4,879.59 | 1,674.00 |

Calculate the correlation coefficient for this data (to 3 decimal places).

| |
| --- |
|  |

# Answers

DO NOT TURN THIS PAGE UNTIL YOU HAVE
COMPLETED MOCK ASSESSMENT 2

1    C    1999  =  120

2002  =  120 × (1.1)³
         =  159.72
         =  160

2    A    2X + 5Y ≤ 500

If you answered B or D, you have the letters the wrong way round and if you answered C, the symbol is greater than instead of less then.

3    B    $10,000 is invested at 5% pa for 5 years.

$10,000 × (1.05)⁵ = $12,763

Option A is incorrect because it has not included the final year's interest payment ($10,000 × (1.05)⁴ = $12,155).

You should have been able to eliminate Options C and D straightaway since commonsense will tell you that $10,000 invested for five years at 5% is unlikely to give such a great return.

4    D    $PV = \dfrac{1}{r}$

$PV = \dfrac{\$15,000}{0.09}$

$= \$166,666.67$

$= \$167,000$

5    | 22 |    $\dfrac{35 + 24 + 2y + 17 + y + 23}{6} = 22$

$\therefore \dfrac{99 + 3y}{6} = 22$

$99 + 3y = 132$

$3y = 33$

$y = 11$

If    $x = 2y$

$x = 2 \times 11$

$= 22$

6    The net present value of Machine A is $ $\boxed{-5,420}$ (to the nearest $).

*Workings*

| Year | Cash outflow $ | Cash inflow $ | Discount factors | Present value $ |
|------|------|------|------|------|
| 0 | −100,000 | | 1.000 | −100,000 |
| 1 | −100,000 | | 0.909 | −90,900 |
| | | | | |
| 1 | | 40,000 | | |
| 2 | | 40,000 | | |
| 3 | | 40,000 | 4.355 | 174,200 |
| 4 | | 40,000 | | |
| 5 | | 40,000 | | |
| 6 | | 40,000 | | |
| | | | | |
| 6 | | 20,000 | 0.564 | 11,280 |
| | | | Net Present Value | −5,420 |

7    C    A macro is used in Excel for automating frequently repeated tasks.

8    C    $\dfrac{\text{Standard deviation}}{\text{Total marks}} \times 100\%$

$\dfrac{2}{20} \times 100\% = 10\%$

9    A

| Year | Cashflow $ | Discount factor 9% | Present value $ |
|------|------|------|------|
| 0 | (25,000) | 1 | (25,000) |
| 1-6 | 6,500 | 4.486 | 29,159 |
| | | NPV = | 4,159 |

Remember to use the cumulative present value tables (and not the present value tables).

10    A    The overall index is an average index and is calculated as follows.

$$\dfrac{(\text{Non-food index} \times \text{weight}) + (\text{food index} \times \text{weight})}{\text{Total weight}}$$

Let x = index for food subgroup

$$\dfrac{(130 \times 7) + (x \times 3)}{10} = 127$$

$910 + 3x = 1,270$

$3x = 1,270 - 910$

$x = 360/3$

$x = 120$

11 ☑ below which 75% of the sample values lie

The point K represents the upper quartile, ie the point below which 75% (300/400 × 100%) of the sample values lie.

12　C　Sample 1 median = average of second and third items in the array, ie $\left(\dfrac{5+5}{2}\right) = 5$

Sample 2 median = the middle (third) item in the array ie 5

The median has the same value, therefore, in both samples.

13 ☑ 50%

$$\text{If}\quad 32 \times (1-r)^4 = 2$$
$$(1-r)^4 = \frac{2}{32}$$
$$1-r = \sqrt[4]{\frac{2}{32}}$$
$$r = 1 - \sqrt[4]{\frac{2}{32}}$$
$$r = 1 - 0.5$$
$$r = 0.5 \text{ or } 50\%$$

14　C　The internal rate of return (IRR) of the investment can be calculated using the following formula.

$$IRR = a\% + \left(\frac{A}{A-B} \times (b-a)\right)\%$$

where　a = first interest rate = 10%
　　　　b = second interest rate = 18%
　　　　A = first NPV = $12,000
　　　　B = second NPV = -$4,000

$$IRR = 10\% + \left(\frac{12,000}{12,000+4,000} \times (18-10)\right)\%$$
$$= 10\% + 6\%$$
$$= 16\%$$

Option B is incorrect since this is simply the average of 18% and 10% = 14%.

Option D is incorrect because no account has been taken of the fact that when –4,000 is subtracted from 12,000 the result is 12,000 – (–4,000) = 16,000 and not 12,000 – (–4,000) = 8,000. Hence the IRR is incorrectly calculated as $10 + \left(\dfrac{12,000}{8,000} \times 8\%\right) = 22\%$.

15        If the net present value of an item of farming equipment is –$9,442 when r = 12% and $2,206 when r = 10%, the internal rate of return of the equipment is $\boxed{10.38\%}$ (to 2 decimal places).

*Workings*

$$IRR = R_1 + \frac{(R_2 - R_1) \times NPV_1}{NPV_1 - NPV_2}$$

where  $R_1$      = 10%
           $R_2$      = 12%
           $NPV_1$  = $2,206
           $NPV_2$  = –$9,442

$$IRR = 10 + \frac{(12 - 10) \times 2,206}{2,206 - (-9,442)}$$

$$= 10.38\%$$

16    D    A simple bar chart is a chart consisting of one or more bars, in which the length of each bar indicates the magnitude of the corresponding data items. This is the best diagram to draw to highlight the differences of typical salaries in different areas.

We are not interested in showing the breakdown of the total salary, therefore a pie diagram and a percentage component bar chart are not really appropriate.

A multiple bar chart is a bar chart in which two or more separate bars are used to present sub-divisions of data. The data available relating to salaries is not subdivided and this type of chart is therefore not appropriate in this situation.

17    B    Expected value = probability × profit

| Contract | Probability | Estimated profits | Expected value |
|---|---|---|---|
| | | $ | $ |
| A | 0.4 | 600,000 | 240,000 |
| B | 0.25 | 700,000 | 175,000 |
| C | 0.2 | 800,000 | 160,000 |
| | | 2,100,000 | 575,000 |

Option A is incorrect because it is just the highest expected value (from Contract A).

Option C is the arithmetic mean of the estimated profits ($2,100,000 ÷ 3 = $700,000)

Option D is the maximum expected profit from any one contract, ie $800,000 from Contract C.

18　　　a = $\boxed{-2.40}$

　　　b = $\boxed{0.31}$

　　　b = $\dfrac{n\Sigma xy - (\Sigma x)(\Sigma y)}{n\Sigma x^2 - (\Sigma x)^2}$

　　　　= $\dfrac{(6 \times 14) - (2 \times 15)}{(6 \times 30) - 2^2}$

　　　　= $\dfrac{84 - 30}{180 - 4}$

　　　　= $\dfrac{54}{176}$ = 0.31

　　　$\overline{y}$ = $\dfrac{15}{6}$ = 2.5

　　　$\overline{x}$ = $\dfrac{2}{6}$ = 0.33

　　　a = $\overline{y} - b\overline{x}$

　　　　= $2.5 - (0.31 \times 0.33)$

　　　　= $2.5 - 0.1023$

　　　　= $-2.40$

19 $\boxed{222.86}$ If $x$ = 4

　　　Value = $(4^{-0.65})^{-6}$

　　　　　= 222.86

20 $\boxed{\checkmark}$ 21

If you successively sum the sales data in groups of 4, there will be 21 four-point moving averages calculated.

The first four-point moving average will be 'situated' between months 2 and 3. The last four-point moving average will be 'situated' between months 22 and 23. Jot down months 1-24, work out where the moving averages would be calculated, and then calculate how many there are if you are unsure how to arrive at the correct answer.

21　D　If C = 2,000 + 300P, then fixed costs are $2,000 and variable costs are $300 per unit.

22　D　Putting a value in the cell, such as 15,710, would mean that the cell would not be automatically updated if changes were later made to the spreadsheet.

23　B　In Excel, placing the $ sign in front of a cell reference makes that reference absolute. When you move or copy a formula, absolute cell references do not change.

24    A    The correct formula is = D28 + D18.

Although D18 + D28 looks the same, because it has no = sign, it is not treated as a formula. Both of the other options count subtotals as well as the cost items.

25 | 0.4225 | $r^2 = 0.65^2$

$$= 0.4225$$

Therefore only just under half of the variation in one variable can be explained by variation in the other.

26    C

$$\text{Coefficient of variation} = \frac{\text{Standard deviation}}{\text{Mean}}$$

$$= \frac{3}{12} = 0.25$$

0.25 as a percentage is 25% ($0.25 \times 100\%$)

If you selected option A, you forgot to multiply the coefficient of variation by 100%.

If you selected option B, you calculated the coefficient of variation as (mean ÷ standard deviation) instead of (standard deviation ÷ mean). You also forgot to multiply your answer by 100%.

If you selected option D, you calculated the coefficient of variation as a percentage as (mean ÷ standard deviation × 100%) instead of (standard deviation ÷ mean × 100%).

27 | ✓ | $\dfrac{V}{R-G}$

$$\text{If} \quad R = \left(\frac{V}{P}\right) + G$$

$$R - G = \frac{V}{P}$$

$$\therefore \quad P = \frac{V}{R-G}$$

28 ☑ 98%

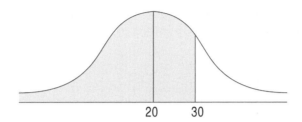

20   30

If $z = \dfrac{x - \mu}{\sigma}$

$= \dfrac{30 - 20}{5}$

$= \dfrac{10}{5} = 2$

Using normal distribution tables, when z = 2, this corresponds to a probability of 0.4772. We must also remember to take into account the area to the left of $\mu$ = 20 which corresponds to a probability of 0.5.

The area that we are interested in shown on the graph above therefore corresponds to a probability of 0.4772 + 0.5 = 0.9772 or 97.72% = 98%

29 ☑ $20,593

Annuity $= \dfrac{PV}{\text{annuity factor}}$

$= \dfrac{\$200,000}{9.712}$

$= \$20,593$

(*Note*. The annuity factor is found by looking in the cumulative present value tables where n=15 and r=6%.)

Alternatively, you could have arrived at the same answer by using the following method.

**Final value of loan must equal sum of repayments**

Final value of loan = $200,000 $\times (1.06)^{15}$ = $479,312

The repayments are a geometric progression. The sum of the repayments can be found by using the formula for the sum of a geometric progression.

$$S = \frac{A(R^n - 1)}{R - 1}$$

where    S = $479,312

R = 1.06

n = 15

$$\therefore \$479,312 = \frac{A(1.06^{15} - 1)}{1.06 - 1}$$

$$\$479,312 \times 0.06 = A(1.06^{15} - 1)$$

$$\$28,758.72 = A(1.06^{15} - 1)$$

$$\therefore A = \frac{\$28,758.72}{(1.06^{15} - 1)}$$

$$A = \$20,593$$

**30** ☑ 1 in 1,000,000

*Workings*

Since the electronic alarms operate independently, the failure of one alarm in no way affects the operation of the other **two alarms**. We need to use the simple multiplication law or AND Law.

$$\therefore \text{Probability of security system failing} = \frac{1}{100} \times \frac{1}{100} \times \frac{1}{100}$$

$$= \frac{1}{1,000,000}$$

**31** ☑ $(10/11)^3 \times \$300$

Interest on $3,000 × 10% = $300

$$\text{Present value of \$300 (in year 3)} = \frac{\$300}{(1.1)^3}$$

$(1.1)^3$ can also be written (as a fraction) as $\left(\frac{11}{10}\right)^3$

$$\therefore \text{PV of \$300 (in year 3)} = \frac{\$300}{(11/10)^3}$$

$$= \$300 \times (10/11)^3$$

32 [✓] 35%

$\quad$ Pr (faulty component ) = 0.1

$\quad$ Pr (no faulty components) = 1 − 0.1 = 0.9

$\quad$ Pr (no faulty components in a box of ten) $= 0.9^{10}$
$$= 0.3487$$
$$= 34.87 \text{ or } 35\%$$

33 [✓] 12%

| Type of fish | A | B | C | D | Total |
|---|---|---|---|---|---|
| Number of fish | 400 | 300 | 200 | 100 | |
| Annual % increase | 10 | 20 | 30 | 40 | |
| Number after one year | 440 | 360 | 260 | 140 | 1,200 |

$\quad$ Percentage of Type D fish in lake after one year $= \dfrac{140}{1,200} \times 100\%$
$$= 11.67\%$$
$$= 12\%$$

34 $\quad$ D $\quad$ Year = 2007

$\quad\quad \therefore$ Trend $\quad = (0.0002 \times 2007^2) + (0.4 \times 2007) + 30.4$

$\quad\quad\quad\quad\quad = 805.6 + 802.8 + 30.4$

$\quad\quad\quad\quad\quad = 1,638.8$

$\quad\quad \therefore$ Forecast $\quad = 1.6 \times 1,638.8$

$\quad\quad\quad\quad\quad = 2,622.08$

$\quad\quad \therefore$ Forecast in whole units = 2,622

35 $\quad$ B $\quad$ In 20X8, t = 8

$\quad\quad$ y = 30t − 10

$\quad\quad$ y = (30 × 8) − 10

$\quad\quad$ y = 240 − 10 = 230

$\quad\quad \therefore$ Forecast profits for 20X8 $\quad = 230 - 25$
$$= 205$$
$$= \$205,000$$

If you selected A, you used t = 9 instead of t = 8. If you selected C, you have used a multiplicative instead of an additive model.

If you selected D, you have added rather than subtracted the cyclical component.

36      The probability that this customer is from the east and over 39 years of age is $\boxed{0.175}$ to 3 decimal places.

*Workings*

Number of customers from the East and over 39 years of age = 65 + 60 + 50 = 175

Total number of customers    = 1,000

$\therefore$ Required probability    $= \dfrac{175}{1,000}$

         $= 0.175$

37      For the North and South, the rank correlation coefficient between sales and age is $\boxed{+1}$ (to the nearest whole number).

| Region/Age | 21-29 | 30-39 | 40-49 | 50-59 | 60 + |
|---|---|---|---|---|---|
| North | 100 | 80 | 50 | 40 | 30 |
| Ranking | 1 | 2 | 3 | 4 | 5 |
| South | 55 | 50 | 45 | 30 | 20 |
| Ranking | 1 | 2 | 3 | 4 | 5 |

The rankings for North and South are identical and therefore the rank correlation coefficient is +1.

38 $\boxed{4.52}$ $y = ax^b$

         $= 8 \times 12^{-0.23}$

         $= 4.51729$

         $= 4.52$ to two decimal places

39    C    $P(A) = 1/4$

         $P(B) = 1/4$

         $P(C) = 1/4$

         $P(D) = 1/4$

         $P(E) = 1/3$

         $P(F) = 2/3$ (twice as likely to go through F)

         $P(A \text{ or } E) = P(A) + P(E) - P(A \text{ and } E)$

                     $= 1/4 + 1/3 - (1/4 \times 1/3)$

                     $= 7/12 - 1/12$

                     $= 6/12$

                     $= 1/2$

The correct option is therefore C.

Option B is incorrect on two counts. Firstly, no account has been taken of the possibility of A *and* E ($1/4 \times 1/3$). Secondly, $1/4 + 1/3 \neq 2/7$!

Option A is incorrect since no account has been taken of P(A) + P(E), only P(A and E) = $1/4 \times 1/3 = 1/12$

Option D is incorrect since the P(A and E), 1/12, has not been subtracted from 7/12

40

A  | $ – |

B  | $12 |

C  | $6 |

D  | $54 |

E  | 0.3 |

*Workings*

A  **Production = 60, demand = 20**

| Revenue | = (20 × $0.5) + (40 × $0.05) |
| | = $10 + $2 = $12 |
| Variable costs | = 60 × $0.2 = $12 |
| Contribution | = Revenue – variable costs |
| | = $12 – $12 |
| | = $nil |

B  **Production = 100, demand = 60**

| Revenue | = (60 × $0.5) + (40 × $0.05) |
| | = $30 + $2 = $32 |
| Variable costs | = 100 × $0.2 = $20 |
| Contribution | = $32 – $20 = $12 |

C  **Production = 140, demand = 60**

| Revenue | = (60 × $0.5) + (80 × $0.05) |
| | = $30 + $4 = $34 |
| Variable costs | = 140 × $0.2 = $28 |
| Contribution | = $34 – $28 = $6 |

D  **Production = 180, demand = 180**

| Revenue | = 180 × $0.5 = $90 |
| Variable costs | = 180 × $0.2 = $36 |
| Contribution | = $90 – $36 = $54 |

E

| Daily demand | 1-39 | 40-79 | 80-119 | 120-159 | 160-199 |
|---|---|---|---|---|---|
| Midpoint | 20 | 60 | 100 | 140 | 180 |
| Number of days | 10 | 20 | 30 | 30 | 10 |

Total number of days = 10 + 20 + 30 + 30 + 10 = 100

Probability of daily demand for 100 cakes = $\dfrac{30}{100}$ = 0.3

41 B As this is a multiplicative model, the seasonal variations should sum to 4 in this case with an average of 1 as there are 4 quarters.

If x = seasonal variation for quarter 4

$$1.3 + 1.6 + 0.5 + X = 4$$
$$X = 4 - 3.4$$
$$X = 0.6$$

42 A T = Y/S for the multiplicative model

| | Quarter | |
|---|---|---|
| | 1 | 2 |
| Seasonal component | 1.3 | 1.6 |
| Actual series | $120,000 | $135,000 |
| Trend (T) | $92,308 | $84,375 |

The trend line for sales has therefore decreased between quarter 1 and quarter 2.

43 | −33 |

| Year | Y − T | Adjustment | Adjusted average |
|---|---|---|---|
| 1 | 16 | 1 | 17 |
| 2 | 32 | 1 | 33 |
| 3 | − 18 | 1 | − 17 |
| 4 | − 34 | 1 | − 33 |
| | − 4 | 4 | 0 |

44 C A shows strong negative correlation, B shows weak positive correlation and D shows weak negative correlation.

45 $\boxed{-0.968}$ $r = \dfrac{n\Sigma xy - (\Sigma x)(\Sigma y)}{\sqrt{[n\Sigma x^2 - (\Sigma x)^2][n\Sigma y^2 - (\Sigma y)^2}}$

$$= \frac{(12 \times 1{,}674) - (137.6 \times 211.5)}{\sqrt{[(12 \times 2{,}101.1) - 137.6^2][(12 \times 4{,}879.59) - 211.5^2]}}$$

$$= \frac{20{,}088 - 29{,}102.4}{\sqrt{(25{,}213.2 - 18{,}933.76)(58{,}555.08 - 44{,}732.25)}}$$

$$= \frac{-9{,}014.4}{\sqrt{6{,}279.44 \times 13{,}822.83}}$$

$$= \frac{-9014.4}{9{,}316.63}$$

$$= -0.968$$

# Mathematical tables

# Logarithms

| | 0 | 1 | 2 | 3 | 4 | 5 | 6 | 7 | 8 | 9 | 1 | 2 | 3 | 4 | 5 | 6 | 7 | 8 | 9 |
|---|---|---|---|---|---|---|---|---|---|---|---|---|---|---|---|---|---|---|---|
| 10 | 0000 | 0043 | 0086 | 0128 | 0170 | | | | | | 4 | 9 | 13 | 17 | 21 | 26 | 30 | 34 | 38 |
| | | | | | | 0212 | 0253 | 0294 | 0334 | 0374 | 4 | 8 | 12 | 16 | 20 | 24 | 28 | 32 | 37 |
| 11 | 0414 | 0453 | 0492 | 0531 | 0569 | | | | | | 4 | 8 | 12 | 15 | 19 | 23 | 27 | 31 | 35 |
| | | | | | | 0607 | 0645 | 0682 | 0719 | 0755 | 4 | 7 | 11 | 15 | 19 | 22 | 26 | 30 | 33 |
| 12 | 0792 | 0828 | 0864 | 0899 | 0934 | 0969 | | | | | 3 | 7 | 11 | 14 | 18 | 21 | 25 | 28 | 32 |
| | | | | | | | 1004 | 1038 | 1072 | 1106 | 3 | 7 | 10 | 14 | 17 | 20 | 24 | 27 | 31 |
| 13 | 1139 | 1173 | 1206 | 1239 | 1271 | | | | | | 3 | 7 | 10 | 13 | 16 | 20 | 23 | 26 | 30 |
| | | | | | | 1303 | 1335 | 1367 | 1399 | 1430 | 3 | 7 | 10 | 12 | 16 | 19 | 22 | 25 | 29 |
| 14 | 1461 | 1492 | 1523 | 1553 | | | | | | | 3 | 6 | 9 | 12 | 15 | 18 | 21 | 24 | 28 |
| | | | | | 1584 | 1614 | 1644 | 1673 | 1703 | 1732 | 3 | 6 | 9 | 12 | 15 | 17 | 20 | 23 | 26 |
| 15 | 1761 | 1790 | 1818 | 1847 | 1875 | 1903 | | | | | 3 | 6 | 9 | 11 | 14 | 17 | 20 | 23 | 26 |
| | | | | | | | 1931 | 1959 | 1987 | 2014 | 3 | 5 | 8 | 11 | 14 | 16 | 19 | 22 | 25 |
| 16 | 2041 | 2068 | 2095 | 2122 | 2148 | | | | | | 3 | 5 | 8 | 11 | 14 | 16 | 19 | 22 | 24 |
| | | | | | | 2175 | 2201 | 2227 | 2253 | 2279 | 3 | 5 | 8 | 10 | 13 | 15 | 18 | 21 | 23 |
| 17 | 2304 | 2330 | 2355 | 2380 | 2405 | 2430 | | | | | 3 | 5 | 8 | 10 | 13 | 15 | 18 | 20 | 23 |
| | | | | | | | 2455 | 2480 | 2504 | 2529 | 2 | 5 | 7 | 10 | 12 | 15 | 17 | 19 | 22 |
| 18 | 2553 | 2577 | 2601 | 2625 | 2648 | | | | | | 2 | 5 | 7 | 9 | 12 | 14 | 16 | 19 | 21 |
| | | | | | | 2672 | 2695 | 2718 | 2742 | 2765 | 2 | 5 | 7 | 9 | 11 | 14 | 16 | 18 | 21 |
| 19 | 2788 | 2810 | 2833 | 2856 | 2878 | | | | | | 2 | 4 | 7 | 9 | 11 | 13 | 16 | 18 | 20 |
| | | | | | | 2900 | 2923 | 2945 | 2967 | 2989 | 2 | 4 | 6 | 8 | 11 | 13 | 15 | 17 | 19 |
| 20 | 3010 | 3032 | 3054 | 3075 | 3096 | 3118 | 3139 | 3160 | 3181 | 3201 | 2 | 4 | 6 | 8 | 11 | 13 | 15 | 17 | 19 |
| 21 | 3222 | 3243 | 3263 | 3284 | 3304 | 3324 | 3345 | 3365 | 3385 | 3404 | 2 | 4 | 6 | 8 | 10 | 12 | 14 | 16 | 18 |
| 22 | 3424 | 3444 | 3464 | 3483 | 3502 | 3522 | 3541 | 3560 | 3579 | 3598 | 2 | 4 | 6 | 8 | 10 | 12 | 14 | 15 | 17 |
| 23 | 3617 | 3636 | 3655 | 3674 | 3692 | 3711 | 3729 | 3747 | 3766 | 3784 | 2 | 4 | 6 | 7 | 9 | 11 | 13 | 15 | 17 |
| 24 | 3802 | 3820 | 3838 | 3856 | 3874 | 3892 | 3909 | 3927 | 3945 | 3962 | 2 | 4 | 5 | 7 | 9 | 11 | 12 | 14 | 16 |
| 25 | 3979 | 3997 | 4014 | 4031 | 4048 | 4065 | 4082 | 4099 | 4116 | 4133 | 2 | 3 | 5 | 7 | 9 | 10 | 12 | 14 | 15 |
| 26 | 4150 | 4166 | 4183 | 4200 | 4216 | 4232 | 4249 | 4265 | 4281 | 4298 | 2 | 3 | 5 | 7 | 8 | 10 | 11 | 13 | 15 |
| 27 | 4314 | 4330 | 4346 | 4362 | 4378 | 4393 | 4409 | 4425 | 4440 | 4456 | 2 | 3 | 5 | 6 | 8 | 9 | 11 | 13 | 14 |
| 28 | 4472 | 4487 | 4502 | 4518 | 4533 | 4548 | 4564 | 4579 | 4594 | 4609 | 2 | 3 | 5 | 6 | 8 | 9 | 11 | 12 | 14 |
| 29 | 4624 | 4639 | 4654 | 4669 | 4683 | 4698 | 4713 | 4728 | 4742 | 4757 | 1 | 3 | 4 | 6 | 7 | 9 | 10 | 12 | 13 |
| 30 | 4771 | 4786 | 4800 | 4814 | 4829 | 4843 | 4857 | 4871 | 4886 | 4900 | 1 | 3 | 4 | 6 | 7 | 9 | 10 | 11 | 13 |
| 31 | 4914 | 4928 | 4942 | 4955 | 4969 | 4983 | 4997 | 5011 | 5024 | 5038 | 1 | 3 | 4 | 6 | 7 | 8 | 10 | 11 | 12 |
| 32 | 5051 | 5065 | 5079 | 5092 | 5105 | 5119 | 5132 | 5145 | 5159 | 5172 | 1 | 3 | 4 | 5 | 7 | 8 | 9 | 11 | 12 |
| 33 | 5185 | 5198 | 5211 | 5224 | 5237 | 5250 | 5263 | 5276 | 5289 | 5302 | 1 | 3 | 4 | 5 | 6 | 8 | 9 | 10 | 12 |
| 34 | 5315 | 5328 | 5340 | 5353 | 5366 | 5378 | 5391 | 5403 | 5416 | 5428 | 1 | 3 | 4 | 5 | 6 | 8 | 9 | 10 | 11 |
| 35 | 5441 | 5453 | 5465 | 5478 | 5490 | 5502 | 5514 | 5527 | 5539 | 5551 | 1 | 2 | 4 | 5 | 6 | 7 | 9 | 10 | 11 |
| 36 | 5563 | 5575 | 5587 | 5599 | 5611 | 5623 | 5635 | 5647 | 5658 | 5670 | 1 | 2 | 4 | 5 | 6 | 7 | 8 | 10 | 11 |
| 37 | 5682 | 5694 | 5705 | 5717 | 5729 | 5740 | 5752 | 5763 | 5775 | 5786 | 1 | 2 | 3 | 5 | 6 | 7 | 8 | 9 | 10 |
| 38 | 5798 | 5809 | 5821 | 5832 | 5843 | 5855 | 5866 | 5877 | 5888 | 5899 | 1 | 2 | 3 | 5 | 6 | 7 | 8 | 9 | 10 |
| 39 | 5911 | 5922 | 5933 | 5944 | 5955 | 5966 | 5977 | 5988 | 5999 | 6010 | 1 | 2 | 3 | 4 | 5 | 7 | 8 | 9 | 10 |
| 40 | 6021 | 6031 | 6042 | 6053 | 6064 | 6075 | 6085 | 6096 | 6107 | 6117 | 1 | 2 | 3 | 4 | 5 | 6 | 8 | 9 | 10 |
| 41 | 6128 | 6138 | 6149 | 6160 | 6170 | 6180 | 6191 | 6201 | 6212 | 6222 | 1 | 2 | 3 | 4 | 5 | 6 | 7 | 8 | 9 |
| 42 | 6232 | 6243 | 6253 | 6263 | 6274 | 6284 | 6294 | 6304 | 6314 | 6325 | 1 | 2 | 3 | 4 | 5 | 6 | 7 | 8 | 9 |
| 43 | 6335 | 6345 | 6355 | 6365 | 6375 | 6385 | 6395 | 6405 | 6415 | 6425 | 1 | 2 | 3 | 4 | 5 | 6 | 7 | 8 | 9 |

# Logarithms

| | 0 | 1 | 2 | 3 | 4 | 5 | 6 | 7 | 8 | 9 | 1 | 2 | 3 | 4 | 5 | 6 | 7 | 8 | 9 |
|---|---|---|---|---|---|---|---|---|---|---|---|---|---|---|---|---|---|---|---|
| 44 | 6435 | 6444 | 6454 | 6464 | 6474 | 6484 | 6493 | 6503 | 6513 | 6522 | 1 | 2 | 3 | 4 | 5 | 6 | 7 | 8 | 9 |
| 45 | 6532 | 6542 | 6551 | 6561 | 6571 | 6580 | 6590 | 6599 | 6609 | 6618 | 1 | 2 | 3 | 4 | 5 | 6 | 7 | 8 | 9 |
| 46 | 6628 | 6637 | 6646 | 6656 | 6665 | 6675 | 6684 | 6693 | 6702 | 6712 | 1 | 2 | 3 | 4 | 5 | 6 | 7 | 7 | 8 |
| 47 | 6721 | 6730 | 6739 | 6749 | 6758 | 6767 | 6776 | 6785 | 6794 | 6803 | 1 | 2 | 3 | 4 | 5 | 5 | 6 | 7 | 8 |
| 48 | 6812 | 6821 | 6830 | 6839 | 6848 | 6857 | 6866 | 6875 | 6884 | 6893 | 1 | 2 | 3 | 4 | 4 | 5 | 6 | 7 | 8 |
| 49 | 6902 | 6911 | 6920 | 6928 | 6937 | 6946 | 6955 | 6964 | 6972 | 6981 | 1 | 2 | 3 | 4 | 4 | 5 | 6 | 7 | 8 |
| 50 | 6990 | 6998 | 7007 | 7016 | 7024 | 7033 | 7042 | 7050 | 7059 | 7067 | 1 | 2 | 3 | 3 | 4 | 5 | 6 | 7 | 8 |
| 51 | 7076 | 7084 | 7093 | 7101 | 7110 | 7118 | 7126 | 7135 | 7143 | 7152 | 1 | 2 | 3 | 3 | 4 | 5 | 6 | 7 | 8 |
| 52 | 7160 | 7168 | 7177 | 7185 | 7193 | 7202 | 7210 | 7218 | 7226 | 7235 | 1 | 2 | 2 | 3 | 4 | 5 | 6 | 7 | 7 |
| 53 | 7243 | 7251 | 7259 | 7267 | 7275 | 7284 | 7292 | 7300 | 7308 | 7316 | 1 | 2 | 2 | 3 | 4 | 5 | 6 | 6 | 7 |
| 54 | 7324 | 7332 | 7340 | 7348 | 7356 | 7364 | 7372 | 7380 | 7388 | 7396 | 1 | 2 | 2 | 3 | 4 | 5 | 6 | 6 | 7 |
| 55 | 7404 | 7412 | 7419 | 7427 | 7435 | 7443 | 7451 | 7459 | 7466 | 7474 | 1 | 2 | 2 | 3 | 4 | 5 | 5 | 6 | 7 |
| 56 | 7482 | 7490 | 7497 | 7505 | 7513 | 7520 | 7528 | 7536 | 7543 | 7551 | 1 | 2 | 2 | 3 | 4 | 5 | 5 | 6 | 7 |
| 57 | 7559 | 7566 | 7574 | 7582 | 7589 | 7597 | 7604 | 7612 | 7619 | 7627 | 1 | 2 | 2 | 3 | 4 | 5 | 5 | 6 | 7 |
| 58 | 7634 | 7642 | 7649 | 7657 | 7664 | 7672 | 7679 | 7686 | 7694 | 7701 | 1 | 1 | 2 | 3 | 4 | 4 | 5 | 6 | 7 |
| 59 | 7709 | 7716 | 7723 | 7731 | 7738 | 7745 | 7752 | 7760 | 7767 | 7774 | 1 | 1 | 2 | 3 | 4 | 4 | 5 | 6 | 7 |
| 60 | 7782 | 7789 | 7796 | 7803 | 7810 | 7818 | 7825 | 7832 | 7839 | 7846 | 1 | 1 | 2 | 3 | 4 | 4 | 5 | 6 | 6 |
| 61 | 7853 | 7860 | 7868 | 7875 | 7882 | 7889 | 7896 | 7903 | 7910 | 7917 | 1 | 1 | 2 | 3 | 4 | 4 | 5 | 6 | 6 |
| 62 | 7924 | 7931 | 7938 | 7945 | 7952 | 7959 | 7966 | 7973 | 7980 | 7987 | 1 | 1 | 2 | 3 | 3 | 4 | 5 | 6 | 6 |
| 63 | 7993 | 8000 | 8007 | 8014 | 8021 | 8028 | 8035 | 8041 | 8048 | 8055 | 1 | 1 | 2 | 3 | 3 | 4 | 5 | 5 | 6 |
| 64 | 8062 | 8069 | 8075 | 8082 | 8089 | 8096 | 8102 | 8109 | 8116 | 8122 | 1 | 1 | 2 | 3 | 3 | 4 | 5 | 5 | 6 |
| 65 | 8129 | 8136 | 8142 | 8149 | 8156 | 8162 | 8169 | 8176 | 8182 | 8189 | 1 | 1 | 2 | 3 | 3 | 4 | 5 | 5 | 6 |
| 66 | 8195 | 8202 | 8209 | 8215 | 8222 | 8228 | 8235 | 8241 | 8248 | 8254 | 1 | 1 | 2 | 3 | 3 | 4 | 5 | 5 | 6 |
| 67 | 8261 | 8267 | 8274 | 8280 | 8287 | 8293 | 8299 | 8306 | 8312 | 8319 | 1 | 1 | 2 | 3 | 3 | 4 | 5 | 5 | 6 |
| 68 | 8325 | 8331 | 8338 | 8344 | 8351 | 8357 | 8363 | 8370 | 8376 | 8382 | 1 | 1 | 2 | 3 | 3 | 4 | 4 | 5 | 6 |
| 69 | 8388 | 8395 | 8401 | 8407 | 8414 | 8420 | 8426 | 8432 | 8439 | 8445 | 1 | 1 | 2 | 2 | 3 | 4 | 4 | 5 | 6 |
| 70 | 8451 | 8457 | 8463 | 8470 | 8476 | 8482 | 8488 | 8494 | 8500 | 8506 | 1 | 1 | 2 | 2 | 3 | 4 | 4 | 5 | 6 |
| 71 | 8513 | 8519 | 8525 | 8531 | 8537 | 8543 | 8549 | 8555 | 8561 | 8567 | 1 | 1 | 2 | 2 | 3 | 4 | 4 | 5 | 5 |
| 72 | 8573 | 8579 | 8585 | 8591 | 8597 | 8603 | 8609 | 8615 | 8621 | 8627 | 1 | 1 | 2 | 2 | 3 | 4 | 4 | 5 | 5 |
| 73 | 8633 | 8639 | 8645 | 8651 | 8657 | 8663 | 8669 | 8675 | 8681 | 8686 | 1 | 1 | 2 | 2 | 3 | 4 | 4 | 5 | 5 |
| 74 | 8692 | 8698 | 8704 | 8710 | 8716 | 8722 | 8727 | 8733 | 8739 | 8745 | 1 | 1 | 2 | 2 | 3 | 4 | 4 | 5 | 5 |
| 75 | 8751 | 8756 | 8762 | 8768 | 8774 | 8779 | 8785 | 8791 | 8797 | 8802 | 1 | 1 | 2 | 2 | 3 | 3 | 4 | 5 | 5 |
| 76 | 8808 | 8814 | 8820 | 8825 | 8831 | 8837 | 8842 | 8848 | 8854 | 8859 | 1 | 1 | 2 | 2 | 3 | 3 | 4 | 5 | 5 |
| 77 | 8865 | 8871 | 8876 | 8882 | 8887 | 8893 | 8899 | 8904 | 8910 | 8915 | 1 | 1 | 2 | 2 | 3 | 3 | 4 | 4 | 5 |
| 78 | 8921 | 8927 | 8932 | 8938 | 8943 | 8949 | 8954 | 8960 | 8965 | 8971 | 1 | 1 | 2 | 2 | 3 | 3 | 4 | 4 | 5 |
| 79 | 8976 | 8982 | 8987 | 8993 | 8998 | 9004 | 9009 | 9015 | 9020 | 9025 | 1 | 1 | 2 | 2 | 3 | 3 | 4 | 4 | 5 |
| 80 | 9031 | 9036 | 9042 | 9047 | 9053 | 9058 | 9063 | 9069 | 9074 | 9079 | 1 | 1 | 2 | 2 | 3 | 3 | 4 | 4 | 5 |
| 81 | 9085 | 9090 | 9096 | 9101 | 9106 | 9112 | 9117 | 9122 | 9128 | 9133 | 1 | 1 | 2 | 2 | 3 | 3 | 4 | 4 | 5 |
| 82 | 9138 | 9143 | 9149 | 9154 | 9159 | 9165 | 9170 | 9175 | 9180 | 9186 | 1 | 1 | 2 | 2 | 3 | 3 | 4 | 4 | 5 |
| 83 | 9191 | 9196 | 9201 | 9206 | 9212 | 9217 | 9222 | 9227 | 9232 | 9238 | 1 | 1 | 2 | 2 | 3 | 3 | 4 | 4 | 5 |
| 84 | 9243 | 9248 | 9253 | 9258 | 9263 | 9269 | 9274 | 9279 | 9284 | 9289 | 1 | 1 | 2 | 2 | 3 | 3 | 4 | 4 | 5 |
| 85 | 9294 | 9299 | 9304 | 9309 | 9315 | 9320 | 9325 | 9330 | 9335 | 9340 | 1 | 1 | 2 | 2 | 3 | 3 | 4 | 4 | 5 |
| 86 | 9345 | 9350 | 9355 | 9360 | 9365 | 9370 | 9375 | 9380 | 9385 | 9390 | 1 | 1 | 2 | 2 | 3 | 3 | 4 | 4 | 5 |
| 87 | 9395 | 9400 | 9405 | 9410 | 9415 | 9420 | 9425 | 9430 | 9435 | 9440 | 0 | 1 | 1 | 2 | 2 | 3 | 3 | 4 | 4 |
| 88 | 9445 | 9450 | 9455 | 9460 | 9465 | 9469 | 9474 | 9479 | 9484 | 9489 | 0 | 1 | 1 | 2 | 2 | 3 | 3 | 4 | 4 |

# Logarithms

| 89 | 9494 | 9499 | 9504 | 9509 | 9513 | 9518 | 9523 | 9528 | 9533 | 9538 | 0 | 1 | 1 | 2 | 2 | 3 | 3 | 4 | 4 |
|----|------|------|------|------|------|------|------|------|------|------|---|---|---|---|---|---|---|---|---|
| 90 | 9542 | 9547 | 9552 | 9557 | 9562 | 9566 | 9571 | 9576 | 9581 | 9586 | 0 | 1 | 1 | 2 | 2 | 3 | 3 | 4 | 4 |
| 91 | 9590 | 9595 | 9600 | 9605 | 9609 | 9614 | 9619 | 9624 | 9628 | 9633 | 0 | 1 | 1 | 2 | 2 | 3 | 3 | 4 | 4 |
| 92 | 9638 | 9643 | 9647 | 9652 | 9657 | 9661 | 9666 | 9671 | 9675 | 9680 | 0 | 1 | 1 | 2 | 2 | 3 | 3 | 4 | 4 |
| 93 | 9685 | 9689 | 9694 | 9699 | 9703 | 9708 | 9713 | 9717 | 9722 | 9727 | 0 | 1 | 1 | 2 | 2 | 3 | 3 | 4 | 4 |
| 94 | 9731 | 9736 | 9741 | 9745 | 9750 | 9754 | 9759 | 9763 | 9768 | 9773 | 0 | 1 | 1 | 2 | 2 | 3 | 3 | 4 | 4 |
| 95 | 9777 | 9782 | 9786 | 9791 | 9795 | 9800 | 9805 | 9809 | 9814 | 9818 | 0 | 1 | 1 | 2 | 2 | 3 | 3 | 4 | 4 |
| 96 | 9823 | 9827 | 9832 | 9836 | 9841 | 9845 | 9850 | 9854 | 9859 | 9863 | 0 | 1 | 1 | 2 | 2 | 3 | 3 | 4 | 4 |
| 97 | 9868 | 9872 | 9877 | 9881 | 9886 | 9890 | 9894 | 9899 | 9903 | 9908 | 0 | 1 | 1 | 2 | 2 | 3 | 3 | 4 | 4 |
| 98 | 9912 | 9917 | 9921 | 9926 | 9930 | 9934 | 9939 | 9943 | 9948 | 9952 | 0 | 1 | 1 | 2 | 2 | 3 | 3 | 4 | 4 |
| 99 | 9956 | 9961 | 9965 | 9969 | 9974 | 9978 | 9983 | 9987 | 9991 | 9996 | 0 | 1 | 1 | 2 | 2 | 3 | 3 | 3 | 4 |

# Tables

## Area under the normal curve

This table gives the area under the normal curve between the mean and the point Z standard deviations above the mean. The corresponding area for deviations below the mean can be found by symmetry.

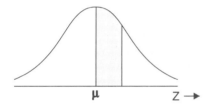

| $Z = \dfrac{(x - \mu)}{\sigma}$ | 0.00 | 0.01 | 0.02 | 0.03 | 0.04 | 0.05 | 0.06 | 0.07 | 0.08 | 0.09 |
|------|------|------|------|------|------|------|------|------|------|------|
| 0.0 | .0000 | .0040 | .0080 | .0120 | .0160 | .0199 | .0239 | .0279 | .0319 | .0359 |
| 0.1 | .0398 | .0438 | .0478 | .0517 | .0557 | .0596 | .0636 | .0675 | .0714 | .0753 |
| 0.2 | .0793 | .0832 | .0871 | .0910 | .0948 | .0987 | .1026 | .1064 | .1103 | .1141 |
| 0.3 | .1179 | .1217 | .1255 | .1293 | .1331 | .1368 | .1406 | .1443 | .1480 | .1517 |
| 0.4 | .1554 | .1591 | .1628 | .1664 | .1700 | .1736 | .1772 | .1808 | .1844 | .1879 |
| 0.5 | .1915 | .1950 | .1985 | .2019 | .2054 | .2088 | .2123 | .2157 | .2190 | .2224 |
| 0.6 | .2257 | .2291 | .2324 | .2357 | .2389 | .2422 | .2454 | .2486 | .2517 | .2549 |
| 0.7 | .2580 | .2611 | .2642 | .2673 | .2704 | .2734 | .2764 | .2794 | .2823 | .2852 |
| 0.8 | .2881 | .2910 | .2939 | .2967 | .2995 | .3023 | .3051 | .3078 | .3106 | .3133 |
| 0.9 | .3159 | .3186 | .3212 | .3238 | .3264 | .3289 | .3315 | .3340 | .3365 | .3389 |
| 1.0 | .3413 | .3438 | .3461 | .3485 | .3508 | .3531 | .3554 | .3577 | .3599 | .3621 |
| 1.1 | .3643 | .3665 | .3686 | .3708 | .3729 | .3749 | .3770 | .3790 | .3810 | .3830 |
| 1.2 | .3849 | .3869 | .3888 | .3907 | .3925 | .3944 | .3962 | .3980 | .3997 | .4015 |
| 1.3 | .4032 | .4049 | .4066 | .4082 | .4099 | .4115 | .4131 | .4147 | .4162 | .4177 |
| 1.4 | .4192 | .4207 | .4222 | .4236 | .4251 | .4265 | .4279 | .4292 | .4306 | .4319 |
| 1.5 | .4332 | .4345 | .4357 | .4370 | .4382 | .4394 | .4406 | .4418 | .4429 | .4441 |

| $Z = \frac{(x-\mu)}{\sigma}$ | 0.00 | 0.01 | 0.02 | 0.03 | 0.04 | 0.05 | 0.06 | 0.07 | 0.08 | 0.09 |
|---|---|---|---|---|---|---|---|---|---|---|
| 1.6 | .4452 | .4463 | .4474 | .4484 | .4495 | .4505 | .4515 | .4525 | .4535 | .4545 |
| 1.7 | .4554 | .4564 | .4573 | .4582 | .4591 | .4599 | .4608 | .4616 | .4625 | .4633 |
| 1.8 | .4641 | .4649 | .4656 | .4664 | .4671 | .4678 | .4686 | .4693 | .4699 | .4706 |
| 1.9 | .4713 | .4719 | .4726 | .4732 | .4738 | .4744 | .4750 | .4756 | .4761 | .4767 |
| 2.0 | .4772 | .4778 | .4783 | .4788 | .4793 | .4798 | .4803 | .4808 | .4812 | .4817 |
| 2.1 | .4821 | .4826 | .4830 | .4834 | .4838 | .4842 | .4846 | .4850 | .4854 | .4857 |
| 2.2 | .4861 | .4864 | .4868 | .4871 | .4875 | .4878 | .4881 | .4884 | .4887 | .4890 |
| 2.3 | .4893 | .4896 | .4898 | .4901 | .4904 | .4906 | .4909 | .4911 | .4913 | .4916 |
| 2.4 | .4918 | .4920 | .4922 | .4925 | .4927 | .4929 | .4931 | .4932 | .4934 | .4936 |
| 2.5 | .4938 | .4940 | .4941 | .4943 | .4945 | .4946 | .4948 | .4949 | .4951 | .4952 |
| 2.6 | .4953 | .4955 | .4956 | .4957 | .4959 | .4960 | .4961 | .4962 | .4963 | .4964 |
| 2.7 | .4965 | .4966 | .4967 | .4968 | .4969 | .4970 | .4971 | .4972 | .4973 | .4974 |
| 2.8 | .4974 | .4975 | .4976 | .4977 | .4977 | .4978 | .4979 | .4979 | .4980 | .4981 |
| 2.9 | .4981 | .4982 | .4982 | .4983 | .4984 | .4984 | .4985 | .4985 | .4986 | .4986 |
| 3.0 | .49865 | .4987 | .4987 | .4988 | .4988 | .4989 | .4989 | .4989 | .4990 | .4990 |
| 3.1 | .49903 | .4991 | .4991 | .4991 | .4992 | .4992 | .4992 | .4992 | .4993 | .4993 |
| 3.2 | .49931 | .4993 | .4994 | .4994 | .4994 | .4994 | .4994 | .4995 | .4995 | .4995 |
| 3.3 | .49952 | .4995 | .4995 | .4996 | .4996 | .4996 | .4996 | .4996 | .4996 | .4997 |
| 3.4 | .49966 | .4997 | .4997 | .4997 | .4997 | .4997 | .4997 | .4997 | .4997 | .4998 |
| 3.5 | .49977 | | | | | | | | | |

# Present value table

Present value of $1 ie $(1+r)-n$ where r = interest rate, n = number of periods until payment or receipt.

| Periods | | | | | Interest rates (r) | | | | | |
|---|---|---|---|---|---|---|---|---|---|---|
| (n) | 1% | 2% | 3% | 4% | 5% | 6% | 7% | 8% | 9% | 10% |
| 1 | 0.990 | 0.980 | 0.971 | 0.962 | 0.952 | 0.943 | 0.935 | 0.926 | 0.917 | 0.909 |
| 2 | 0.980 | 0.961 | 0.943 | 0.925 | 0.907 | 0.890 | 0.873 | 0.857 | 0.842 | 0.826 |
| 3 | 0.971 | 0.942 | 0.915 | 0.889 | 0.864 | 0.840 | 0.816 | 0.794 | 0.772 | 0.751 |
| 4 | 0.961 | 0.924 | 0.888 | 0.855 | 0.823 | 0.792 | 0.763 | 0.735 | 0.708 | 0.683 |
| 5 | 0.951 | 0.906 | 0.863 | 0.822 | 0.784 | 0.747 | 0.713 | 0.681 | 0.650 | 0.621 |
| 6 | 0.942 | 0.888 | 0.837 | 0.790 | 0.746 | 0.705 | 0.666 | 0.630 | 0.596 | 0.564 |
| 7 | 0.933 | 0.871 | 0.813 | 0.760 | 0.711 | 0.665 | 0.623 | 0.583 | 0.547 | 0.513 |
| 8 | 0.923 | 0.853 | 0.789 | 0.731 | 0.677 | 0.627 | 0.582 | 0.540 | 0.502 | 0.467 |
| 9 | 0.914 | 0.837 | 0.766 | 0.703 | 0.645 | 0.592 | 0.544 | 0.500 | 0.460 | 0.424 |
| 10 | 0.905 | 0.820 | 0.744 | 0.676 | 0.614 | 0.558 | 0.508 | 0.463 | 0.422 | 0.386 |
| 11 | 0.896 | 0.804 | 0.722 | 0.650 | 0.585 | 0.527 | 0.475 | 0.429 | 0.388 | 0.350 |
| 12 | 0.887 | 0.788 | 0.701 | 0.625 | 0.557 | 0.497 | 0.444 | 0.397 | 0.356 | 0.319 |
| 13 | 0.879 | 0.773 | 0.681 | 0.601 | 0.530 | 0.469 | 0.415 | 0.368 | 0.326 | 0.290 |
| 14 | 0.870 | 0.758 | 0.661 | 0.577 | 0.505 | 0.442 | 0.388 | 0.340 | 0.299 | 0.263 |
| 15 | 0.861 | 0.743 | 0.642 | 0.555 | 0.481 | 0.417 | 0.362 | 0.315 | 0.275 | 0.239 |
| 16 | 0.853 | 0.728 | 0.623 | 0.534 | 0.458 | 0.394 | 0.339 | 0.292 | 0.252 | 0.218 |
| 17 | 0.844 | 0.714 | 0.605 | 0.513 | 0.436 | 0.371 | 0.317 | 0.270 | 0.231 | 0.198 |

| Periods | | | | | Interest rates (r) | | | | | |
|---|---|---|---|---|---|---|---|---|---|---|
| (n) | 1% | 2% | 3% | 4% | 5% | 6% | 7% | 8% | 9% | 10% |
| 18 | 0.836 | 0.700 | 0.587 | 0.494 | 0.416 | 0.350 | 0.296 | 0.250 | 0.212 | 0.180 |
| 19 | 0.828 | 0.686 | 0.570 | 0.475 | 0.396 | 0.331 | 0.277 | 0.232 | 0.194 | 0.164 |
| 20 | 0.820 | 0.673 | 0.554 | 0.456 | 0.377 | 0.312 | 0.258 | 0.215 | 0.178 | 0.149 |

| Periods | | | | | Interest rates (r) | | | | | |
|---|---|---|---|---|---|---|---|---|---|---|
| (n) | 11% | 12% | 13% | 14% | 15% | 16% | 17% | 18% | 19% | 20% |
| 1 | 0.901 | 0.893 | 0.885 | 0.877 | 0.870 | 0.862 | 0.855 | 0.847 | 0.840 | 0.833 |
| 2 | 0.812 | 0.797 | 0.783 | 0.769 | 0.756 | 0.743 | 0.731 | 0.718 | 0.706 | 0.694 |
| 3 | 0.731 | 0.712 | 0.693 | 0.675 | 0.658 | 0.641 | 0.624 | 0.609 | 0.593 | 0.579 |
| 4 | 0.659 | 0.636 | 0.613 | 0.592 | 0.572 | 0.552 | 0.534 | 0.516 | 0.499 | 0.482 |
| 5 | 0.593 | 0.567 | 0.543 | 0.519 | 0.497 | 0.476 | 0.456 | 0.437 | 0.419 | 0.402 |
| 6 | 0.535 | 0.507 | 0.480 | 0.456 | 0.432 | 0.410 | 0.390 | 0.370 | 0.352 | 0.335 |
| 7 | 0.482 | 0.452 | 0.425 | 0.400 | 0.376 | 0.354 | 0.333 | 0.314 | 0.296 | 0.279 |
| 8 | 0.434 | 0.404 | 0.376 | 0.351 | 0.327 | 0.305 | 0.285 | 0.266 | 0.249 | 0.233 |
| 9 | 0.391 | 0.361 | 0.333 | 0.308 | 0.284 | 0.263 | 0.243 | 0.225 | 0.209 | 0.194 |
| 10 | 0.352 | 0.322 | 0.295 | 0.270 | 0.247 | 0.227 | 0.208 | 0.191 | 0.176 | 0.162 |
| 11 | 0.317 | 0.287 | 0.261 | 0.237 | 0.215 | 0.195 | 0.178 | 0.162 | 0.148 | 0.135 |
| 12 | 0.286 | 0.257 | 0.231 | 0.208 | 0.187 | 0.168 | 0.152 | 0.137 | 0.124 | 0.112 |
| 13 | 0.258 | 0.229 | 0.204 | 0.182 | 0.163 | 0.145 | 0.130 | 0.116 | 0.104 | 0.093 |
| 14 | 0.232 | 0.205 | 0.181 | 0.160 | 0.141 | 0.125 | 0.111 | 0.099 | 0.088 | 0.078 |
| 15 | 0.209 | 0.183 | 0.160 | 0.140 | 0.123 | 0.108 | 0.095 | 0.084 | 0.074 | 0.065 |
| 16 | 0.188 | 0.163 | 0.141 | 0.123 | 0.107 | 0.093 | 0.081 | 0.071 | 0.062 | 0.054 |
| 17 | 0.170 | 0.146 | 0.125 | 0.108 | 0.093 | 0.080 | 0.069 | 0.060 | 0.052 | 0.045 |
| 18 | 0.153 | 0.130 | 0.111 | 0.095 | 0.081 | 0.069 | 0.059 | 0.051 | 0.044 | 0.038 |
| 19 | 0.138 | 0.116 | 0.098 | 0.083 | 0.070 | 0.060 | 0.051 | 0.043 | 0.037 | 0.031 |
| 20 | 0.124 | 0.104 | 0.087 | 0.073 | 0.061 | 0.051 | 0.043 | 0.037 | 0.031 | 0.026 |

# Cumulative present value table

This table shows the present value of $1 per annum, receivable or payable at the end of each year for n years $\dfrac{1-(1+r)^{-n}}{r}$.

| Periods | | | | | Interest rates (r) | | | | | |
|---|---|---|---|---|---|---|---|---|---|---|
| (n) | 1% | 2% | 3% | 4% | 5% | 6% | 7% | 8% | 9% | 10% |
| 1 | 0.990 | 0.980 | 0.971 | 0.962 | 0.952 | 0.943 | 0.935 | 0.926 | 0.917 | 0.909 |
| 2 | 1.970 | 1.942 | 1.913 | 1.886 | 1.859 | 1.833 | 1.808 | 1.783 | 1.759 | 1.736 |
| 3 | 2.941 | 2.884 | 2.829 | 2.775 | 2.723 | 2.673 | 2.624 | 2.577 | 2.531 | 2.487 |
| 4 | 3.902 | 3.808 | 3.717 | 3.630 | 3.546 | 3.465 | 3.387 | 3.312 | 3.240 | 3.170 |
| 5 | 4.853 | 4.713 | 4.580 | 4.452 | 4.329 | 4.212 | 4.100 | 3.993 | 3.890 | 3.791 |
| 6 | 5.795 | 5.601 | 5.417 | 5.242 | 5.076 | 4.917 | 4.767 | 4.623 | 4.486 | 4.355 |
| 7 | 6.728 | 6.472 | 6.230 | 6.002 | 5.786 | 5.582 | 5.389 | 5.206 | 5.033 | 4.868 |

| Periods | | | | | Interest rates (r) | | | | | |
|---|---|---|---|---|---|---|---|---|---|---|
| (n) | 1% | 2% | 3% | 4% | 5% | 6% | 7% | 8% | 9% | 10% |
| 8 | 7.652 | 7.325 | 7.020 | 6.733 | 6.463 | 6.210 | 5.971 | 5.747 | 5.535 | 5.335 |
| 9 | 8.566 | 8.162 | 7.786 | 7.435 | 7.108 | 6.802 | 6.515 | 6.247 | 5.995 | 5.759 |
| 10 | 9.471 | 8.983 | 8.530 | 8.111 | 7.722 | 7.360 | 7.024 | 6.710 | 6.418 | 6.145 |
| 11 | 10.368 | 9.787 | 9.253 | 8.760 | 8.306 | 7.887 | 7.499 | 7.139 | 6.805 | 6.495 |
| 12 | 11.255 | 10.575 | 9.954 | 9.385 | 8.863 | 8.384 | 7.943 | 7.536 | 7.161 | 6.814 |
| 13 | 12.134 | 11.348 | 10.635 | 9.986 | 9.394 | 8.853 | 8.358 | 7.904 | 7.487 | 7.103 |
| 14 | 13.004 | 12.106 | 11.296 | 10.563 | 9.899 | 9.295 | 8.745 | 8.244 | 7.786 | 7.367 |
| 15 | 13.865 | 12.849 | 11.938 | 11.118 | 10.380 | 9.712 | 9.108 | 8.559 | 8.061 | 7.606 |
| 16 | 14.718 | 13.578 | 12.561 | 11.652 | 10.838 | 10.106 | 9.447 | 8.851 | 8.313 | 7.824 |
| 17 | 15.562 | 14.292 | 13.166 | 12.166 | 11.274 | 10.477 | 9.763 | 9.122 | 8.544 | 8.022 |
| 18 | 16.398 | 14.992 | 13.754 | 12.659 | 11.690 | 10.828 | 10.059 | 9.372 | 8.756 | 8.201 |
| 19 | 17.226 | 15.679 | 14.324 | 13.134 | 12.085 | 11.158 | 10.336 | 9.604 | 8.950 | 8.365 |
| 20 | 18.046 | 16.351 | 14.878 | 13.590 | 12.462 | 11.470 | 10.594 | 9.818 | 9.129 | 8.514 |

| Periods | | | | | Interest rates (r) | | | | | |
|---|---|---|---|---|---|---|---|---|---|---|
| (n) | 11% | 12% | 13% | 14% | 15% | 16% | 17% | 18% | 19% | 20% |
| 1 | 0.901 | 0.893 | 0.885 | 0.877 | 0.870 | 0.862 | 0.855 | 0.847 | 0.840 | 0.833 |
| 2 | 1.713 | 1.690 | 1.668 | 1.647 | 1.626 | 1.605 | 1.585 | 1.566 | 1.547 | 1.528 |
| 3 | 2.444 | 2.402 | 2.361 | 2.322 | 2.283 | 2.246 | 2.210 | 2.174 | 2.140 | 2.106 |
| 4 | 3.102 | 3.037 | 2.974 | 2.914 | 2.855 | 2.798 | 2.743 | 2.690 | 2.639 | 2.589 |
| 5 | 3.696 | 3.605 | 3.517 | 3.433 | 3.352 | 3.274 | 3.199 | 3.127 | 3.058 | 2.991 |
| 6 | 4.231 | 4.111 | 3.998 | 3.889 | 3.784 | 3.685 | 3.589 | 3.498 | 3.410 | 3.326 |
| 7 | 4.712 | 4.564 | 4.423 | 4.288 | 4.160 | 4.039 | 3.922 | 3.812 | 3.706 | 3.605 |
| 8 | 5.146 | 4.968 | 4.799 | 4.639 | 4.487 | 4.344 | 4.207 | 4.078 | 3.954 | 3.837 |
| 9 | 5.537 | 5.328 | 5.132 | 4.946 | 4.772 | 4.607 | 4.451 | 4.303 | 4.163 | 4.031 |
| 10 | 5.889 | 5.650 | 5.426 | 5.216 | 5.019 | 4.833 | 4.659 | 4.494 | 4.339 | 4.192 |
| 11 | 6.207 | 5.938 | 5.687 | 5.453 | 5.234 | 5.029 | 4.836 | 4.656 | 4.486 | 4.327 |
| 12 | 6.492 | 6.194 | 5.918 | 5.660 | 5.421 | 5.197 | 4.988 | 4.793 | 4.611 | 4.439 |
| 13 | 6.750 | 6.424 | 6.122 | 5.842 | 5.583 | 5.342 | 5.118 | 4.910 | 4.715 | 4.533 |
| 14 | 6.982 | 6.628 | 6.302 | 6.002 | 5.724 | 5.468 | 5.229 | 5.008 | 4.802 | 4.611 |
| 15 | 7.191 | 6.811 | 6.462 | 6.142 | 5.847 | 5.575 | 5.324 | 5.092 | 4.876 | 4.675 |
| 16 | 7.379 | 6.974 | 6.604 | 6.265 | 5.954 | 5.668 | 5.405 | 5.162 | 4.938 | 4.730 |
| 17 | 7.549 | 7.120 | 6.729 | 6.373 | 6.047 | 5.749 | 5.475 | 5.222 | 4.990 | 4.775 |
| 18 | 7.702 | 7.250 | 6.840 | 6.467 | 6.128 | 5.818 | 5.534 | 5.273 | 5.033 | 4.812 |
| 19 | 7.839 | 7.366 | 6.938 | 6.550 | 6.198 | 5.877 | 5.584 | 5.316 | 5.070 | 4.843 |
| 20 | 7.963 | 7.469 | 7.025 | 6.623 | 6.259 | 5.929 | 5.628 | 5.353 | 5.101 | 4.870 |

# Probability

$A \cup B$ = A **or** B. $A \cap B$ = A **and** B (overlap). P(B/A) = probability of B, **given** A.

# Rules of addition

If A and B are *mutually exclusive*: $P(A \cup B) = P(A) + P(B)$

If A and B are **not** mutually exclusive: $P(A \cup B) = P(A) + P(B) - P(A \cap B)$

# Rules of multiplication

If A and B are *independent*:  $P(A \cap B) = P(A) * P(B)$

If A and B are **not** independent:  $P(A \cap B) = P(A) * P(B/A)$

$E(X)$ = expected value = probability * payoff

# Quadratic equations

If $aX^2 + bX + c = 0$ is the general quadratic equation, then the two solutions (roots) are given by

$$X = \frac{-b \pm \sqrt{b^2 - 4ac}}{2a}$$

# Descriptive statistics

## Arithmetic mean

$$\bar{x} = \frac{\sum x}{n} \text{ or } \bar{x} = \frac{\sum fx}{\sum f}$$

## Standard deviation

$$\sqrt{\frac{\sum (x - \bar{x})^2}{n}}$$

$$SD = \sqrt{\frac{\sum fx^2}{\sum f} - \bar{x}^2} \text{ (frequency distribution)}$$

# Index numbers

Price relative = $100 * P_1 / P_0$

Quantity relative = $100 * Q_1 / Q_0$

Price: $\dfrac{\sum W \times P_1 / P_0}{\sum W} \times 100$  where W denotes weights

Quantity: $\dfrac{\sum W \times Q_1 / Q_0}{\sum W} \times 100$  where W denotes weights

# Time series

Additive model: Series = Trend + Seasonal + Random

Multiplicative model: Series = Trend * Seasonal * Random

## Linear regression and correlation

The linear regression equation of Y on X is given by:

$$Y = a + bX \text{ or}$$

$$Y - \overline{Y} = b(X - \overline{X}), \text{where}$$

$$b = \frac{\text{Covariance}(XY)}{\text{Variance}(X)} = \frac{n\sum XY - (\sum X)(\sum Y)}{n\sum X^2 - (\sum X)^2}$$

and $a = \overline{Y} - b\overline{X}$,

$$\text{or solve} \quad \sum Y = na + b\sum X$$

$$\sum XY = a\sum X + b\sum X^2$$

## Coefficient of correlation (r)

$$r = \frac{\text{Covariance}(XY)}{\sqrt{\text{VAR}(X).\text{VAR}(Y)}}$$

$$= \frac{n\sum XY - (\sum X)(\sum Y)}{\sqrt{[n\sum X^2 - (\sum X)^2][n\sum Y^2 - (\sum Y)^2]}}$$

$$R(\text{rank}) = 1 - \left[\frac{6\sum d^2}{n(n^2 - 1)}\right]$$

## Financial mathematics

### Compound Interest (Values and Sums)

Future Value of $S_1$ of a sum X, invested for n periods, compounded at r% interest:

$$S = X[1 + r]^n$$

### Annuity

Present value of an annuity of £1 per annum receivable or payable, for n years, commencing in one year, discounted at r% per annum:

$$PV = \frac{1}{r}\left[1 - \frac{1}{[1+r]^n}\right]$$

### Perpetuity

Present value of £1 per annum, payable or receivable in perpetuity, commencing in one year discounted at r% per annum

$$PV = \frac{1}{r}$$

## Review Form & Free Prize Draw – Paper C3 Fundamentals of Business Mathematics

All original review forms from the entire BPP range, completed with genuine comments, will be entered into one of two draws on 31 July 2006 and 31 January 2007. The names on the first four forms picked out on each occasion will be sent a cheque for £50.

Name: _____  Address: _____

_____

_____

**How have you used this Kit?**
*(Tick one box only)*

☐ Home study (book only)

☐ On a course: college _____

☐ With 'correspondence' package

☐ Other _____

**Why did you decide to purchase this Kit?**
*(Tick one box only)*

☐ Have used the complementary Study text

☐ Have used other BPP products in the past

☐ Recommendation by friend/colleague

☐ Recommendation by a lecturer at college

☐ Saw advertising

☐ Other _____

**During the past six months do you recall seeing/receiving any of the following?**
*(Tick as many boxes as are relevant)*

☐ Our advertisement in *CIMA Insider*

☐ Our advertisement in *Financial Management*

☐ Our advertisement in *Pass*

☐ Our brochure with a letter through the post

☐ Our website www.bpp.com

**Which (if any) aspects of our advertising do you find useful?**
*(Tick as many boxes as are relevant)*

☐ Prices and publication dates of new editions

☐ Information on product content

☐ Facility to order books off-the-page

☐ None of the above

*Which BPP products have you used?*

| | | | | |
|---|---|---|---|---|
| Text ☐ | Kit ☑ | | i-Pass ☐ | |
| Passcard ☐ | CD ☐ | | | |
| Big Picture Poster ☐ | Virtual Campus ☐ | | | |

*Your ratings, comments and suggestions would be appreciated on the following areas.*

| | Very useful | Useful | Not useful |
|---|---|---|---|
| *Effective revision* | ☐ | ☐ | ☐ |
| *Exam guidance* | ☐ | ☐ | ☐ |
| *Multiple choice questions* | ☐ | ☐ | ☐ |
| *Objective test questions* | ☐ | ☐ | ☐ |
| *Guidance in answers* | ☐ | ☐ | ☐ |
| *Content and structure of answers* | ☐ | ☐ | ☐ |
| *Mock assessments* | ☐ | ☐ | ☐ |
| *Mock assessment answers* | ☐ | ☐ | ☐ |

*Overall opinion of this Kit*    Excellent ☐    Good ☐    Adequate ☐    Poor ☐

**Do you intend to continue using BPP products?**    Yes ☐    No ☐

The BPP author of this edition can be e-mailed at: julietgood@bpp.com

**Please return this form to: Nick Weller, CIMA Range Manager, BPP Professional Education, FREEPOST, London, W12 8BR**

**Review Form & Free Prize Draw (continued)**

**TELL US WHAT YOU THINK**

**Please note any comments and suggestions/errors below**

**Free Prize Draw Rules**

1  Closing date for 31 July 2006 draw is 30 June 2006. Closing date for 31 January 2007 draw is 31 December 2006.

2  Restricted to entries with UK and Eire addresses only. BPP employees, their families and business associates are excluded.

3  No purchase necessary. Entry forms are available upon request from BPP Professional Education. No more than one entry per title, per person. Draw restricted to persons aged 16 and over.

4  Winners will be notified by post and receive their cheques not later than 6 weeks after the relevant draw date.

5  The decision of the promoter in all matters is final and binding. No correspondence will be entered into.